To Light the Sabbath Candles

TO LIGHT THE SABBATH CANDLES

Reconciling One New Humanity at the Lord's Table

Christine Graef

WIPF & STOCK · Eugene, Oregon

TO LIGHT THE SABBATH CANDLES
Reconciling the One New Humanity at the Lord's Table

Copyright © 2018 Christine Graef. All rights reserved. Except for brief quotations in critical publications or reviews, no part of this book may be reproduced in any manner without prior written permission from the publisher. Write: Permissions, Wipf and Stock Publishers, 199 W. 8th Ave., Suite 3, Eugene, OR 97401.

Wipf & Stock
An Imprint of Wipf and Stock Publishers
199 W. 8th Ave., Suite 3
Eugene, OR 97401

www.wipfandstock.com

PAPERBACK ISBN: 978-1-5326-5656-9
HARDCOVER ISBN: 978-1-5326-5657-6
EBOOK ISBN: 978-1-5326-5658-3

Manufactured in the U.S.A. 09/11/18

Revised Standard Version of the Bible, copyright © 1946, 1952, and 1971 the Division of Christian Education of the National Council of the Churches of Christ in the United States of America. Used by permission. All rights reserved.

And he said to them, "Come away by yourselves to a secluded place, and rest a while." (Mark 6:31)

Contents

1. **Light** | 1
2. **Breath** | 24
3. **Nerot** | 47
4. **Fire** | 70
5. **Challah** | 93
6. **Haman** | 117
7. **Niddah** | 140

Bibliography | 165

1

LIGHT

> Everything is in the hands of heaven except the fear of heaven
> —Maimonides

BEFORE CREATION WAS MADE, the Word resided in a throne room high above the heavens. White hot lightning refracts all around him, flashing like crystals brighter than sunlight. He is as untouchable as fire. No one can approach him without the flames lighting his eyes piercing the soul. Cloaked in white, whiter than snow, he is haloed in lightning, with hair like pure wool (Dan 7:9). The imperial robe draped over his shoulders fills heaven's temple with glory (Isa 6:1). His body shines like the alluring gem beryl, his arms and feet gleam like bronze burnished in a furnace of fiery trials. When he speaks, the sound of rushing water thunders through the heavens (Dan 10:6; Rev 1:14).

Thousands upon thousands of angels hover around him. Six-winged seraphim chorus to each other, "Holy, holy, holy is the Lord of hosts." With two wings, the faces of the fiery angels are hidden. With two they cover their feet, and with two they fly (Isa 6:2-3). In front of the throne seven lamps burn with the eternal fire of the seven spirits of God (Rev 4:6-8).

Smaller than the majestic seraphim, cherubim radiate heaven's raging brightness as they move in whirlwinds, glowing in the midst of brilliant light (Ezek 1:4-24). Each have four wings, two wings of each touch one another and two cover their bodies. Their legs are straight and their feet are like calves' feet. They move in flashes of lightning upon wheels within wheels, whirling by the spirit of God, raising the divine chariot, which goes everywhere to pursue those lost in darkness.

When the pulse in man swells against captivity, with prayer pressing to shatter the atmosphere, the angelic beings help his words reach the Beloved in his glory in heaven. Known as columns of smoke in the Zohar, a collection of insights on heaven's light, the angels are present in the incense of burnt offerings coming into the throne room.

Ablaze with heaven's protectiveness, the cherubim each are bestowed with four different faces. A face of a lion is on the right side, one like an ox on the left side, a third face is like a man, and the fourth like an eagle (Ezek 1:4–14).

The lion would symbolize fortitude that "does not turn away from any" (Prov 30:30), with wrath like the fire of a king that should not be provoked (Prov 20:2).

The ox's strength would bear burdens, steadily laboring to increase growth upon earth (Prov 14:4). The ox would be well-laden (Ps 144:14) and recognize its owner (Isa 1:3). God brought his people out of Egypt; they have the strength of a wild ox (Num 24:8).

The firelight flooding heaven penetrates to lift wearied souls on eagle's wings, strengthened to rise and see beyond the storms (Isa 40:31). Faith would renew like the eagle's flight (Ps 103:5). Eagle's wings would carry the people to God when oppressors surrounded them (Exod 19:4). At the end of time, God's people would be given the two wings of a great eagle to flee from the enemy, the serpent, into the wilderness, and be nourished for a time, and times, and half a time (Rev 12:14).

The face of man on the cherubim represents traits inspired in both men and women to yearn for the transcendent light of the Lord's powerful glory. Representing the intellect and emotions endowed on humanity, the face represents man being given purpose.

The angels of the wheel move so quickly that no one sees the flashing light moving the unknowable mystery through the realms of the beautiful worlds of the firmament (Ezek 1:14). Above the living creatures is heaven, the stunning colors of the awesome crystal (Ezek 1:22).

When the holy one said "Let there be light" (Gen 1:3), he pronounced sovereign reign over darkness and the angelic beings appeared with choruses of worship echoing across the universes. Shining with his majesty, pervading everywhere between heaven and the outer rim of all creation, every particle of their light burns toward God, receiving his command to share in the story that begins in a garden swept down an eddie of sin, a descent stopped by an ancient rock to ascend to a city of peace.

Under their wings, cherubim have the hands of a man, reflecting God's hand extended from his throne to bestow wisdom, victory, understanding, and glory. He opens his hand to welcome those who return to the source of life. His hand also metes out justice on those who do not return. He sees all, holds all in his hand, hears the crying, sings over his people; his heart weeps when we go astray. The entire spectrum of God's hidden features enable man to restrain unbounded emotions, balancing judgment that would be unspeakable if kindness did not cover all iniquity.

The Word dwelling with the Father of light was named before the stars, before the angels or any created thing. Nothing was made without him (John 1:1–3). When he opened the gates of heaven and said, "Let there be light," the brightness from heaven would translate into the first of the ten commandments citing the one holiness. "I am the Lord your God, have no other god before me," then again when he spoke the words "I am the light," and fulfilled his light, returning to dwell with man.

God saw that the light was good (Gen 1:4). The word *zohar* (brightness) designates *nekuda reshima*, the origin of the ray of light that manifests the Divine, where he abides in the glorious temple. Its brightness vibrated to shape the colors, textures, and sounds of the universe. In it is reserved the time of judgment that will unleash a roaring inferno through the atmosphere and melt the elements.

The Word told his disciples they will see heaven open and the angels of God ascending and descending upon him (John 1:51). He is the gate that bridges heaven and earth throughout the perpetual ascent and descent of life's journey toward God.

Every valley will be exalted, every hill made low, and the glory of the Lord will be revealed, and all people will see it together (Isa 40:4–5). Our humility is elevated, and our high places are put under him.

Jacob glimpsed this in a dream revealing a ladder set on earth extending all the way to the heights of God's dwelling. He saw angels descend and ascend on Mount Moriah. Enthralled by the vision, he built an altar, and all his hope lifted as he went on his way into an unknown journey. He was given a new name, "Israel," to live as a bridge between the will of heaven being done on earth. Jerusalem would be built in this place, serving as an altar for the joy of the whole earth (Ps 48:2).

The Word created souls as flames of heaven's fire, and when the confusion of darkness covered his people in heavy anguish, the soul still burned, reaching toward heaven. He strengthened the direction in a burning bush, in flame traveling with an ark, in a brightness bursting in the sky to announce when the Word came to dwell on earth. On the palms of his hands are engraved all those who belong to him, securely inside the borders of his light (Isa 49:16).

"I give them eternal life, and they shall never perish, and no one shall snatch them out of my hand" (John 10:28). His hands became bloodied and bruised, scarred with piercing, but the Word would rise from the grave still holding his beloved safely in his palms.

He is the only Son of the living God, coming to finish the work of his Father after the creation was made. "It is finished," he said, as he hung dying on the stake of execution.

The Father first shared his holy name in the book of Genesis, saying, "In the day that the Lord God [YHVH] made the earth and the heavens" (2:4). This holy name is unpronounceable except as the sound of breathing. Often spoken as Yahveh, the true sound is unutterable because it has no vowels, spelled with Yod Hey Vay Hey, meaning "he exists," encompassing the unified dimensions of eternity and all past, present, and future. The name YHVH is descriptive of God in his supernatural awesome power above. The name *Elohim* is God's power in the physical creation of nature, God in the body, guiding the sea; God of the sunlight, the stars, and the dewdrops on lilies.

When darkness was upon the surface of the deep, the Father of light sent his flames to instill every atom with radiance and purpose, causing them to flutter into an organized cohesive creation. The heat and flame from heaven's light formed life-giving seeds, establishing the laws of nature that would govern every layer of creation. All the glory of his aspects display in the sky's flashing thunder, the massive planets moving across a wide universe, the renewal of refreshing rainfall, high winds, soft breezes, and all the work of his staggering wisdom in the majestic mountains and tiniest microcosms.

But his mercy was not shown in these things.

To reveal his great mercy, God separated a people and gave them his name as part of their name, which contains within it *El*. They would be called Israel, children of light entrusted with the high calling of bringing God's mercy from behind the veil that separates heaven from the physical world of creation. Birthed through Abraham, "Israel is my firstborn" (Exod 4:22), they are "a chosen race, a royal priesthood, a holy nation, God's own people, that you may declare the wonderful deeds of him who called you out of darkness into his marvelous light" (1 Pet 2:9).

God's indivisibility formed the elements to move every sphere as one living vision. His Spirit moved on the surface of the deep waters (Gen 1:1–2). The Spirit vibrated on the water, fluttering its particles with God's breath, and the surface dove into the deep—the depths rose to the surface, beginning the continuous cycle of water's life.

He instructed angels to conduct the measure of his winds. The sea and wind compressed the shells and corals of its sea creatures into rocks, in turn compacting into limestone.

These stones would build Jerusalem and glow with rosy golden hues as the sun set at the end of the day. For the Lord has chosen Zion; he has desired it for his habitation (Ps 132:13). To show the world his great mercy, he gave instructions to pray for the peace of Jerusalem, because from here, words would revive the dead, pouring out song with the fragrance of spices. From here cascades of tears would advance the way to guard the soul.

The infinite light shone into finite creation emitting in celestial nebulas and bursting blazing stars out of nothingness, shooting meteorites in the deep sky, quasars and blazers, pulsars and meteor showers, lightning and sprites, a display of aurora australenis in the south sky and aurora borealis in the north.

The Word poured light into chemical reactions to affect light in chemiluminescence. Bioluminescence brought light from within living organisms such as Antarctic krill, foxfire and glowworms, parchment worms and piddock, as well as natural phenomena such as cavitation.

He stretched the atmosphere into the galaxies to participate in the earth by uniting to the heaven beyond. The setting sun and appearance of stars transition the days. The Word made the moon to mark the seasons; the sun knows its time for setting (Ps 104:19).

> Boundless One, the concealed of all concealments, without beginning and without end, the great invisible center and fount of all life and motion existent in worlds known and unknown, careering in their mighty orbits in the fathomless abysses of space, the Great Being the smallest portion of whose glory and might and majesty is reflected and seen in sun and moon and the splendid galaxies of stars and constellations, all glittering and flashing in a midnight sky, and in the mystic music of the spheres are forever singing as they shine: "The hand that made us is divine."[1]

The sun faithfully completes its ecliptic through the constellations every twenty-eight years, returning to the place where it was first created. Known as *machzor gadol* ("the great cycle"), when its light returns to its first dawn, Israel's people recite profound appreciation for the Creator, acknowledging the awe of his handiwork. He made the sun to shine light on

---

1. "Zohar," 110.

everyone, whether wicked or fair, sorrowful or joyful. Seeing the sun at this turning point, whether standing alone or in the company of a gathering, the special blessing, the *Birkat Ha'chamah*, is spoken to thank God for making the sun. Blessed are You, Lord our God, Ruler of the universe, who does the work of creation.

The moon's path is narrower, carrying the sun's light in circles 238,855 miles around earth through a background of constellations gathering his splendor to minister to every corner. The aspects of the moon include phases, lunar days, void-of-course periods, eclipses, and apogee and perigee moments; in the moon's orbit, it returns to its original cycle every 8.85 years, 3,232.6054 days, as it spins with earth's rotation.

The Midrash states, "There is no blade of grass that does not have a constellation [*mazal*] over it, telling it to grow." Wishing someone "*mazal tov*" contains the wish for God to align the constellations and planets favorably, but consulting the stars and planets, astrology and horoscopes, to determine influence over a life is forbidden. The Talmud states, "*Ein Mazal LeYisroel*" (there is no *mazal* [constellations] for Israel's people), meaning that the people have been lifted above the stars when they received the Torah from the angelic realm and became connected to the power far above the physical world. Those who are wise will shine like the brightness of the heavens (Dan 12:3) because their wisdom is from God.

The moon rises, a shepherdess leading the people to gather in festivals, recalling all that God has done for them. Her light moves across the rugged rocky hills, bending to touch dry sandy deserts, seeking out the depths of valleys where the carob and sage grow and alighting on the heights of snow-capped mountaintops. She wades in the shallows to assure with prophetic redemption, witnessing to the Lord's name in heights the earth cannot contain. Yet he made a dwelling for himself in the minds of his people.

When moonlight blooms full in the middle of Nisan as springtime renews, each generation witnesses to Passover, the story of a people led through water to a mountain covered with the cloud of God's glory, the red marks on doorposts that were a sign to an angel, the rock that gave them water, families of slaves becoming a nation as they gathered around a pillar of fire.

On Passover's night of moonlight, for thousands of years, the door to millions of homes closes on the world—inside, a new child wonders at the items passed from parent to child to hold, because history began in a home in a garden. The gathering recalls the gift of creation being made by God's will as family surround the table within a sanctuary of thanksgiving. The table is laid from God's commandment to let the land produce fruit of various kinds. Because God said "let us make mankind in our image" (Gen

1:26), Passover binds the generations as the teachings are passed in parent's prayers, heard like rushing waters carried by the river of life.

Matzah, which the Israelites made as they readied to leave Egypt, is passed around, the sweetness of honey replacing the taste of bitter memories as faith watches for the return of the Word, their Messiah. For nearly 1,500 years, the women lit the candles for Passover before the coming one appeared and the fallen creation beheld the Lamb of God.

The cherished history of the people who bear God's name is strewn with mass graves, embedded with fear of what will come next, yet still burns with the ancient flame begun in heaven's temple. The people would talk of cruelties so unimaginable that they would wish to follow the angels up Jacob's ladder. Persecuted "because you are Jewish," God's treasured possession, they have always been different.

The world sees a grief-stricken plight of Israel. Never entering their door, they don't realize what their story tells us. Look instead at what God can do, Jesus told his disciples when they asked who was to blame for an affliction. To be part of a traumatized people who God's holy power is bringing together with those he called from the world (who never lost their humor, their generosity toward the poor, or their dream of Jerusalem), is to be alive in his great voice.

God commanded the moonlight to signal Passover, in order to remember that God keeps his covenant by giving the people *emunah*, faith that trusts him in captivity as well as in being freed, a light shining in darkness, reminding that the darkness has not overcome it (John 1:5). The moon wanes on the Shabbat after Passover, after the crucifixion of the Lord, when his people celebrate the Feast of Unleavened Bread, the bread of life, who takes away the sin of the world.

The Day of First Fruits comes next, celebrating the harvest presented to God (Lev 23:10–11). When the voice of Jesus was heard again raised from the dead, he became the first fruit of the resurrection (1 Cor 15:20; 2 Tim 2:6–8) as the barley sheaf was waved in the temple during the morning's offering.

The day passes into the Omer to count the forty-nine days that journey the soul to Shavuot, also called Pentecost. This brings thanks for the giving of the Torah on Mount Sinai that infused the physical deliverance on earth with the spiritual redemption of heaven. The lightning of heaven thundered that day, over three million people standing in the stillness of awe at the bottom of the mountain, and they became witnesses to the time that God gave the commands. On the day of Pentecost, Paul got up and quoted Joel, who prophesied to Israel, saying that after the Lord pours his Spirit on people around the world, their children will begin prophesying, seeing visions and dreaming dreams (Joel 2:28; Acts 2:17). His Spirit would baptize around the world and return to Jerusalem to open floods of blessings.

The ingathering of the exiles from the four corners of the earth, a stream of millions coming back to live in Israel, is guided by God leading toward the time of the Lord's return. An eternal people, Jewish believers converge on the land, prophesying the Messiah's return, telling of the Lord's vision for the one new humanity.

The Spirit moves on every name written in the Book of Life; in incomprehensible light they would breathe the Spirit's words. The Lord again gathers the scattered knowledge in the way he moved his apostles to weave the parts of the body to each other, establishing the relationship of souls burning in expectation.

> The Lord is in his holy temple; let all the earth keep silence before him. (Hab 2:20)

As to the times and the seasons, brethren, you have no need to have anything written to you (1 Thess 5:1). The people of Abraham understood the significance of the festivals in the turning sky which God appointed, telling us what is important to his heart. The summer sky passes into autumn to gather Israel for the three feasts declaring Messiah's second coming—the Feast of Trumpets, the Day of Atonement, and the Feast of Tabernacles.

They wait as the sun lights the moon's lamp, commencing autumn's Feast of Trumpets telling of the Word coming down from heaven to win the battle for those upheld in the palm of his hand. When God's Son appears, coming in glory on the clouds of heaven, he will send out his angels with a loud trumpet call (Matt 24:30–31); "For the trumpet will sound, and the dead will be raised imperishable, and we shall be changed" (1 Cor 15:52).

The atmosphere's pressure, fog, and humidity along the path of light make it impossible to predict the hour of the day the moonlight will first appear in the night sky and the trumpets be blown. No one knows the day or hour (Mark 13:32).

The prophets had foretold him. Isaiah spoke of the wounds of God's rebellious children, recorded in the first chapter. In Isaiah 53, the prophet then saw the suffering Savior, who would come and be wounded for them. He foresees the bruising placed on God's Son after seeing the raw wounds of Israel's children in chapter 1. He looks at his people struck down and smitten, then in chapter 53 sees that the smiting is put on the back of God's Son to heal us.

Seven hundred and fifty years later, Acts 8 would reveal what Isaiah had seen. He was led to slaughter like a sheep. He did not open his mouth to defend himself because it was the will of God.

Light

Who is the Word in heaven's throne who created all things? "The Lord created me at the beginning of his work, the first of his acts of old. Ages ago I was set up, at the first, before the beginning of the earth" (Prov 8:22–23). The Word became flesh and made his dwelling among us (John 1:14), and they beheld his glory, full of grace, the truth of the only begotten of the Father. His birth was announced with a blazing light over Bethlehem in language that could mean this was an angel revealing itself or a star's light announcing the scepter rising out of Israel (Num 24:17). "I am the light of the world; he who follows me will not walk in darkness, but will have the light of life" (John 8:12). He brought God's glory to earth to light the path for footsteps to follow toward heaven (Ps 119:105).

The Word chose to be born through a Jewish woman on the rugged valley hills of the lower Jordan, an enclosed basin between the Dead Sea and the Mediterranean where an abundance of walnuts, figs, and palms flourished. "But you, O Bethlehem Eph'rathah, who are little to be among the clans of Judah, from you shall come forth for me one who is to be ruler in Israel, whose origin is from of old, from ancient days" (Mic 5:2). His name comes from a far place, calling him Wonderful Counselor, Lamb of God, Lion of Judah, Prince of Peace, Yeshua, meaning YHVH Saves.

Abraham, Isaac, and Jacob knew him as Shaddai, the covenant maker who would multiply the light. The Midrash explains that "dai" comes from the idea that when God created the universe it expanded until he said "Dai!" (enough, sufficient). Guardian of the doors of Israel, God begins and ends the boundaries for times of harm and repair. The years of weeping under the persecutor's lies, betrayals, and divisions among people cause the heart to cry out to a distant God. But the mystery of the cross means tears will end, and when the Lord appears, we will be like him.

"The secret things belong to the Lord our God; but the things that are revealed belong to us and to our children for ever, that we may do all the words of this law" (Deut 29:29).

He bestowed humanity with his words to trust in the way to walk. He alone is refuge, coming to earth in the song of angels bestowing peace to men of good will. The stars sang when he descended to earth, the earth rejoiced from her suffering, and the Lord of the Shabbat had come.

Luke would pen pages in chronological detail as he witnessed the life of the King of kings, the Lord of lords, who came out of heaven, where he dwelt in holy light. Matthew would record his Jewish ancestry. John would trace the coming of Jesus, the Son of the Blessed One, to the time before creation when the Word lived in eternity surrounded by spectacular holy fire. Together they would tell the world of the divine Word, whose identity existed with the Father in the beginning. The apostle Paul would say, "For us there is one God, the Father, from whom are all things and for whom we exist, and one Lord, Jesus Christ, through whom are all things and through whom we exist" (1 Cor 8:6).

Jesus proclaimed himself to be the "Alpha and Omega" (Rev 1:8; 21:6; 22:13), the first and last letters of the Greek alphabet, identifying himself with the God who sustained Israel in the Old Testament. Isaiah scripted his being: "Who has performed and done this, calling the generations from the beginning? I, the Lord, the first, and with the last; I am he" (Isa 41:4); "I am the first, and I am the last; apart from me there is no God" (44:6); "I am he, I am the first and I am the last" (48:12). His light would author and complete faith (Heb 12:2), bringing the grace of sanctifying his people. Those who are victorious will be clothed in white and their name never blotted out of his Book of Life (Rev 3:5).

Amid the leaping, flashing streams of flame blazing from the throne room, amid the thousand thousands of angels standing before him, the book will be opened and the dead will be judged by what is written on the pages of God's remembrance (Rev 20:15; Dan 7:10). The apostles' names are written here, along with those of their fellow workers (Luke 10:20; Phil 4:3), all the assembly of the firstborn (Heb 12:23), and all those whose names God breathed into being from the foundation of the world and which have not been blotted out by the Lamb.

The Talmud explains that before the world was founded, the Lord made seven things—the Throne of Glory, the garden of Eden, the Torah, Sheol's darkness that covers over the names of those banished from the Book of Life, the temple, the Name of the Messiah, and repentance.

As he traced out his plan, God found that the foundation would not stand firm until he created repentance.

The ten days between the Feast of Trumpets (Rosh Hashanah) and Yom Kippur are appointed Days of Awe because everyone needs a way to begin again. They are days of looking inward to appraise how we are serving God with all our heart. There are special prayers, called *S'lihot* prayers, during the Days of Awe, meaning "forgive me" in Hebrew.

The Word spoke to the water, directing it to carve out rivers and lakes which shimmer with light to reflect the true self of anyone looking into it. Separating into currents to carry away transgressions, he made a way for people to know they could be rid of their past mistakes. A ceremony called *Tashlich*, meaning to cast or to throw, symbolizes God casting sins into the deepest sea by standing at a river's edge and throwing leavened bread into moving water.

Micah said that God will hurl the wrongs into the depth of the sea, similarly to when his people came out of Egypt and sang to the Lord because he hurled their enemies into the sea. The past and the guilt with it may come chasing after us to hold us back, but God will stand and hurl the taunts into the depths. More than forgiveness, this is deliverance that gives a new way of being.

The holiest day of the year, Yom Kippur (or Day of Atonement) is a day when the soul comes nearest to God. "For on this day he will forgive you, to purify you, that you be cleansed from all your sins before God" (Lev 16:30). Yom Kippur is a day to fast. The day honors God from one evening to the next by men lighting a candle called *dos lebidikeh licht* ("the living light") in Yiddish, or *dos gezunteh licht* ("the healthy light").

Yom Kippur connotes a return along a known road. It is not just repenting from regrets. It is a turning to behold the beauty of the Lord that has existed from the beginning, when there were no transgressions.

Whoever does not afflict his soul on this day shall be cut off from their people (Lev 23:29). When John stood in the river Jordan calling to the people to repent, he said "*teshuvah*," meaning to stand in the same place again and be given the opportunity to make a different choice. Jesus came from heaven and repeated the gift of repentance, saying that those who recognize they are poor in spirit and mourn wrongs will be blessed with comfort and inherit the earth and the kingdom of God.

Repentance would restore the image of God within people. The lit candle reflects the souls of man (which Proverbs 20:27 calls "candles" or "lamps"), giving light to all in the house. There was disorder and darkness without light. In light, the mind learns the way God wants us to approach him, and this knowledge stands firm against the enemy of the Word, who attempts to invent false beliefs.

He made prayer a delight just to know him, bringing desires of the heart (Ps 37:4). "Desire" comes from the Hebrew word *mishalot*, derived from *shaal*, which means to seek council in prayer. The intimate flame of the soul rises to burn with God's own desires and align with God's purposes. Thy will be done, on earth as it is in heaven.

Pouring through the heavens in ordered arrangements, divine light sends his messages of mercy or warns of impending judgment. Angels move with God's appointed times to extend his covenant with Israel to others. Coming from the holy place, an angel has been given the eternal gospel to proclaim to every nation, tribe, language, and people (Rev 14:6). Embodying eternity's light, they are present when righteousness prevails. They are bright when someone enters the meeting place with God by studying his word, following the divine will in humble approach of the throne room.

Luminous in a world of darkness, angelic beings resonate in worship, of whom Scripture says, "He makes winds his messengers, flames of fire his servants" (Ps 104:4).

All of Israel was called to sing with these angels.

> This is none other than the house of God, and this is the gate of heaven. (Gen 28:17)

Moses descended Mount Sinai clothed in sufficient brightness to define their mission to understand the light. "Show me your glory!" Moses beseeched God, thirsting to be nearer to God. Paul, even after decades of serving the Lord, still thirsted for more.

Jesus announced that no one knows the Father except those who the Son chooses to reveal him, and he chose to first reveal God to Israel.

Isaiah saw the Lord high and exalted (Isa 6:1). They saw the God of Israel (Exod 24:10). The glory of the Lord appeared (Num 16:42). Like the appearance of the bow that is in the cloud on the day of rain, so was the appearance of the brightness round about (Ezek 1:28). The radiance of the Lord's glory surrounded them (Luke 2:9). When he was stoned, Steven shone with the light of a present angel, in the special mercy given to those who stand for the Lord at all cost.

"God, it seems you've been our home forever, long before you brought earth itself to birth," Moses discerned in Psalm 90.

The Lord hears when those who fear him speak to each other and respect his name (Mal 3:16). During the autumn days of Rosh Hashanah, the day of remembrance, *Unetanneh tokef* ("let us speak of the awesomeness") is chanted in a stirring liturgy while the ark of the covenant is open and the congregants are standing.

The first paragraph of *Unetanneh tokef* speaks of the judgment day. The angels in heaven tremble at this, inferring that man should approach this day in humility. Paul reminded us to continue to work out our salvation with fear and trembling (Phil 2:12).

> Let us now relate the power of this day's holiness, for it is awesome and frightening. On it Your Kingship will be exalted; Your throne will be firmed with kindness and You will sit upon it in truth. It is true that You alone are the One Who judges, proves, knows, and bears witness; Who writes and seals, Who counts and Who calculates. You will remember all that was forgotten. You will open the Book of Remembrances—it will read itself—and each person's signature is there. And the great shofar will be sounded and a still, thin voice will be heard. Angels will hasten, a trembling and terror will seize them—and they will

say, "Behold, it is the Day of Judgment, to muster the heavenly host for judgment!"—for even they are not guiltless in Your eyes in judgment. All mankind will pass before You like a flock of sheep. Like a shepherd pasturing his flock, making sheep pass under his staff, so shall You cause to pass, count, calculate, and consider the soul of all the living; and You shall apportion the destinies of all Your creatures and inscribe their verdict.

It is said that, on Rosh Hashanah, names and events for the year will be inscribed, and on Yom Kippur it will be noted how many will pass from the earth and how many will be created, who will rest and who will wander, who will be impoverished and who will be enriched, who will be degraded and who will be exalted.

The soul's thirst to unite flame with heaven restores the people to the Lord. The sons of Korah wrote Psalm 42, as a deer longing for flowing streams, a soul thirsting for the living God, longing to behold his face. But Korah had rebelled, accusing Moses and Aaron and wanting to take a position of leadership. The ground swallowed him, yet his descendants knew themselves to need God. Through the introspection of self and repentance, the prayer teaches of judgment being changed for each individual:

> For Your Name signifies Your praise: hard to anger and easy to appease, for You do not wish the death of one deserving death, but that he repent from his way and live. Until the day of his death You await him; if he repents You will accept him immediately. It is true that You are their Creator and You know their inclination, for they are flesh and blood. A man's origin is from dust and his destiny is back to dust, at risk of his life he earns his bread; he is likened to a broken shard, withering grass, a fading flower, a passing shade, a dissipating cloud, a blowing wind, flying dust, and a fleeting dream. But You are the King, the Living and Enduring God.

The days of sunlight and nights of moonlight lead the way to the last of the year's pilgrimage feasts, the Feast of Tabernacles, also known as Sukkot, when the men journeyed to the temple to present themselves before the Lord (Exod 23:14; 34:22; Deut 16:16). All of Israel is to move into hand-built shelters, called *sukkah*s, for a week in remembrance of their wandering in the desert when God dwelt with them in a cloud of glory.

Under commandment to rejoice before the Lord after the days of introspection, branches of palm, willow and other trees are waved in celebration to the Lord (Lev 23:40) to give thanks so that, in our awareness of all we've been given, we are freed to live joyous, selfless lives from within our souls.

The feast is held at the end of the harvest, symbolizing the gathering of God's people for the marriage supper of the Lamb when Jesus returns and the divine light first spoken dwells in the world again.

Zechariah described the coming day as living water flowing out from Jerusalem, which will never again be destroyed. The Lord will be king over earth and his name alone will be worshiped (Zech 14:1–21). In Revelation 21, the city of Jerusalem has no need of sun or moon because of his light.

Zechariah prophesied that in the world to come, people from all nations will go up year after year to worship the king and celebrate the Feast of Tabernacles. Anyone not participating will have no rainfall (Zech 14:16–17).

Both wicked and righteous are ripening, strengthening, and intensifying as time moves toward the sound of the trumpet. Women who light the Lord's candles during these menacing times will be the most righteous in all of creation's history. Their finest hour will be amid threats, massacres, beheadings, hunger, and prisons, as they hold themselves as flames of God through the most perilous of generations.

In the telling of the time in the desert, the book of Numbers begins at Mount Sinai as the Israelites are prepared to possess the promise and cross the Jordan River into their land. It is here that the first "Amen" appears, spoken by women who agree to yield to the Lord's examination of their purity. "Then the woman is to say, 'Amen. So be it'" (Num 5:22). She is saying what God says is true, expressing her agreement with the Lord and strengthening her people's faith.

Leadership is to come from these homes, raised to be patient, honest, able to nourish children to walk with light, holding the mystery of the faith, to be a faithful husband of one woman (1 Tim 3:3–9). They will be found among all nations, among the rich living in comfort and the poor seeking a sip of clean water, in homes, deserts, mountains, valleys, and seashores. Theirs will be a minority voice called to stand in a world desecrating all that is decent and just.

The great mystery of God never concerns his plan with a majority of people. All the birds, animals, the sun and stars, and all creation go on as they were made to do because it is his will for them, uncaring about the changing politics of churches and governments. His living waters are pristine flowing down from above to enter a world polluting his words, yet continue in his purpose to seek out a small faithful group.

When the Israelites arrived at the hills and valleys full of pomegranates filled with jewels of seeds, figs, and heavy with clusters of grapes, they wept, feeling outnumbered and unable to enter the promised land. They mourned when they listened to those who said it would be impossible because, even after the long journey led by God's glory, their faith did not see tomorrow.

Joshua and Caleb tore their clothes when they saw how they doubted, lamenting as if someone was about to die. God said he would do this and he will fulfill what he said, they told the people. Believe the Lord. Don't fear the people in that land. Their protection has departed from them. The Lord is with us.

Who has believed our report? And to whom has the arm of the Lord been revealed (Isa 53:1)?

Those who thirst have believed (Matt 5:3–12).

Those who murmured doubt were left in the wilderness to die (Num 14).

Moses broke the first tablets that God's finger had written because the people stopped trusting in God and made an image to worship. Three thousand people died that day. Moses went back up the mountain and interceded again, demonstrating the need for Yom Kippur, the chance to return again to the Lord. Still God refused to go with Israel. Moses refused to lead without the Lord's presence. The Lord said he would send an angel with them, but he would not go because the people reflected their lack of belief.

The east wind that caused the sea to roll back for the Israelites blasted them through the wilderness with withering gusts of heat (Gen 41:6; Job 1:19; Jer 4:11; Exod 14:21). Yet God sustained them. They knew his works, but those who died did not yet know his ways.

Moses pressed: "Lord, teach me your ways that I may know you and find favor with you. Teach us to live wisely," he prayed, imploring the Lord to come to his people, and they would dance and their eyes sparkle again if his loveliness rested on them. The Lord told Moses he would go with him and give him rest.

Moses called upon heaven and earth as witness to his people, setting before them life and death, reiterating the choice between the tree of life or the tree forbidden by God in the garden of Eden. He knew that he was speaking the last words he was given and would no longer be able to lead the people. He said, "Give ear, oh heavens and I will speak, and hear, oh earth, the words of my mouth" (Deut 30:19; 31:28; 32:1). He called for God's Spirit to continue testifying to them. Paul too charged his people "in the presence of God and Jesus and the elect angels" to continue the instructions because it was meant for all generations (1 Tim 2:21).

The Lord walks among his gardens, gathering flowers, sweet-scented herbs, burning from a bush to call his friends to him. He follows his people across oceans to other lands, seeking each one to bring them home again. Those struggling to sing with angels prevailed and entered his rest.

> And God saw everything that he had made, and behold, it was very good. (Gen 1:31)

The Lord separated the light of day from the dark of night on the fourth day. In his fourth commandment, he separated the day of Shabbat from the rest of the week, beginning in darkness through daylight to the next evening. Keep my Sabbaths, the Lord instructed, that "you may know that I am God who makes you holy." On the seventh day, all that had been created is to be enjoyed.

All of the Word's creations entered a banquet of plenty prepared for them before they were made. In the throne room, the Father, Son, and Holy Spirit acting together shaped the forms, hues, and purposes in an intricate alliance propagating offerings to sustain health. The lilies are so beautiful to the Word that he clothed them in splendor (Matt 6:28). The birds were colored with soft feathers, so precious that each one is held by God's presence when it falls (Matt 10:29).

The raven was graced with the commission to bring food and water to God's prophet Elijah where he rested by the stream Cherith. We're not told where the raven went when it was sent from the ark. Observations of Rabbi Hezekiah ben Manoah in the thirteenth century suggest that the raven naturally cleans up the environment. If the water was subsiding, the bird would land on all that was strewn on ground around the ark.

The glossy-feathered raven was not suited to be a sacrifice, but the Lord is so near he hears their cry and gives food to their young birds when they hunger. Consider the ravens, for they neither sow nor reap, and yet God feeds them (Luke 12:24).

Each part of creation was prepared to blaze with God's breath and bring the whole into a celebrated oneness. By the sixth day of creation, harmony was brought out of darkness and the angels, the sons of the morning, sang joyously throughout the universes. The waters were brought together to nourish life. The cycle of creative events set in motion the ability to receive renewing life from heaven. Starlight continued with new births. The time givers, the sun and moon and winds (all of which determine temperature), brought each of the six days of creating nearer to the Lord, and man into the serenity of the Shabbat day.

Plants first appeared on the third day, Tuesday, thought to be renewed every Tuesday ever since. Their fragrance carries the aroma of the garden of Eden, calming the soul with the blessing of restoration. Around the Shabbat table, the spices delight the spirit and body, drawing in the strength of the Lord.

The earth brought forth grass, the herb yielding seed (Gen 1:12) for the cattle, the herb for man to bring food from the earth (Ps 104:14). The plants would aid man in their prayer offerings. The light would delight in their growth for the palate of food. Treasures cradled in the changing seasons developed gifted fragrance, aloes to soothe skin, anise to cool high fevers, balsam trees to offer balm, horseradish and coriander to be present on the Passover table. Sweetly scented hyssop would be used for cleansing and to mark the doorposts of those whose names were written in the Book of Life. Myrrh anoints the dead, treats a sore throat so song can be sung, and purifies a woman to beautify her for her king.

A tall evergreen with long leaves, the myrtle brings the scent of Eden. The starlike flowers give round berries with seeds dispersed by birds. The myrtle is one of the four sacred plants of Sukkot. During the temple times, worshipers waved a myrtle leaf with boughs of willow and palm to rejoice before the Lord on each day of the festival (Lev 23:40).

Cinnamon is cultivated for flavor as well as its properties of lowering blood pressure and bringing remembrance of God's goodness. When the holy Shabbat comes, the soul aches for the infinite purpose of God's ways to confirm their work, the scents of paradise bring certainty that mistakes can be fixed.

Broad-leafed grasses grew high on smooth stems called to gather together along estuaries to build up the ground for shrub to grow and otters and beavers, bitterns and warblers to find shelter. Fields of reed grew to slow rushing water to a trickle as the root systems purify the water in a clean effluent.

Strong winds blow on the reeds and people trample through them. Weakened and unable to stand tall in the sunlight or receive rain through a bent stalk into their leaves, they become vulnerable, knowing there's no strength left. The Lord will not break a bruised reed. His hand holds up its weight, sustaining it. "I will make a way for you to fulfill my will for you," he says (Phil 2:13–14). Hard-pressed on every side but not crushed, struck down but not destroyed, the life he willed would prevail (2 Cor 4:8–9). Knowing our frame, he remembers that we are only reeds in a storm all around us (Ps 103). All his billows and waves pass over us, so heavily the wound is felt in our bones, yet his song is with us (Ps 42).

God gave part of his name to land bordered by the Mediterranean Sea, a country called Israel enjoined with the people in mutual well-being to continue their generations. Just as he chose the garden of Eden for a home for the first people, here is where he will bless them.

The Lord speaks to the land, mountains of Israel, you will sprout your branches and bear your fruit for my people Israel. I will turn toward you and you will be tilled and sown. I will multiply the house of Israel and the cities will be inhabited, the ruins rebuilt. I will cause my people Israel to possess you and you will be their inheritance. Never again will you make them childless (Ezek 36:8–12).

The land responds to the people (Isa 27:6). Moving to Israel, ascending to Jerusalem, is referred to as *aliya*, "going up." Leaving is going down. With each wave of *aliya*, or Jewish people returning to Israel, there has been an increase in rainfall, waking and blossoming the land with fruit to fill shops around the world. Seeds left by a palm tree two thousand years ago were discovered by archaeologists in Masada. They were set in a drawer until 2005 when they were planted by the Arava Institute for Environmental Studies at Kibbutz Ketura in Israel. Astonishing everyone, the palm tree sprouted and grew to pollinate a female palm tree, which has produced the fruit of dates.[2]

The land flourishes with fig trees, producing two harvests a year. Holding the smooth fresh fig in the hand, its fresh green scent smells like the day creation was first blessed by the sun's warmth. Biting into its sweet juice is synonymous with God's promise. The early crop comes in spring around the time of Passover, even before the leaves have unfurled. The fruits come again in the fall as the people draw near to Rosh Hashanah, Yom Kippur, and Sukkot.

Blossoming became a symbol of security and shade from the heat throughout Scripture. "Like the first fruit on the fig tree, in its first season, I saw your fathers" (Hos 9:10). The growth of the fig covered shame: "Then the eyes of both were opened, and they knew that they were naked; and they sewed fig leaves together and made themselves aprons" (Gen 3:7).

Jesus anticipates the time when Judah and Israel live in safety, every man under his vine and his fig tree (1 Kgs 4:25). He calls to Nathanael, who was sitting under a fig tree "like a true Israelite" (John 1:48–50). The nation is warned of destruction through Habakkuk and Haggai with the image of fig trees stripped of their fruit. The fig flourishes in times of restoration and withers in times of judgment. The Lord would curse a fig tree for having no fruit (Mark 11:12–21) and use the fig as a metaphor for recognizing the times. "From the fig tree learn its lesson: as soon as its branch becomes tender and puts forth its leaves, you know that summer is near" (Matt 24:32). Be watchful of the people's return to Israel. It tells us the time of Messiah's return is nearing.

Before the flood came, Noah left the door of the ark open to welcome others should they be called. Noah's Hebrew name is Noach, meaning "rest" or "comfort." The Zohar tells us that Noah's family withstood the temptations

---

2. Roach, *Methuselah*, paras. 1–2, 5.

of the world around them because they kept the Shabbat rest and heaven's power came down to uphold them.

After the flood, when the dove returned with an olive branch, Noah and all his crew were reassured that life would continue. The olive branch became the symbol of the peace the Lord offers, and the bird of the prophetic vision of the Spirit coming on Jesus after his baptism by John, the certain hope of a better tomorrow. The dove found a place to rest the third time it was sent from the ark. The nation of Israel faced countless exiles, inquisitions, pogroms, and genocide, but like the dove they return to find rest among Israel's groves of olive trees.

When his ministry was nearly completed, Jesus prayed on the Mount of Olives, east of Jerusalem, where he knelt in a garden shaded by olive trees and prayed for the light in heaven to prevail over his own wish to be spared (Matt 26:39). There beneath the olives he entered God's will that he be the Shabbat light, drawing lives to him.

For he is our peace, who has made us both one, and has broken down the dividing wall of hostility, by abolishing in his flesh the law of commandments and ordinances, that he might create in himself one new man in place of the two, so making peace, and might reconcile us both to God in one body through the cross, thereby bringing the hostility to an end (Eph 2:14–16).

Paul spoke of the olive tree growing from a seed to illustrate heaven's work among humanity. He spoke of the fullness of Israel and the people of other nations flourishing together under God's holy light. Non-Jews are wild branches grafted into the tree to share its root. "Don't boast as if you were better than the natural branches," he warned. "Remember that you are not supporting the root. The root is supporting you."

In God's design, the Israelites and those of other nations who know God could never be whole without each other. They were each a single note of a song, an instrument part of a great orchestra. One God made them all. His light would dawn as the morning sun rising gradually, gently illuminating a way for them to have devotion together as more truths brighten the day before night falls. The olive tree's roots grow deep, drinking of the living water's righteousness, sanctifying, purifying, enabling a rebirth to see God's way to peace.

"Rejoice, O Gentiles, with his people!" (Rom 15:10).

The transformations means cutting the stems so they will bind together.Both the wild and natural become aware of the day's sunlight, the raindrops, and the movement of song around them in great gratitude to God. If unwound or unpruned, nothing binds, nothing grows. A branch withers, choked by arrogance.

When the days drew near for Jesus to be taken up to heaven, he set his face toward the stones that built Jerusalem (Luke 9:51). The stone the builder despised emerges as the cornerstone (Ps 118:22), once again shedding light on all the nations of the world. As the days draw near for his return, God's people in every corner of earth turn toward the holy city as the Holy Spirit brings to mind the things the Word spoke.

"To what will you compare me?" the Lord asks. He is there in the flashing storm and in the calm sea. He's expressed in the bird feeding her chicks from his banquet. There in the cleansing fire and the fire that consumes with judgment, he commands us to "have no other gods," and to create no other truth to follow.

The light from the throne above beckons, still a burning light encompassing the heritage of Jerusalem. For David's sake, the Lord gave him a lamp in Jerusalem (1 Kgs 15:4), the city where God chose to put his name (11:36). For Jerusalem's sake, the prophets would not be silent until her righteousness went forth like brightness and her salvation like a burning torch (Isa 62:10). No battle could extinguish the lamp of Israel for her heirs (2 Sam 21:17).

The light came from the Word. "And we have the prophetic word made more sure. You will do well to pay attention to this as to a lamp shining in a dark place, until the day dawns and the morning star rises in your hearts" (2 Pet 1:19).

Adonai Tz'va'ot, God the ruler of the angelic hosts of heaven, had spoken. The Lord has not forgotten (Lev 25:13). Through his Son, each olive has needed oil. Every member, Jew or gentile, is credited with righteousness if they believe; a good example is Abraham, who righteously listened to the Lord even before he was circumcised a Jew.

In his letter to his people, Jesus told of God and the angels watching over the church, angels going throughout the world and reporting back to Jesus. Jesus tells the church of Sardis that what they began has not yet been fulfilled. It has not yet produced mature fruit. They had a reputation of being alive, pouring energy into activities, but not finishing the work of Jesus.

"Wake up!" he says. Be alert to all the Word had given to them. Hold fast to the few good things remaining, because Jesus sees this dying among the people. He tells them to remember their first love. He urges them to discern God's concerns (Rev 3:1–6).

The called brought offerings to the Creator. Frankincense was offered on a special incense altar in services of the tabernacle and the temple. Its fragrance perfumed the sanctuary (Exod 30:34) and accompanied the meal offering (Lev 2:1). Presented with the showbread (Lev 24:7), it symbolized the prayers of the people (Rev 5:8). Frankincense and myrrh were gifted to the infant Jesus because of his willingness to offer himself as a sacrifice for the innermost prayers of the people.

David vowed he would not bring any offering to the Lord his God that cost him nothing (2 Sam 24:24). *Minchah*, a meal offering, devoted the fruits of man's work to God.[3] A representative piece was burnt on the fire of the altar and the rest eaten by the priests. The offerings were made from domestic animals trained to submit to instruction. The offering is a substitution for the person needing purification by fire and requiring training to submit, a "soothing aroma to the Lord." Every family sent someone to Jerusalem with an offering, where they would learn more of God's word.

Now they bring themselves, the first fruits of the harvest offering the whole of their lives. Honor the Lord with your first fruits. *Karbanot*, translated as "offering," comes from the root qof-resh-bet, meaning "to draw near."

So fierce is the love of God's appointed for their people that both Moses and Paul would offer to be blotted out of God's book for their sake (Exod 32:32; Rom 9:3). "For your sake . . . I am poured out like a drink offering," Paul said as he finished the race (2 Tim 4:6).

Israel is described as the "first fruits of God's harvest" (Jer 2:3). Firstfruits are the first to come in time, dedicated to God, who by faith we know will provide more for the greater harvest to follow. Israel was the beginning of the redemption harvested among all nations, brought forth by the word of truth (Jas 1:18).

Scripture first records a drink offering when God changed Jacob's name to Israel, telling him that a nation and community of nations shall come from him and kings shall spring from him. Jacob set up a stone pillar, poured out a drink offering, and poured oil on it (Gen 35:11–14).

Pouring out a drink offering foreshadowed the blood Jesus spilled on the cross. "This cup which is poured out for you is the new covenant in my blood" (Luke 22:20). The tithe God asks is for the whole self to be presented to live for him. Test me in this, he says, "and see if I will not throw open the floodgates of heaven and pour out so much blessing that there will not be room enough to store it" (Mal 3:10). Further,

> For you are all sons of light and sons of the day . . . But, since we belong to the day, let us be sober, and put on the breastplate of faith and love, and for a helmet the hope of salvation (1 Thess 5:5, 8)

---

3. Jewish Virtual Library, "Jewish Practices and Rituals," para. 16.

To enter a temple built of stones made by the sea and tapestry from the hands of skilled women, the high priest was prescribed to sew the design of the pomegranates to the hem of his robe in blue, purple, and scarlet yarns, with bells of gold between them (Exod 28:33–35). Aaron would wear the robe when he ministered. As he moved, the sound of the bells was heard when he entered the holy place before the Lord, so that he would not die.

The robe is a sign of the glory of God, unstained by sin or condemnation. It is a high honor for a man to be arrayed by this robe, this truth displayed with fringes (*tzizith*), referring to the justice of the Creator's laws. The bells sewn between the pomegranates serve as reminders to listen to the danger of approaching God's holiness without first seeking the mercy of his covenant. Insincere hearts are pursued by destroying angels. "Her pursuers have all overtaken her in the midst of her distress" (Lam 1:3), therefore pray that he is merciful and forgiving of iniquities (Ps 78:38).

Rows of four hundred pomegranates adorned Solomon's Temple and its pillars, declaring God's promised covenant. The seeds of the covenant would be carried into all the world through the words of the high priest Jesus. The prophet Ezekiel would announce, "Then all the princes of the sea will step down from their thrones, and remove their robes, and strip off their embroidered garments; they will clothe themselves with trembling" (Ezek 26:16). Embroidered with worldly knowledge, the robes will be cast away. Jesus warned that the scribes and Pharisees do their work to be seen of men and enlarge the borders of their robes (Matt 23:5). They expand their own eloquence.

The Word brought the law from the desert, inscribed with the heart of God blooming in a dry thirsty land, to be carried in the hands of a man who saw a glimpse of God that no one else would know. The story of the many footsteps pressed into the sand leading to the holy habitation was shared with the world. Some never made it, left dead in the desert sun. The Word brought strength for those who entered his Shabbat peace.

Throughout the Scriptures, God calls for his people to rise up and throw off their old selves, and his creation reflects this theme. "Little girl I say to you arise!" the Lord said to the daughter of a ruler of the synagogue who was thought to be dead (Matt 9:25). "Rise, take up your bed and walk," he said to the man at the pool of Bethesda (John 5:8). "Awake O sleeper, and arise from the dead, and Christ shall give you light" (Eph 5:14);" "Awake, awake, put on your strength, O Zion; put on your beautiful garments" (Isa 52:1). Because the creations "will all grow old like a garment" (Heb 1:11), he will roll up the universe like a robe, and then spread it out as a new garment (Psalm 102:26).

Light

In the book of Revelation, John writes: "Then I saw a new heaven and a new earth; for the first heaven and the first earth had passed away... I saw the holy city, the new Jerusalem, coming down out of heaven from God, prepared as a bride beautifully dressed for her husband... One of the seven angels... spoke to me, saying, 'Come, I will show you the Bride, the wife of the Lamb'" (Rev 21:1, 2, 9). And according to King David, those who persist to accuse and reject, though they were prayed for, will be clothed with a coat of cursing soaked into their body like water, a garment of shame and isolation soaked like oil into their bone (Ps 109:18–19).

The years descend through narrow paths pressed in by grief, passing remembrance of sun-warmed skies bringing tall trees with shade, the cool splash of raindrops scenting the wind, a table set for family, the dependable moon outside the window, a hand to hold, laughter that never worried. Watching it pass away, nothing more to long for, there appears no belief ahead in the world's ways, only yearning brought low into the hard place where the song of the angels has no singers to join them.

God's heart is that each name he calls will see their place at his table, which has been prepared from the fruits of creation. The Shabbat candlelight invites into eternal life.

The betrothed waits for her bridegroom, preparing with incense and myrrh, watching the sky as the moon passes through her phases, listening for his voice as the new is unrolled, swallowing up mortality and putting on immortality.

Jerusalem, the city that will provide peace, still rises above the sun in the minds of her people. Unfolding down out of heaven, the holy city will cascade the bright glory of God, its brilliance shining like a precious jewel. An angel has measured the city, its gates, and its walls, which are as pure as glass. The glory of God gives it light, and Jesus is its lamp. The glory of the nations will ascend here and walk by its light. There will be no night, so the gates will never be shut.

Only those whose names are written in the Book of Life will enter (Rev 21:10–27).

2

BREATH

> It is the spirit in a man, the breath of the Almighty,
> that makes him understand. (Job 32:8)

WHEN GOD BREATHED, TIME began to vibrate and hearts began to beat. The whole of creation was ordered through God breathing light, heavens, and earth into being. On the evening and morning of the sixth day, God in his throne room tenderly took earth and carefully formed man. He breathed his own breath, the breath of life, into man and put him in the well-watered garden in the east called Eden.

God called the man Adam, the first of mankind, *min ha'adamah* in the Hebrew language (formed from the earth). *Adamah* means cultivatable soil because, as man grows, God gardens seeds of light within him and prunes man so that he can cultivate both earth and souls to produce fruit.

The Lord said, "Let us make man in our image, after our likeness" (Gen 1:26). Maimonides, the influential Torah scholar of the middle ages, points to the fact that God does not have a physical body. There is nothing that resembles God, who is beyond comprehension. Maimonides wrote that making man in his image references a much deeper reflection of the characteristics of the living God:

> All these worlds send forth reflections of their light upon the earth which they receive from other worlds higher and more glorious than themselves, which in their totality form the Grand Archetypal Man, whose image, all who bear it, are called Man.

Until Eve was separated and built into a woman, man did not realize his capacity to love, commit, and care for something. Eve elicited the protectiveness in man and inspiration to build and prepare for tomorrow. She radiated with the union of marriage. Presented to her husband by her father, God, she resonated in the way a father and mother prepare their daughter and bring her to her wedding, establishing the way of marriage. "They are no longer two, but one flesh" (Mark 10:8).

Adam recognized she was part of him and said, "this at last is bone of my bone and flesh of my flesh" (Gen 2:23), words that cherished Eve and drew her to him. He took her into his heart, saying she shall be called woman. "Therefore a man leaves his father and his mother and cleaves to his wife, and they become one flesh" (2:24).

Commanding not to break the bond between those he joins together, the Lord says that "he who finds a wife finds a good thing, and obtains favor from the Lord" (Prov 18:22). It was God who decided if Adam needed a wife. God presented her and defined their relationship, each of them a flame burning with his purpose, walking in the light of his lamp. He set the precedent of waiting for God to choose and form relationship in shared fellowship with the Lord. Believers would be told not to bond to unbelievers. They are told not to lie to or about each other, because they bear the image of God.

The mysteries of heaven were experienced by the first of mankind in the garden of Eden. The Lord illuminated the complexity of ecology, the animal kingdoms he so tenderly made, the purpose of plants, rocks, currents of the river, and the wisdom that founded the heavens. The couple basked in the hymns of the angels praising the Creator.

The Word walked with them in Eden and stood with them as they enjoyed the refreshing river. He shared the map of the constellations, the movement of the sun and moon, and the calculation of seasons and cycles. He taught them that every particle is integrally entwined into one harmonious energy because he, the Lord, is one.

"Because the Lord your God walks in the midst of your camp, to save you and to give up your enemies before you, therefore your camp must be holy, that he may not see anything indecent among you, and turn away from you" (Deut 23:14). To welcome the Lord's presence, everywhere we occupy is to be preserved as holy in body and in action, no unclean thing found there and no obscene language used because, like the garden of Eden, the glory walks where relationship with him creates an oasis of grace.

As anxious to be with his disciples as he had been to walk with his new creation in the garden of Eden, the Lord delights in those searching his knowledge. In biblical language, *orah* and *simhah* ("light" and "joy") are synonymous. It was the gift to Adam and Eve, a light and joy from heaven that brought them together.

> How you are fallen from heaven, O Day Star, son of Dawn! How you are cut down to the ground, you who laid the nations low! (Isa 14:12)

But the enemy of God disliked this union. Subtle and manipulative, the moment Adam and Eve became a unified couple, the serpent appeared.

In a fit of rebellion, he made war with the angels of light. Satan was cast out of heaven. Jesus said, "I saw Satan fall like lightning from heaven" (Luke 10:18), and in the book of Revelation, Satan is seen as "a star that had fallen from the sky to the earth" (Rev 9:1).

The wonder of it was recorded as an enormous red dragon whose tail swept a third of the stars out of the sky and flung them to earth. The great dragon was hurled down, the ancient serpent called Satan who leads the world astray. Satan was stripped of his garment of light. He could not replicate the image of God, so he hid himself in the serpent.

Before Adamah was separated into male and female, the Lord told Adamah that he could eat from every tree in the garden of Eden, but commanded him not to eat from the tree of the knowledge of good and evil. This fruit brings death. After saying this, the Lord said it isn't good for the man to be alone. Then he brought Eve out of the structure of Adam's bones to be a suitable companion for him.

At an opportune moment, Satan found Eve under rustling leaves dappled by the sun's rays, there where the first flowers scented the land and she heard the first melodic birds sing, the grasses whisper, and the river ripple with fresh water. Satan enticed the woman to take the forbidden fruit. She reached out her hand and grasped its fruit. Biting into its juice, she ate from the tree bringing death.

Eve was now changed; she turned to offer it to Adam, bone of her bone, and he ate it. The river's gurgling seemed to silence, and the songs of birds sounded suddenly distant. The rustling leaves seemed a disarray of growth they no longer understood. The soft breeze they were accustomed to carried foreboding as they heard the Lord's voice call and tremble their hearts with fear.

The struggle between the forces ruling heaven and those hurled out of heaven became internalized in both man and woman. Adam and Eve had to leave the garden of Eden and toil to make a living before returning as dust into the ground, and their breath returned to God, who had given it (Eccl 12:7). As it is said of woman, "A garden locked is my sister, my bride, a garden locked, a fountain sealed" (Song 4:12).

A cherubim with the faces of a man, a lion, an ox, and an eagle drew a sword and posted at the entrance of the garden of Eden. Now, the way to the tree of life is guarded so no one who is not cleansed and restored to God can live eternally with heaven. Satiated in heaven, the flaming sword turns in every direction to keep the way of the tree of life.

Still knowing that God had joined them together, Adam and Eve accepted the terrifying loss of walking intimately with the Lord in his garden of Eden and built a new life. Heaven had been an open vault, a continuation of their daily world. But now the celestial atmosphere became a place Satan swarmed in search of souls he could devour. The descent of man hurled into a maelstrom of downward falling, rushing winds pulling every created thing downward into the pit. Shame came upon Adam and Eve and all of their future progeny. There was nothing man could do to fix it.

The Lord brings beauty up from ashes, refining silver and jewels out of dust. He used the descent into death opened by the tree of knowledge to bring about the ascent to the glory of heaven. He would reach down into the maelstrom and gather male and female, young and old, recorded in the Book of Life in his throne room and raise them to the light. Those seeing through the dimmed glass, knowing in part, shall know face to face (1 Cor 13:12).

The Lord told of his plan for a redeemer to the grieving Adam and Eve, whose mistake cost their children the delight of heaven. The Midrash Rabbah Breishis 18:4 says that God spoke with Adam and Eve in the Hebrew language, and they spoke it to their descendants. In that language, there is no word for coincidence. There is knowledge that God is in heaven delivering and repairing.

Adam and Eve kept the traits of the language. They understood *mitzvah*, which came to be understood as "command," but literally means "directions for the journey." Every *mitzvah* is an act that binds thought and action to the will of God. *Rasha*, often used to mean "wicked," literally means "lost from the path." There was no word for "fair" because unfair things would continue happening, even to the best of humanity, that in time God would work for the good of all mankind.

When God breathed, he brought about union of lives. The very first human relationship was between man and woman. After they were made, God said it is very good, and he made rest on the next day (Gen 2:1–3). When Adam and Eve left paradise, they retained longing for its pristine world. Their souls sought Shabbat to find opportunity to return to their source, having to find peace within its future hope. Spending time with the Lord means seeing a future comforted by the champion, who would come and restore relationship with heaven.

On Shabbat, God stopped creating and asserting changes on his world. On Shabbat, man enters the gate with melodies of praise and joins God, leaving the work world to rest and stop interfering with nature. His deepest soul is freed to come into his destiny with the inheritance of rest in God's oneness.

Adam and Eve remembered heaven and passed the knowledge to their offspring. At the time of Adam and Eve's grandson, Enosh, born to their son Seth, the people began to call upon the name of the Lord (Gen 4:26). Seven generations after Adam, Enoch walked with God. He exalted God, knowing the movements of the creation which God had taught to Adam and Eve. He knew about ministering angels and the light of heaven, where the Holy One resides. His parents told him of the garden of Eden that is guarded by a sword, and made him aware of the promised redeemer.

"You will seek me and find me; when you seek me with all your heart, I will be found by you" (Jer 29:13). Adam and his wife Eve were the first to experience exile. Like Adamah, the Lord's people were formed and then brought into a land God had prepared for them. They too were given commands to protect them, and if these commands were not obeyed, they would die. They too were exiled from their land and told that the Lord would make a way to return.

Children of Israel parted to thread throughout the earth, each a soul bringing the nation's tenets, now bringing their children to learn of the faces in the distant past. The stories rise from the ground like flowers after long winter frosts, speaking to every generation, refusing to be silenced, saying no, it is not a crime to know the Lord, whose light glows even under the cloak of a lowly servant.

The snake could not divide them from God. Nothing silences the words; no cruelty, threat, or grave. They speak with a torch lit by the thunderous flames breathed from heaven. Yea, thou dost light my lamp; the Lord my God lightens my darkness (Ps 18:28; 2 Sam 22:29).

With the task of restoring mankind to his image, the Word spoke to Abraham, who received the knowledge and believed him. He wrote upon Moses' heart, and the majestic light in the Torah came down from the angelic realm. Moses told Israel that God would raise a prophet from among them. "You must listen to him," he said (Deut 18:15). The redeemer's words breathed through every experience of man, his kings and shepherds, his prophets and prisoners, breathing through their depths of sorrow with billowing winds, making a way for flights of soaring praise.

The words of the apostle defined these kinsmen. They are Israelites, and to them belong the sonship, the glory, the covenants, the giving of the law, the worship, and the promises; to them belong the patriarchs, and of their race, according to the flesh, is the Christ (Rom 9:4–5).

Delighting to hear their prayer, the Lord told them to turn to him and he would abide with them. From the practices, gentiles would understand sacredness of God abiding in the home. In the domain of home, the gifts of each individual are brought forth to find what moves them to come together with others to bring wholeness to the world.

Family lines continued as the heavens separated and the boundary between holiness and earth hardened, separating mankind from the knowledge of the Word's presence. Humanity would search deep into the blue sky, but heaven is veiled. The world spun around the light of the sun and populations expanded with less sensitivity to God's presence, asserting themselves against God's ways, and looking to the created worlds to satisfy their happiness.

The human race began feeling that there never had been a Creator who cared, as the unison of light throughout creation shattered into fragments. Humanity's common language splintered into many foreign tongues. The enemy of God pursued the chosen nation into a long history among those professing God's name yet turning their back on the people of Israel, leaving them to stand alone as their deaths rose in smoke to heaven's highest realms.

The Lord was grieved. What he had joined together was divided. The Lord determined it would be better for the hearts of people to be brought back together. Bringing the people back into his inner dimension of holiness would release the mercy within the image of God and our soul desire, separated from its fulfillment, would be realized.

Solomon dedicated the temple with extended prayer to all people who are not Israelites but have turned to the Lord so that all the people of the earth would know his name (1 Kgs 8:41–43). The invitation to non-Jews was reiterated when God sent light to rise in the sky and lead foreigners in the east to come to Jerusalem to ask, "Where is the one who has been born king of the Jews?"

Jesus' death tore the veil that separated the Holy of Holies and Jews and gentiles streamed into one flock under one shepherd, fulfilling God's plan for humanity. His purpose was to create in himself one new man out of the two, thus making peace, and in one body to reconcile both of them to God through the cross (Eph 2:15–16).

He manifests himself to those who love him so that the works of the devil are destroyed (John 14:21; 3:8). The Word raised apostles from his chosen nation to appeal to humanity. He breathed out Scripture and sent those who would handle the holy words with genuine care. Avoid godless chatter, Paul wrote to Timothy, because those who indulge in it will become more and more ungodly. Their teaching will spread like gangrene (2 Tim 2:16–17).

In his 1959 book *The Jewish World in the Time of Jesus*, Charles Guignebert wrote:

> The very hostility of the early church to the synagogue, and the tenacity with which the Christian clergy sought to guard against any possible invasion of the Jewish spirit or of Jewish propaganda, were often determining factors in the decisions and even in the development of the institutions of the Christian church.[1]

Cut off from being nourished by the flow of living water, entire parts of the body of Jesus withered. Forgetting that the message is forgiveness and restoring to God, the Crusades used force to capture the holy place of Jerusalem. Slaughtering Muslims, Jews, and other Christians in Jerusalem in 1099 AD, one hundred thousand men held the city for nearly a hundred years. The thinking persisted across oceans into indigenous lands, still remembered in perception of the Christian religion crushing national identity.

God does not forgive those who do not turn back to him. Are we to freely forgive the persecutors, the Hamans, the Nazis, the church that did not stand with Jews, the violence against daughters, the obscene mockery against sons? God says to forgive those who acknowledge their mistakes (Luke 17:3–37).

The heavens opened to John when he was a captive, and he saw the four living creatures with the faces of a lion, an ox, a man, and an eagle. He watched as they gave glory, honor, and thanks to the one who sits on the throne for all eternity. When they sang "holy holy is the Lord God Amighty," the twenty-four elders fell and worshiped toward the Lord, "Worthy art thou, our Lord and God, to receive glory and honor and power, for thou didst create all things, and by thy will they existed and were created" (Rev 4:8, 11).

Inside the mysteries of heaven, the choir of the angelic beings triggers the church to praise, bow, and behold the Lord. From the descent into divisions, the Spirit of God works in unknown dimensions, opening his palms with words perfumed by the tree of life, uncovering the awaited promises as heaven's anticipation amplifies on earth. Who can comprehend the breadth and reach, the length, or rise to the height and plumb to the depth of the Lord (Eph 3:18).

His Spirit moved across the Jewish and gentile believers who, for nearly two thousand years, worshiped in worlds apart. Unparalleled in all

---

1. Guignebert, *Jewish World*, 2.

of history, now seeing the ways the teachings had been wrongly distributed at the expense of heritage, they saw how it breaks the heart of the Lord who had borne all this on the stake of execution. The Lord gave his peace as he prepared the Shabbat, a peace that will continue guarding Shabbat as a holy day on the new earth (Isa 66:23).

He called his own into a space where they can leave the world outside and meet with him. Coming from many backgrounds, from the north and south, drawn from the east and west, presenting themselves before the Lord to feel his light on their faces, they sought the concerns of the Lord. "For we are his workmanship, created in Christ Jesus for good works, which God prepared beforehand, that we should walk in them" (Eph 2:10).

God accomplished union between people by first making the human to need others. If he was made alone, man would have thought himself self-sufficient. By creating the human being, God created yearning, giving, needing, and affection. By making them with different attributes and various gifts among the nations, they would learn to give and receive with understanding, broadening their own experience to bring balance to growth.

In traditional Hebrew, there is no concept for independence because, apart from God, nothing can be done. He is the source of everything. The Lord commanded his Israelites to love strangers who came to God because they too knew what it is to have been exiled and foreigners when they were in Egypt (Deut 10:19). In addition, do not abandon the teaching of your mother (Prov 1:8), as national identity is upheld in the home.

The Greco-Roman world differed. Roman society was shockingly brutal and sexualized. Under Greco-Roman law, it was common to drown a newborn baby, or to expose it to the elements until it died or was devoured by animals. In Ashkelon, the Lawrence E. Stager excavation uncovered a sewer large enough for a person to stand up in that ran under a bathhouse. It had become clogged in the sixth century by the bones of nearly a hundred newborn babies killed and thrown into the sewer. Infanticide among Greeks and Romans was considered birth control. Revealing the attitude is a letter written from a father, Hilarion, on June 17, 1 BC, to his pregnant wife Alis:

> Know that I am still in Alexandria. And do not worry if they all come back and I remain in Alexandria. I ask and beg you to take good care of our baby son, and as soon as I receive payment I will send it up to you. If you are delivered of child [before I get home], if it is a boy keep it, if a girl discard it. You have sent me word, "Don't forget me." How can I forget you. I beg you not to worry.[2]

---

2. Lewis, *Life in Egypt*, 54.

Ashkelon is a Mediterranean seaport bringing in trade flows of olive oil, timber, wine, wool, textiles, garden crops, fish, and wheat from other ports and nearby valleys. A villa overlooking terraced gardens was also excavated to discover hundreds of sherds from a collection of ceramic oil lamps in a small room. These were etched with erotic and mythological motifs made from molds arousing hetero- and homosexual thoughts as they burned their false flames. The lamps show that sodomy and pederasty were acceptable as long as the initiator was of privileged social status.

Greco-Roman attitudes toward human sexuality differed markedly from the attitudes of those who knew Scripture and held the relationship between man and woman as sacred, established by God before they entered creation's first Shabbat rest. Fidelity was held highly among believers and celibacy considered a devotion to God surpassing all earthly relationship.

Husbands of the time could force wives into the deadly risk of abortion. There was no knowledge of bacteria. Infection or ingesting poison to cause miscarriage caused many deaths of both mother and child. The Jewish teaching that declared killing a child as a sin equivalent to murder was considered irrelevant.

In his second-century letter, A Plea for the Christians, Athenagoras of Athens addressed the emperors saying these women who bring on abortion commit murder and will have to give an account to God.

> For it does not belong to the same person to regard the very foetus in the womb as a created being, and therefore an object of God's care, and when it has passed into life, to kill it; and not to expose an infant, because those who expose them are chargeable with child-murder, and on the other hand, when it has been reared to destroy it.[3]

He begins his letter by saying,

> In your empire, greatest of sovereigns, different nations have different customs and laws; and no one is hindered by law or fear of punishment from following his ancestral usages, however ridiculous these may be. A citizen of Ilium calls Hector a god, and pays divine honours to Helen, taking her for Adrasteia. The Lacedaemonian venerates Agamemnon as Zeus, and Phylonoe the daughter of Tyndarus; and the man of Tenedos worships Tennes. The Athenian sacrifices to Erechtheus as Poseidon.[4]

---

3. Athenagoras, "Athenagoras of Athens," para. 76.
4. Athenagoras, "Athenagoras of Athens," para. 1.

But for us who are called Christians, you have not in like manner cared, he says. "You allow us to be harassed, plundered, and persecuted, the multitude making war upon us for our name alone."[5]

He laid his statement before the emperor beseeching him to understand the truth of what they believe. "If, then, Zeus is fire, and Hera the earth, and Aidoneus the air, and Nestis water, and these are elements—fire, water, air—none of them is a god, neither Zeus, nor Hera, nor Aidoneus; for from matter separated into parts by God is their constitution and origin: 'Fire, water, earth, and the air's gentle height, And harmony with these.'"[6]

The faith made streams into the world, flowing because Constantine responded to the growing multitude of binding relationships that held life as sacred. In his book *The Rise of Christianity*, Rodney Stark explored how Christianity gained ascendancy over paganism in first-century Rome, where a diversity of languages and more than a dozen gods were worshiped, requiring viciously sacrificial appeasement.

Stark writes that the Christian relationship grew strong because it responded to fear and brutalities by binding the unity of efforts that connected individuals together. Even under persecution, the faith could not be destroyed by killing off its leaders. Epidemics in the year 165 and again in 251 AD took the lives of thousands in the Roman Empire. The people's spirit weakened as they were left to die alone with their stone-faced gods and the stars shining down unresponsive to their cries. However, the relationship with Christ was personal, shared around the table of communion.

God's laws given through Moses are living words to teach what it means to be created in the image of God. They are words for life, concerned with how we live in hardships, joy, poverty, and blessings. Those knowing God brought light shining into the darkness, taking care of the sick, taking care of each other in faith that faced terrible deaths, and praying in agony for the birth of the divine flame of the soul to emerge in the thinking of the persecutors.

The stories of the matriarchs taught women that God held them in high esteem. Widows were honored and not forced to find a man so they would survive. Young girls were not forced to marry at the age of eleven or twelve. Women cleaved to the God of Israel and shared the faith with neighbors. Paul commended Phoebe, who helped many of the people, including him. He greets both Aquila and Priscilla, who risked their lives for him, and thanks them on behalf of all the gentile churches; he also expresses gratitude to Mary, Tryphena, Tryphosa, and Persis, all of whom worked hard for the

---

5. Athenagoras, "Athenagoras of Athens," para. 2.
6. Athenagoras, "Athenagoras of Athens," para. 47.

people). The mother of Rufus had been a mother to him too (Rom 16:1–15). Peter reached out and took the hand of Tabitha, a woman who spent her days sewing clothing for widows, after his prayers resurrected her from the dead (Acts 9:36–42).

Eve's Hebrew name is Chavah, the mother of all living, making all lives in the future possible. Created immediately before the first Shabbat, having the purpose of being a helpmate, women would have days when the support needed most is to stand beside a partner's effort. Other times the help most needed is to position against what a man is doing. Woman was to do this for her husband, her children, her family, friends, and congregants with gifts intended to strengthen each other. Scripture's Woman of Valor lists her many descriptions, including wisdom of a teacher, the beauty of supporting honor, loyal, comfort, and light, all of them to bring strength to her community. "Many women have done excellently, but you surpass them all" (Prov 31:29).

The men and women were encouraged to live a quiet life (1 Thess 4:11), poised with modesty, guarding the privacy of personal matters, and, as Isaiah described the Servant, not loud in the streets or trying to dominate others. The Servant moves quietly through lives, bringing meaning to emotion. The Son of God delivered his foundation through these thoughts regarding preserving the family through the words of Paul (1 Cor 7:2–7).

The Romans saw these women as fellow workers, important in the new faith, and martyred them along with the church's male leaders. But the faith gained ascendancy and Jesus triumphed. Disciples of Jesus brought a new concept, *agape*, which is a spiritual, divine love equated to God alone and defined throughout Scripture. After giving instructions for the household to wives, husbands, and children, whether free or slaves, Paul says that whatever you do, in every part of life, you must work at it with all your heart in your every waking hour because it is the Lord you are serving (Col 3:18–24).

By this we perceive the love of God because he lay down his life for us, and we ought to lay down our lives for the brethren. In this was manifested the love of God, that God sent his only begotten Son into the world. Not that we loved God, but that he loved us first. He who loved us and washed us in his own blood. We are to follow after love, do everything in love, serve each other in love, speak the truth in love, put on love, spur one another on to more love, and fervently love one another from the heart.

After Christianity was made the official religion of the empire, the law made infanticide illegal. It failed to stop the fathers and mothers who discarded their babies in the sewers of Ashkelon. But having been deprived of seeing themselves as part of God's plan, women increasingly wanted what the new believers offered and began learning the tenets. They brought in their neighbors and family members. They brought their husbands and sons into the faith, and they were urged to become men trusted with the word of God. By the end of the second century, Jewish laws were changing society's laws and influencing family structure as faith in Jesus opened doors through Asia Minor and North Africa. Jesus was taking down the walls.

The break between the gentile and Jewish believers took centuries.

And God blessed the seventh day, and sanctified it. (Gen 2:3)

Because of her great influence since the time of Eve, woman was given Shabbat responsibilities, the very first thing that God sanctified as holy (Gen 2:3). He called the day his law long before the Ten Commandments were given, telling Moses that the people were to gather twice as much manna on Friday because on Saturday there was to be rest, "that I may prove them, whether they will walk in my law or not. . . . The Lord has given you the sabbath, therefore on the sixth day he gives you bread for two days; remain every man of you in his place, let no man go out of his place on the seventh day. So the people rested on the seventh day" (Exod 16:4–5, 29–30).

The Shabbat existed from the beginning. After setting the process of creation into motion, God blessed the Shabbat with the plenty that grew during the week. You shall call to the Shabbat delight (Isa 58:13), inviting it into the home.

The writings do not say how Adam and Eve observed Shabbat as the day of rest, but they knew that God created rest after he made them. They knew that the earth, being fertile and offering the blessing of sustenance, depends on God's cycles and, as parents, passed the story to the generations to come. They began the work of peacemakers, counseling others into relationship with God.

After being rescued from slavery, the Jews were told to remember the rest God had made. Repeated by Moses in Deuteronomy, Shabbat continually recalls that we are in slavery, and the Lord our God brings us out with an outstretched hand. Jesus, the Lord who made Shabbat, stretched out his arms and invited all into his rest. "Peace I leave with you; my peace I give to you," he said (John 14:27).

The non-Jewish stranger who keeps the Shabbat holy will be blessed (Isa 56:1–8). The Shabbat is the only one of the ten commandments that God calls holy. "Remember the sabbath day, to keep it holy" (Exod 20:8), so it does not lose its importance. Knowing that the world would try to obscure this day, it is the only commandment that God reminds to "remember." God's promise to "make you ride upon the heights of the earth; I will feed you with the heritage of Jacob your father" (Isa 58:14) is dependent on gathering each person into his Shabbat rest.

Sunset on Friday until sunset on Saturday brings the people from the ordinary into the holy and back to the ordinary. Beginning a week of achieving work inspired by God's holy day is to be patterned within the power moving God's entire universe. Without this, no one partakes of the *Oneg Shabbat*, the delight of the day that reinforces the identity of children of God.

Preparing for Shabbat is similar to the way a person prepares to meet an honored guest, before the light of day has set and there is no more time to get ready. It is a moment of reflection in greeting the world to come when the Lord of the Shabbat, Jesus, returns. Activity and striving come to a halt in that moment, just as we remain as we are when he returns. Whatever achievement is lacking cannot be changed.

In temple days, the shofar was sounded from the roof of the courtyard of the Temple Mount to let the people know when to put down their work and get ready for Shabbat. The final breaths of who we are in God means that each week we can strive to become closer, no matter the past's mistakes. Putting down the work, stopping the building, coming alongside God as he rested from his work, is to begin a new week with growth renewed.

The land too is to be given a Shabbat rest every seven years if the people are to enjoy its support (2 Chr 36:21). The species created by the Word would be sustained and won't go extinct. The seven land cycles, forty-nine years, were to be followed by a Year of Jubilee. Every fifty years, slaves were to be set free and debt be forgiven. All lands are to be returned to their original people, and each person to their original clan. The day is to sound with a trumpet proclaiming the Lord's favor.

After seven hundred years, fourteen Jubilees that had not yet been fulfilled, the people's hearts stirred, recalling how God spoke to Isaiah about the one who would make the Jubilee possible. Then Jesus appeared, emerging out of his time in the wilderness. He stood in the synagogue of Nazareth to read a haftorah portion, Isaiah's words: "The Spirit of the Lord is upon me . . . He has sent me . . . to proclaim the acceptable year of the Lord." Today, he said, this Scripture is filled (Luke 4:16–21).

All eyes were on him. The congregation marveled at the knowledge with which Jesus spoke of the Lord's favor. Nearly everywhere, sermons would be preached about how we are to behave for God as pews emptied because someone did not want to be told another way to live their life. When Jesus stood and spoke, he told about what God wants to give to the people.

His story began with his earthly father, Joseph, being assured that Mary had not betrayed him. Joseph could trust his betrothed. She stood silently, remembering the angel of God, who had spoken privately to her, holding the prophetic knowledge quietly in her heart, regardless of what others spoke. The Son of the Father of light came into existence in that important trust between man and woman. It was a commandment to honor each other because Satan would expand his ploy to disrupt God's designed union between people, put in place so that humans would not be alone.

A woman who fears the Lord is to be praised. (Prov 31:30)

By the twenty-first century, finding the Shabbat rest in the Lord became the most difficult commandment. People struggled with priorities pressuring to control their time. The teachings of God became disordered. The Roman emperor Constantine had substituted Sunday with state control over religion, and the church left the table of discussion. Soon forgetting much of the mystery God wants to reveal to us by giving Shabbat rest, the world fell prey to the influence of the god of this age (1 John 5:19; 2 Cor 4:4) preventing people from fulfilling their destiny of joining as family with their Creator.

It became unthinkable to just stop and let go for a day, wrongly perceived as only a list of what cannot be done. Thoughts of rest come in images of advertisements of sunbathed beaches, remote islands, and mountains to climb, always with phones and email in reach. Rest became viewed as only for those who can afford it and don't need to work hours every day just to pay bills. But the Jews were brought out from that kind of slavery in Egypt, and Jesus wanted his rest shared with everyone. "Delight yourself in the Lord" (Ps 37:4) is the reason to cease the activities that consume our time for the hours inside his Shabbat.

Women would forget what Eve knew as she fulfilled her potential to return the Lord's presence on earth with her family. When asked what they do, women would respond by telling of their career, defining themselves as a doctor, secretary, waitress, school teacher, or other role. The six days God gave to work express our creativity to live in the image of God, who created everything. It brings us dignity, a calling to the work we are to do within relationship with God. But the work of all life culminates in Shabbat.

Shabbat belongs to the *eidut mitzvah*s (*eidut* is the Hebrew word for "testimony"). When Shabbat is kept, the people are giving testimony to the blessing of the first light of creation bringing life out of darkness, and the light that prevails in the world to come. Ushering in the day at sunset affirms the belief that God remains the world's creator and continues breathing light into darkness.

The sudden light of the Shabbat candle flames joins together those God calls to his table. The command of the Lord is radiant, giving light to the eyes. The light extends its circle to new friends, driving away chaos and loneliness, deepening insights, and widening awareness.

It was from such homes that the apostles came to Jesus. Paul told Timothy to "continue in what you have learned and have become firmly believed, knowing from whom you learned it and how from childhood you have been acquainted with the sacred writings which are able to instruct you for salvation through faith in Christ Jesus" (2 Tim 3:14-15). Further teaching includes Philippians 4:6, "Have no anxiety about anything, but in everything by prayer and supplication with thanksgiving let your requests be made known to God," and Matthew 6:32 and Ephesians 2:12, which speak of gentiles having no hope due to being apart from God, and yet pursuing his peace. Finish strong with the teachings first begun in your ancestors.

Shabbat releases control to God, who is trustworthy. In the Lord's Prayer, Jesus addresses the dimensions of present, past, and future as welcoming the will of God for the future, asking for provision for the present day, and the forgiveness that delivers from the past (Luke 11:1-4). Prayer is for our sake.

Sarah, Rebekah, Rachel, and Leah were all barren women who God chose to be mothers of the nation, and were commanded to pray only to God. It is said that God longed to hear them speak to him of the desires of their hearts and waited to hear their voices. Their prayers were God's will, and he answered, becoming an example of coming to God in relationship with heaven's will.

Rabbi David Aaron, an author and teacher in Jerusalem inspiring renaissance in Jewish living, says that "prayer is probably one of the more difficult aspects of Judaism. To study Torah is intellectually engaging, challenging, to have engaging discussions is not so difficult to do. But to stand before God and to start opening my heart and speaking to what appears to be thin air is really very difficult."[7]

Praying, called davvening, must enunciate the words, Rabbi David says. Until we speak what we want, we're not ready to receive it. When we're praying, we shouldn't be focusing on trying to change God, he says. We should focus on trying to change ourselves, consciously filling our hearts with the capacity to think his thoughts, dream his dreams. What is it we are waiting for and envision? "The question that we should ask is not "Did God hear my prayer?"; the first question I really should ask is, "Did I hear my prayer?" Rabbi Aaron says. "Through my prayer did I change my relationship with God, which will change my experience."[8]

Prayer requires tremendous trust. "I think a great part of our survival is that we really, in a lot of ways, knew what we wanted," Rabbi Aaron notes.

---

7. Aaron, "Secrets to Powerful Prayer," 7:21.
8. Aaron, "Secrets to Powerful Prayer," 16:11, 17:04..

"We dreamed and we continue to dream . . . We have to have an understanding of what is really good."[9]

It brought the prophet Jeremiah into a posture of despair. When the temple and the paths leading up to the appointed gatherings to meet with God lay in ruins, Jeremiah wept over his people, unable to bear seeing how they suffered. How will God meet with them now?

The walk ascending toward heaven is accomplished through generations of tears full of heartbreak. There is incredible sadness coming up against the failures of the church. Jeremiah's tears come out of his passion over the work of God. When he approached Jerusalem, Jesus wept over how hidden from her eyes was the way to peace (Luke 19:41–44). Paul wrote to the Corinthians in great anguish (2 Cor 2:4). David implored the Lord to record his tears on his scroll (Ps 56:8).

These are tears which yearn for the work of God, witnessing the enemy trampling what is good. The apostles said that the work of the Lord would be a struggle, bringing hardship as it brought life and joy. "He that goes forth weeping, bearing the seed for sowing, shall come home with shouts of joy, bringing his sheaves with him" (Ps 126:6). Sowing in tears, reaping in joy. God may not change circumstance, but he does change how we identify with his plan.

Leah, whose name is derived from "weary," was stuck in a dysfunctional family. Her father manipulated people. She was in love with Jacob, but Jacob did not value her. She was unwanted, unloved, and trapped in circumstances that would not change.

When her first son, Reuben, was born, she said, surely now my husband will love me. Her next son, Simeon, was born, and she said that God has heard that she is hated. When Levi was born, she said that now her husband would join her because she had given birth to three sons for him. She longed for God to change the dynamics. But when her fourth son, Judah, was born, it was she who transformed. She said, "This time I praise God." She became the mother of Judah, through whom the promises to the entire world would come (Gen 29:31–35).

My ways are not your ways, the Lord says (Isa 55:8).

When God made Israel "like a desert, [turned] her into a parched land, and [slayed] her with thirst," the Lord guided them through the wilderness; "There she will respond as in the days of her youth, as in the day she came up out of Egypt" (Hos 2:3, 14–15).

It is a return to rejoicing to accomplish his will.

---

9. Aaron, "Secrets to Powerful Prayer," 53:21.

Circumstance may not change. Sorrow may remain, but God breathes into us to draw out songs of praise unveiling our true identity. "Listen, my beloved brethren. Has not God chosen those who are poor in the world to be rich in faith and heirs of the kingdom which he has promised to those who love him?" (Jas 2:5). The Lord drew song from the Israelites wandering for thirty-eight years through the desert. He drew faith from a man paralyzed for thirty-eight years. With no strength and no understanding, the Lord's called were given light and, gathering to the light, were given rest.

Jeremiah could not see how the Lord would ever fix this. But he calls to mind that "the steadfast love of the Lord never ceases, his mercies . . . are new every morning; great is his faithfulness. 'The Lord is my portion,' says my soul. . . . It is good that one should wait quietly for the salvation of the Lord" (Lam 3:22–26).

Isaiah said those who wait on the Lord will renew their strength. He speaks to a people in mourning, oppressed, who are redeemed yet are feeling that God is far from them. Isaiah tells them that God understands his people (Isa 40). He knows that to find him and fulfill his will, they need to set aside a time to meet with him.

Children of his unknowable depth breathe within its bounds sustained by light, becoming a firmament of constellations first uttered from heaven.

> Did God say, "You shall not eat of any tree of the garden"? (Gen 3:1)

The first commandment given to humankind was about food. Eat freely of every tree in the garden, but don't eat the tree of the knowledge of good and evil, because you will die (Gen 2:16–17). Of all things people are told to do and not do, being told what not to eat is irritating because it is such an invasion on personal choice.

Even God regulating the diet of Adam and Eve was met with a rebellion for their own choices. The serpent entered the garden of Eden, intelligent and perceptive of this weakness. Made in the image of God, Adam and Eve had traits of creativity and wanted to leave their own distinctive mark on the world. Eve is the mother of all living with desire to be wise and share what she found. Did God really say that?

The question echoes through society, especially in personal matters of sustenance. God is to be recognized as sovereign, but the Word does not limit the freedoms of the intellect to consider decisions. The command was about relationship with heaven.

The Israelites were told to be "a people dwelling alone, and not reckoning itself among the nations" (Num 23:9). Choosing the foods that God provides and avoiding the ones he said not to eat reminds the people and the children around them that they have an incontestable national identity that honors the living God. It tells God that they remember the covenant that sustains life. When foods are chosen for the home, it is an act of choosing God's commands, bringing into balance the action of Eve and Adam ignoring the instruction. It is a statement that the Lord's foundation still stands firm.

Just after traveling through the Red Sea, where God spectacularly displayed his power, the people are told to assemble. God then speaks about practical ways for families to live and be healthy through the generations. Moses' final words were a warning to guard both yourself and your soul. Both are needed to bring the fulfillment of God's purpose. "If you will diligently hearken to the voice of the Lord your God . . . I will put none of the diseases upon you which I put upon the Egyptians; for I am the Lord, your healer" (Exod 15:26).

In one breath, God told them to guard and remember the Shabbat. His word opened time to be in the presence of family and be completely optimistic in worries of necessities, clothing, eating, and relationship. The space is a gift assuring that the Lord will overthrow the enemy with the breath of his mouth when his splendor returns (2 Thess 2:8).

Living by being faithful is asking, "Did God really say that?"; otherwise, we are left clinging to either the material world for nurturance or the spiritual world to obliterate physical need. The first heresy of the church was not in denying Jesus was God. It was in denying that he was man with all the same tactile senses and responses as any person. He became physical, touchable, woundable, with human nature. He had a human soul, feeling, thinking, relating to the world around him. Jesus grew in wisdom, he learned Scripture, knelt to pray, craved good health, and was tempted. There were places he liked to go, such as visiting the home of Martha, Mary, and Lazarus or going off by himself to the sea. He chose disciples whose hearts centered on the knowledge of Jerusalem, wanting them with him. The Lord Jesus was troubled (John 11:33). He was in anguish (Luke 22:44). He was deeply distressed (Mark 14:33–34). He knows our experience in inner dimensions which no friend is able to comprehend.

Feeling that Jesus was as far away as God, some denominations elevated Mary or saints because they seemed nearer to approach, although when his mother was blessed for giving birth to him, Jesus responded by saying, "more blessed are those who heed the word and obey it." Praying to a dead person is idolatry. Hardship is intended to turn us toward him, not to seek someone else to take away the challenges.

By the fifth century, instead of preserving the Lord's days, the church created different holidays like Christmas and Easter, exhibitions of art, the use of icons painted on wood representing saints, and implemented statues. The church accumulated teachers that tickled their itching ears. The time had begun that Paul warned of people not wanting the truth of sound doctrine (2 Tim 4:3). Emerging traditions began to move the church away from communion with Israel.

Breaking bread together remained part of every culture, whether a black-tie event or a picnic on green grasses. God knows that food can bring people together and affect the entire sense of self worth. Eating disorders, illness from dieting, shame from failure to lose unwanted pounds, sickness from not eating healthy food; all can hinder seeing the inestimable beauty of the soul. The choice is between the two kinds of water: the teachings of his words as the source of living water, or false teachings (called broken wells that contain bitter, stagnant water).

Jesus came saying he is the bread of life. Those who hunger will be filled. Serving the bread on Shabbat translates the law into an act of trusting him to overcome habits that ruin a life. Follow me, he says, up the aliyah to the place he meets with his people. Taking this bread is believing that God blesses the sustenance he created for our well-being and imparts responsibility to care for it in his ways.

This command is to act in the image of God passing on a healthy earth from generation to generation, an earth that is tended with the responsibility first given to Adam and Eve. In the book of Deuteronomy, the Israelites were told not to destroy the fruit-bearing trees during battle. The sages extended the law to peacetime and other objects that may benefit someone. He will bless our bread and water for health in every cell in the body (Exod 23:25). The land will be healthy, producing harvest, which follows the Lord's ways. Water, the foundation of life, will be clean—without it, there is no health. Sustaining and repairing the world requires respect to know that it is God who assigned roles to each member of creation to fulfill the whole.

The light of a flame was first needed by Adam and Eve when they were banished from the garden of Eden. They brought the garden with them in their soul, desirous of wisdom and dreams beyond the margins of this world. It seeded in the knowledge of indigenous communities knowing God's way to derive health from nature blooming around them. Burdock, standing tall in fields with its burr roots, was used for purifying and strengthening the immune system. Echinacea's cone-shaped flowers bloom in summer in North America, offering relief from wounds, insect bites, and infection. Out in the bush of Australia, tea tree oil provides topical balm.

When we enter an indigenous community that shares knowledge of medicinal plants in the turning seasons and gathers to give thanks in appreciation for the fields and forests continuing to bear fruit for all generations, we enter an aspect of Shabbat that brings rest in God-sustaining life. We enter knowledge of his living word, which gives the peace Moses spoke to his people, saying, "The Lord your God is providing you a place of rest, and will give you this land" (Josh 1:13).

The parts of the body not receiving the knowledge will hurt. Jesus wants the knowledge flowing through the body, a river cleansing the toxins, removing misunderstandings for the sake of our homes and the strength of our mind to better understand the ways of God.

Dietary laws (*kashrut*) guide decisions every day about what to eat and how to prepare the food. The prohibition against mixing meat from the death of an animal with milk that sustains a living animal keeps the people a distinguished people. Charity is embedded in the commandments to leave food for the poor. Shopping at kosher stores continues a sense of community that stands against assimilation tarnishing the Word.

God's ways see the human as a spiritual being joined with a physical body. Battles of appetite are appeased by trusting the Word to supply needs, overcoming the anxiety of addiction by giving sincere thanks for everything he provides. Coping with the stresses of the world and the conflicts within ourselves are to be balanced by coming aside to rest and be with the Lord, acknowledging the transcendence that is beyond understanding in thanking God.

But salvation was gradually reduced to mean being saved from an unfulfilling personal or professional life. The reality of being redeemed from the wrath of hell was buried under conforming to sets of behavior. When Jesus was asked what people were to do, the first word he said was "repent." When Peter was asked, he repeated Jesus and said "repent." This is what the church spoke when it began to grow. Then the church began to change and said that it is only faith that saves, though the apostles had revealed what we need, turning back to God, empowered with the Spirit in every aspect of the day.

Denominations formed and treated the symptoms. When Saul was tormented by dark spirits because he had disobeyed God's light, counselors brought David to relieve his depression with music. It eased Saul only momentarily. Saul needed to turn back to God. He needed to open the repentance in his heart and follow the path of sanctification. The message became diluted, teaching that the Lord is only about love and acceptance, but without confession and redemption, the schism widened, even among believers.

We need to be asking where exactly in God's word is something being said. The many divisions of believers each state they're doing it right. They agree on Jesus as Lord, but the disjoint in thinking comes when a member fails the personal responsibility that longs for him in the secret place, where we search for Jesus' gentle voice and we sing from our soul's burning light. Then we'll be marching together up the aliyah, riding his high winds.

Turning toward God begins a lifetime of transformation that will take captive every thought as every aspect of a life is brought to relate to his goodness. Even when we don't fully understand the healthful reasons behind it, "trust in the Lord with all your heart, and do not rely on your own insight. In all your ways acknowledge him, and he will make straight your paths" (Prov 3:5–6).

Before the people of Israel even heard what God was going to ask of them, they all responded together, saying "All that the Lord has spoken we will do" (Exod 19:8), because they knew it was from God. They had come out of Egypt on eagle's wings. They had been given the prophetic messages for their people. Knowing that it is from God is enough.

We've been given the vision of what to want. Do not be glad over someone's downfall because the holy Lord never felt glad over someone suffering the consequence of a sin. Look further, he says. He's already begun doing his work. Patiently, persistently he builds up his people from his own body. He is bringing more Jewish people from the far ends of the earth to return to Israel. There will be weeping and praying as God brings them, returning by streams of water on smooth paths so they won't stumble (Jer 31:9). "Hear the word of the Lord, O nations, and declare it in the coastlands afar off; say, 'He who scattered Israel will gather him, and will keep him as a shepherd keeps his flock'" (Jer 31:10).

Thousands of years after Jeremiah foresaw it happening, Jews began seeing Jesus at the right hand of the Father interceding to bring about the promises to Abraham. They bring the message to follow the Messiah to where he ascended to be crowned. They come standing in the shoes of peace because God chose Israel by sovereign love. He keeps Israel by this love. "I have loved you with an everlasting love," he told the people (Jer 31:3).

For generations, the Israelites set the table for Shabbat, foreshadowing the generous hospitality of the Messiah who laid the bounty of creation. Welcoming Jesus as the Messiah has opened the table to the world.

In the 1960s, Messianic rabbis felt very alone. There was no unifying movement yet. In the 1970s and 1980s, people began forming groups, readapting themselves back into the culture that first framed its message. They plowed the ground, seeking the words of the root of David. As of 2012, population estimates of Messianic Jews in the United States were nearly two hundred fifty thousand members, for Israel between ten thousand and twenty thousand members, and an estimated worldwide membership of more than three hundred fifty thousand.

The coming together of Jews and gentiles declares Jesus victorious in his atoning work, breaking down the partition that separated them, and marking the nearing of the time of his return when all will be Shabbat. Stepping through centuries of mistakes, they see the Messiah spoken of in more than one thousand prophecies in the Old Testament. They saw the horrific price he paid for the Jews to welcome others under the shelter of the living God. Their hearts worshiped as they repeated the psalm: "In his hand are the depths of the earth; the heights of the mountains are his also. . . . he is our God, and we are the people of his pasture" (Ps 95).

Romans 8:37 says, "In all these things we are more than conquerors through him who loved us." Conquering the divisions between people and God, between nation and nation, between Israel and gentiles, through difficulties and opposition, there is nothing that can separate the people from the Lord's victory for them.

More than a hundred years after the exile of the north, the prophet had a vision of Rachel mourning over her children, the people of Israel. "Rachel is weeping for her children; she refuses to be comforted" (Jer 31:15). The apostle Matthew explained the fulfillment of this when Herod murdered the infant sons of Israel in his attempt to kill the newborn Jesus (Matt 2:18). Rachel wept until the Lord spoke comfort reiterating the promise to her people: "Keep your voice from weeping, and your eyes from tears; for your work shall be rewarded . . . and they shall come back from the land of the enemy" (Jer 31:16).

Jacob met Rachel at a well, tending her father's sheep. He kissed her, and lifted his voice and wept (Gen 29:1–6, 10–11). But he had to first marry Leah, the older sister, in a marriage of treachery he did see coming. The Midrash explains that because Jacob pretended to be Esau to deceive his father, he now had two wives because he had been two men. Leah is said to have told him, "Did not your father call you Esau, and you answered him! So did you too call me and I answered you!" (Gen 70:19, LXX).

It is said that only the children of Rachel can defeat the offspring of Esau and his grandson Amalek, whose name contains the doubt that plagues the faith in every generation. Enemies who are the spiritual offspring of Amalek threaten the Jews' return to Israel and their reconciliation with the church, but they will be left empty of any beauty in themselves, powerless and thirsting for the divine water of life.

When Rachel died in the month of Cheshvan, Benjamin was born, completing the tribes of Israel. The last son of Jacob and patriarch of the twelfth tribe, Benjamin is the only son to be born in Israel; through him Saul would be their first king, and Mordechai and Esther would bring about the miracle of Purim immediately before the people returned to Israel to build the second temple.

Rachel died a young woman, having built up the house of Israel together with Leah (Ruth 4:11). She is thought of as a mother whose name embodies the entire force of creation interceding with God on behalf of her children. In Rachel's tears, the mother guards and continues the spiritual identity of her people. Culture at home is seeded and nurtured so they are able to return again and to defend their borders, both spiritually and physically.

It is to this grace that the people return as the days descend into the dark, cold rainy season. Cheshvan is the month that the world was flooded in Noah's time (Gen 7:10–11) and a rainbow given over every land for every people where everywhere lives are instilled with love of homeland.

It is a time when leaves fall and the earth sleeps under winter's low gray sky. Yet when the rainy season begins, the water is sowing future growth in seeds hidden beneath the surface. In the moment Rachel passed on, shadows of sorrow fell to be lifted by a new birth. There is hope for the end. Your children will return to their borders.

The seeds are being watered, the roots quietly grow unnoticed as they thirst. There is future life that waits in the moment, a spring ascending with bounty because God breathes life.

3

NEROT

Whatever Sarah says to you, do as she tells you. (Gen 21:12)

THE WOMEN SURROUNDING JESUS listened quietly as they learned theology, supporting his needs and those of his apostles. Mary, who found shelter under his light; Joanna, who had resources to offer; Peter's mother-in-law, who was healed and rose to serve him; rich or poor, they gathered around his light and kept it blazing.

He touched those who were not noticed by society. He restored a woman afflicted by internal bleeding for twelve years. He bent over a crippled woman and said, "Woman, you are freed from your infirmity" (Luke 13:10–17). He returned the dead to their women. A widow in a small hillside town in Galilee was about to bury her son when Jesus commanded the boy to rise and gave him back to the embrace of his mother (Luke 7:11–17).

> Jesus sees them, identifies their need and, in one gloriously wrenching moment, He thrusts them on center stage in the drama of redemption with the spotlights of eternity beaming upon them, and He immortalizes them in sacred history.[1]

These are women who lit the Shabbat candles.

When God chose a people who would tell his story, he gave the fourth commandment as a sign of his covenant with Israel. "You shall keep my sabbaths, for this is a sign between me and you throughout your generations,

---

1. Bilezikian, *Beyond Sex Roles*, 82.

that you may know that I, the Lord, sanctify you" (Exod 31:12–13). No work is to be done on this day because the Israelites, all their families, servants, and animals are to live within the rhythms God established when he set life in motion bringing creation from darkness into light.

Observing Shabbat has preserved the Jewish people as a distinguished group for thousands of years. It has protected them from losing their identity to the world. Even far from their homeland, the day remembers God is always present by building the home around communion with God.

Nerot, the candle lights, is one of the rabbinical *mitzvot* ("instructions") that are the privilege of women to bring blessing. The other two, *challah* ("separating a portion of dough") and *niddah* ("family purity") also relate to home and family.

The first woman to light Shabbat candles was Sarah, the matriarch of Israel. Abraham and Sarah were the first Jews and became the father and mother of nations when their names were changed from Abram to Abraham, and Sarai to Sarah (meaning a "recognized princess").

Sarah would light the candles on the evening of Shabbat, Friday evening, in the tent she shared with Abraham. It is said that the light from the candles would glow from one Friday to the next as they greeted the many guests who visited during the week.

When Sarah died, Abraham had to ask the people of the land for a grave site. He was well-known to them and they said, "You are a mighty prince among us. Bury your dead in the choicest of our sepulchres." But Abraham refused the offer. He wanted to place Sarah in a nearby cave (Gen 23:1–9).

Sarah died in Hebron in Canaan. When God called Abraham out of his dwelling, Abraham moved his tent to Canaan and built an altar to the Lord. It was in this beautiful desert place that God spoke to him about descendants who would be as numerous as the stars. It was here God entered a covenant with Abraham that would change his name from Abram, father of a nation, with the letter *hei*, making him father of many nations. It is here that Hagar became pregnant, where Abraham hosted angels, and where Isaac marries Rebekah; it is a place important to God and to Abraham.

The rabbis refer to Sarah in the verse "a good wife is the crown of her husband" (Prov 12:4). She is honored as a woman who spiritually recognized Abraham as a man of God's choosing. There were no synagogues or churches, no Scripture yet to guide her choices, but she was gifted with discernment. Peter noted that "Sarah obeyed Abraham, calling him lord. And you are now her children if you do right and let nothing terrify you" (1 Pet 3:6). If Sarah had moments of reluctance, she stood with Abraham anyway because she had faith.

Reminding us that his power can multiply light throughout earth from just one flame burning, God said, "Look to Abraham your father and to Sarah who bore you; for when he was but one I called him, and I blessed him and made him many" (Isa 51:2).

Abraham and Sarah never saw the promises of God. Their faith endured as nomads, wandering for years with their sight fixed on the heavenly city beyond this world, a city called "The Lord is there" (Ezek 48:35). They waited for both a place and a people that they greeted from afar. Their pilgrimage witnessed Sarah conceiving beyond the natural time of life, knowing the vision of the many born through them. The Lord told Abraham, "by you all the families of earth shall bless themselves" (Gen 12:3).

Abraham considered his own body and Sarah's womb as dead, but because God had spoken, he was assured (Rom 4:19–21). His hope without any visible possibility was credited to him as righteousness and millions of people were born through this power to trust. Nothing is too difficult for God, Sarah and Abraham were told, repeated again to Mary who would give birth to Jesus. Sarah said, "God has made laughter for me" (Gen 21:6). The waiting for God to create her son marked Isaac as a divine gift.

When he lost Sarah, Abraham lost his life's partner. This great man who inspired so many was suddenly "old [and] well advanced in years" after she died (Gen 24:1). Sarah was a woman who made her husband feel young and still attractive, a woman who stayed at his side as they pioneered into a new land. She had left the city of Ur where there was commerce, treasures of silver, precious stones, and educated people revealed in the tablets of writings found there. She left this home to travel with her husband into the sun's heat, which blazed over an unknown desert, because the Lord had told Abraham to leave his father's house for a new place he would be shown.

Though they lived as nomadic tent dwellers, they did possess Canaan. The presence of their faith occupied the land for the birth of entire peoples who would believe the promise without yet having seen it. "Your father Abraham rejoiced that he was to see my day; he saw it and was glad," Jesus told the Jews who questioned his identity (John 8:56).

Sarah perceived that Ishmael, Abraham's son with Hagar, was a bad influence on Isaac, so she told Abraham to send them away. Although Abraham was grieved to do this, God told him to listen to her voice. Sarah's prophetic knowledge was at the foundation of the people becoming a nation, as would Rebekah, who perceived that Jacob (not Esau) should receive the blessing.

Isaac would recognize the anointing of his wife, Rebekah, when years later the same miracle of Shabbat candlelight burning throughout the week was given to her. Lighting the candles on the eve of Shabbat became a tradition to illuminate the same hospitality in the homes of their descendants.

The flame of the Shabbat candle recalls God saying, "Let there be light." Before light there was no fulfillment of creation. Light associates with the hallowed glory of God. In bright clouds, a burning bush, a pillar of fire, a symbol of Torah, God is always with them. The psalmist wrote, "The Lord is my light and my salvation" (Ps 27:1). The prophet spoke, "the Lord will be your everlasting light" (Isa 60:19).

The candlelight is also a symbol of the human soul. Representing the light we are appointed to bring to the world (Isa 49:6), the flame burns always upward, reaching to connect to the holy flames of heaven. Shabbat seeks the Lord's presence in answer to the soul's restless desire for heaven's fulfillment. Hunger is sated in letting his praises pour from us. Fear of him makes life secure. Falling to bow low before him lifts us. We are free only when we enslave ourselves to serve him.

The moment the flame lights, a window into the *olam habah* (world to come) opens when the light of the Lord will rule the nations and all creation is given relief and rejoices. The Messiah's coming was prophesied as light from heaven. "Arise, shine; for your light has come, and the glory of the Lord has risen upon you" (Isa 60:1).

Every day invites people to prepare for the Lord's return. The sun blushes the sky, a last glance on the day, and fades to let blessing come. The gate of heaven opens to give the day a glimpse of the future of man and God in harmony. On that day, the Lord shall give "rest from your pain and turmoil and the hard service with which you were made to serve" (Isa 14:3).

Israel inherited the flames and bestowed the honor on women to guard and remember to observe the two biblical principles (Deut 5:12; Exod 20:8) as they light two candles to pierce the dark. Paul would bring the words "remember" and "guard" into the Messiah's teachings. His peace will guard hearts that bring concerns with thanksgiving to God. We are to remember what is true, noble, pure, lovely, praiseworthy, and keep them in thought (Phil 4:6–8).

Scripture instructs us "to keep the Sabbath" (Exod 31:16). Every person must ready themselves. The Lord said, "remember the Sabbath day, to keep it holy." Keeping it holy means remembering it during the week, as if preparing to greet an honored guest, the holiness that made all of creation. A special fruit, a unique recipe, a new blouse, or a story about what God has done during the week are brought to the day.

The women give meaning to what God spoke by placing the candles (or oil lamps and matches) on a table near where they will eat the Shabbat meal, and it won't need to be moved until after Shabbat. The best tablecloth and silver are used. A grandmother's china and a mother's recipe weave strands of the past into a future, holding a promise made at the beginning of time.

The house has been cleaned, floors washed, carpets vacuumed, laundry folded and put away. Men, women, and children around the world put on their most beautiful clothing before the sun leaves the sky to usher in the Shabbat. Family gather at the table, fulfilling God's will for them to enjoy a good meal. From ancient days, herbs and spices appeared in a fragrant kitchen with bread baking in the oven.

Eighteen minutes before sunset, the mystery of light flares into the room when the women turn their attention to light the candles. If no woman of age is present, a man may do this.

The Lord's glory is assigned to the moment the light flares. The woman sets the match down to burn itself out, extends her hands over the radiance of the candles, and draws them inward in circular motions. Because God has no image, and he said to Moses that no one can see him and live, her hand covers her eyes as she meets the Shekhinah and recites the blessing. Pronouncing each word with the breath of life, bringing all the body's harmony into pathways of melody, she says:

> *Baruch ata Adonai Eloheinu melech ha olam asher kidisha-nu bi-mitz-vo-tav vi-tzi-va-noo li-had-leek ner shel Shabat kodesh.*
>
> Blessed are you, Lord our God, King of the universe, who has sanctified us with His commandments, and commanded us to kindle the light of the Holy Shabbat.

In this private moment, speaking to the Lord is a time to tell him her desires for her children to grow in the ways of the Lord. The prayer for the re-establishment of the temple in Jerusalem is often spoken at this time.

> May it be your will, Lord, our God and God of our fathers, that the Temple be speedily rebuilt in our days, and grant our portion in your Torah. There we will serve you with awe as in days of old and as in ancient years. And may the offerings of Judah and Jerusalem be as pleasing to you as ever and as in ancient times.

Here is the woman coming to the God of Israel, the force and light of the universe, the strength and power of goodness. Shadows are quietly chased from the room by light spreading gently, not aggressively, but with intimate words to God. "Not by might, nor by power, but by my Spirit, says the Lord of hosts" (Zech 4:6).

It is out of these homes that the leaders come who carry the heritage of light to the nations. In privacy, they are being prepared, like David's time in the fields tending sheep taught him to be aware, protect, and lead before he confronted Goliath. Another example is that of Jesus, who defeated the enemy's temptations in the wilderness before he walked into the community and faced the temptation of his own will in the garden.

After the woman finishes, she greets everyone with blessings for a good Shabbat. It is this day that many customarily place coins in a box for charity, since the temple is no longer there for offerings.

The wine has been prepared for *kiddush*, the prayer traditionally spoken by men over the wine before blessing the *challah*. *Kiddush* means to make a distinction, to elevate the physical in the day into the spiritual realm. Two loaves of *challah* are served to remember the double portion of manna gathered in the wilderness, when God showed that he will provide if we honor his day of rest.

> If you turn back your foot from the sabbath, from doing your pleasure on my holy day, and call the sabbath a delight and the holy day of the Lord honorable; if you honor it, not going your own ways, or seeking your own pleasure, or talking idly; then you shall take delight in the Lord, and I will make you ride upon the heights of the earth; I will feed you with the heritage of Jacob your father, for the mouth of the Lord has spoken. (Isa 58:13–14)

Conversation speaks of the blessings God has directed during the week. Scripture reinforced this instructing to keep the mind on "whatever is true, whatever is honorable, whatever is just, whatever is pure, whatever is lovely, whatever is gracious, if there is any excellence, if there is anything worthy of praise" (Phil 4:8). Further, "Let your speech always be gracious, seasoned with salt, so that you may know how you ought to answer every one" (Col 4:6).

Rest gives healing with a chance to recuperate by embracing the whole of the mind, body, and spirit. There is time to sit quietly with God and ask the purpose of being here. Time is given for finishing books, taking walks outside, and having uninterrupted conversations with children. Shabbat gathers family and friends from the isolating work of the week to share companionship, sing songs, and tell stories.

Light brings about communication as they gather in its clarity to interact and understand each other. Light unifies those in its glow, but darkness likes confusion, because we will not see the vast gap between the soul and God to realize our need to be restored. In the dark, the distinctions among peoples are not discerned until the light reveals that each comes with gifts bestowed by God.

It is a time to learn from each other. Brought inside from the world's rhetorical arguments, there is space to deliberate the words of the Scripture in common desire because of respect to advance learning.

After being severely beaten without a trial and thrown into prison, Paul and Silas were taken into prison, and a guard was ordered to fasten their feet in the stocks. As the apostles sang hymns to the Lord, an earthquake shook the prison, loosened the chains of the prisoners, and opened the door. The guard was terrified, thinking he needed to die rather than face Roman punishment for losing prisoners. But Paul called out to him. The jailer called for lights to be lit and rushed, trembling, to Paul and Silas. "What must I do to be saved?" he asked. The jailer brought them to his house, washed their wounds and sat them at a meal at his table. There they talked of the word of the Lord and all in the home were redeemed (Acts 16:16–40).

Listening to other views enlarges understanding. Because only God can see the whole of a truth, Scripture has been gathered from the perspectives of different voices, followed by many written commentaries. Many, from Abraham and Moses through the prophets, questioned God about the other side of an issue. Moses asked, "Why did you send me?" Abraham asked, "Shall the judge of all the earth not do justice?" Jeremiah wanted to know why the faithless live at ease. Habakkuk asked God why he was tolerating the wicked.

"Come, let us reason together," God said. His law considers all sides because the oppressors need redemption as much as the oppressed. Present at the Shabbat table, God encourages sharing views that lead to knowing his ways.

The language used in Hebrew is *Shabbat Vayinafash*, meaning that the soul in our body stops, refreshes, and enjoys the work created during the week. The physical pleasure of sharing a meal at a beautifully laid table disconnects from life's continual changes and becomes a dependable space to be with God, who never changes. The blur of tears that veil the face during the week's challenges fall away and, turning to the light, stretching out hands to speak the blessings, the women invite others to stand in God's sight, knowing they live because of him.

Issues between parents and children melt away in the candle glow. Whatever has happened during the week comes under Shabbat descending to bless the home. Men are freed of the week in order to be fully attentive to their family. A father lays hands on his child's head and speaks the ancient words of forefathers. If his child is a son, he says, "May God make you a symbol of blessing as he did Ephraim and Manasseh." Ephraim and

Manasseh were born and grew up in Egypt surrounded by the practices of the diaspora, away from the holy land. But they held onto the ways of God. Throughout ages, parents have prayed that their children would be able to withstand the temptations of exile and keep a strong identity.

If his child is a daughter, he says, "May God make you a symbol of blessing as he did Sarah, Rebekah, Rachel, and Leah." The Shabbat blessing pours through parents over children, as they ask the Lord to "command his messengers to guard over you wherever you go," hug the child, and say something about a special moment in their lives that week that affirms God's presence, even through our stressful days.

When Shabbat ends, this inner heart becomes of no importance to the world. The light Sarah kindled burned from Friday to Friday, a glow of remembrance kept through the hard times when struggling with emotions, especially for the young learning to be on their own. The blessings say, be gentle with yourself as you move through the days. Even the weather returns to sunlit times and so will your heart. Make no decisions in storms that will become a distant memory. You are learning to stand strong.

The book of God is opened, and youth witness how its light breaks the silence that holds the words of God captive. It marks the home as sacred space. Girls growing to an age when they become self-conscious with how they look, magnifying flaws and forgetting their value, hear the depth of loveliness in keeping the practices, called *halakhah*, that uphold the ways of God.

Halakhah is often translated as Jewish law, but more literally means "the path that one walks." There is risk that this could reduce a spiritual relationship with God to legalism, but every one of the 613 *mitzvahs* listed in the Mishneh Torah are drawn from Scripture to clarify what God spoke for our good. The acts of eating, getting dressed, lighting Shabbat candles, praying after meals, and guarding against outside influence turn the days of life into meaningful connection with the Lord.

The Shabbat rest draws the divine spark within that gives life to all things, uniting with ancestors and carrying responsibility to coming generations. The day anticipates the time when the church's work will be done and we enter into the rest of the Lord of the Shabbat.

The Lord told Abraham that whoever blesses the people of the covenant will be blessed (Gen 12:3). The covenant endures forever (Ps 100:5). How a people group approaches the Shabbat table or instead supports Israel's enemies determines the very future of their children.

> Likewise when a foreigner, who is not of thy people, comes from a far country for thy name's sake. (1 Kgs 8:41)

Waiting for the consolation of Jerusalem, Simeon prophetically announced the child Jesus as "a light for revelation to the Gentiles, and for glory to thy people Israel" (Luke 2:32). Jesus opened his home in heaven to all who come through his door. Pouring gifts of spiritual strengths into each life, he welcomes strangers with generous hospitality.

"I tell you, many will come from east and west and sit at the table with Abraham, Isaac, and Jacob in the kingdom of heaven," Jesus announced (Matt 8:11). Jesus let the people know that the welcoming invitation of the Lord of the Shabbat is for all the world.

The day of rest was commanded, yet Jesus healed a man on the Shabbat. Sin had disturbed his garden and made good works necessary every day. Rest was created on the seventh day, but the work of the Father was not yet finished. "I came to finish the work of the Father," Jesus said (John 4:34). "Come to me and I will give you rest." On the cross as he hung dying, he said, "It is finished" (19:30). The work of the Father was now completed. Then he sat down at the right hand of the Father. He rested and brought his people into his rest through forgiveness, bringing them into one humanity.

"The new man is a Jew. The new man is a Gentile. The new man is a male, the new man is a female, young and old," said Ari Sorko-Ram, sharing the Shabbat service at Baruch HaShem Congregation in Texas in the fall of 2016.[2] "Ezekiel 36:26 says 'I will give you a new heart and a new spirit.' This is critical for all of us to operate in unity. The body of the Messiah, the commonwealth of Israel, all emphasize the new man, the new kingdom identity."[3]

Ari and Shira Sorko-Ram founded Maoz Israel (Stronghold of Israel) in Tel Aviv, Israel in 1976, participating in many projects with the messianic Jewish movement. Their congregation, Tiferet Yeshua (The Glory of Yeshua), is continually expanding its tent for the growing number of believers in Israel.

Ari explained that, instead of the one new man, what happened has been used by many to confuse or eliminate the Jewish people with theologies teaching that there is no identity in nation or heritage. "These were established before we were born," he said. "He met each and every one of us in the womb, wrought in secret parts of the earth, fearfully and wonderfully made. In his book our names are all written."[4] Scripture says to train up a child in the way he should go, the way God appointed in the womb, to accomplish their part in God's overall plan. What nation, what gender, what

2. Sorko-Ram, "Guest Speaker," 43:55.
3. Sorko-Ram, "Guest Speaker," 43:13.
4. Sorko-Ram, "Guest Speaker," 42:07.

time of history a person is born into as part of a particular heritage is in God's detailed plan.

The new covenant did not change our national heritage, Ari said.[5] Paul taught that anyone at the time of salvation who was circumcised should remain circumcised, and anyone uncircumcised should remain uncircumcised. Being born again is what matters, not national affiliation. It is about being grafted into the olive tree and learning to put on the new man with access to God through Jesus.

"There is no nation created by God that is not an effective function of the body of Jesus," Ari said.[6] Ephesians 2:14 wants us to understand the crucifixion tore down the dividing wall between Jews and non-Jews, making them one through his peace. He prayed to his Father for all who believe in him, that they may be one (John 17:20–21).

"He's the king of nations," Ari said. "We are all members of different nations under the kingship of Jesus. We don't lose our national identity. We are members of a commonwealth."[7]

The first non-Jewish evangelist told of in the Bible was not only a woman, but a sinful woman who had five former husbands and was living with a man who wasn't her husband. Jesus saw her as a soul deeply thirsting to bring the divergent parts of her life into wholeness. He did not hesitate to ask the Samaritan woman at the well for a drink so that he could offer her heaven's living waters.

Salvation is of the Jews, he told her, coming to the Samaritans with the vessel of salvation. She may have wondered if she should be talking about this, acquiescing to the void of identity in the light of Israel's God. Jesus' answer was a confident yes: "I chose you and I claim you." She immediately became a disciple, proclaiming Jesus to other Samaritans who, learning of him, came to know him to be the savior of the world. She brought many Samaritans to faith in Israel's Messiah (John 4:39; see the full story in 4:1–42).

At the first encounter, the woman began by arguing about denominations. Jews worship on Mount Zion, she said. Samaritans worship on another mountain. Jesus responded by telling her that the Father seeks true worshipers who worship in spirit and in truth. Worshiping in the right way is not about temples made with hands. In 1 Corinthians, Paul says the body is the temple for the Lord to dwell in. Worship dwells within us. We are to come together to bless the Lord, and bless him with all that is within us. The woman thirsted no more—thirst is quenched by blessing the Lord.

---

5. Sorko-Ram, "Guest Speaker," 41:04.
6. Sorko-Ram, "Guest Speaker," 36:40.
7. Sorko-Ram, "Guest Speaker," 18:40.

A Syrophoenician woman fell at his feet pleading for her daughter, who was possessed by an impure spirit. Reflecting back her own thoughts on the teachings of gentiles in comparison to the Israelites, he tells her, "Let the children first be fed, for it is not right to take the children's bread and throw it to the dogs" (Mark 7:27). He brought the thinking into the light, and she acknowledges that he is the Messiah, a recognition that transcends every segregation (Mark 7:24–30).

Solomon asked God to hear the prayers of non-Jews who came to the holy temple, "for they shall hear of thy great name, and thy mighty hand, and of thy outstretched arm" (1 Kgs 8:41–43). The prophet Isaiah refers to the temple as a "house for all nations." During the festival of Sukkot, at the temple, seventy bulls were offered on behalf of the seventy nations of the world. The Talmud states that if Romans had realized the benefit they were receiving, they would not have destroyed the temple.

Israelites knew that God had provided a path for others when he sealed a covenant with Noah (Gen 9). The covenant instructed all of humanity:

Do not deny God. Relationship between humanity and its Creator is under requirement to know God. The 613 commandments for Jews and seven for all of mankind unify to acknowledge that God is One.

Do not blaspheme God. Speech distinguishes people who show gratitude for all that the Lord has given, or those who speak ingratitude in their bitterness. What is spoken of God either acknowledges his sovereignty or denies it by both Jews and non-Jews.

Do not murder. Humans are made in God's image. Laws against murder and the consequences of prison, banishment, or death are established in every nation.

Do not engage in illicit sexual relations. Taboos against adultery, incest, homosexuality, and bestial relations forbid desecrating the divine sanction of marriage between a man and woman that enhances not only family, but also the communities of entire nations.

Do not steal. God's law protects property, forbids taking what we have no right to, and builds respectful business practices.

Do not eat a live animal. Life is in the blood. Observing the way God treasures his creations not only preserves an environment, but protects human health.

Establish courts and legal systems for justice. The Talmud says, "War comes to the world through the delay of justice, the perversion of justice, and the teaching of Torah out of accordance with its legal meaning." When justice rectifies, God's light is brought into the ways of peace and care of the needy and oppressed. This is recognized by the United States Congress in its

Declaration endorsing the Noahide laws (H.J. Res. 104, Public Law 102–14, March 1991).

The most shared commandment between the peoples is the one that sanctifies God's holy name. He alone is to be worshiped.

All regulations enacted by God to govern art, music, gardening, and caring for newborns and social groups were taught to Noah's sons and grandchildren who passed the words to their children as the nations formed. They were to bless their Creator and honor their parents. Any, no matter what heritage, who cursed his father or his mother would extinguish their own light into pitch darkness (Prov 20:20).

Gentiles living in the land of Israel who honored the Noahide covenant were known as *ger toshav* (stranger/resident). After convening in Jerusalem, the council of apostles fully agreed that gentiles honoring the Noahide laws are acceptable in the new covenant's ekklesia (Acts 15:19–20). Jesus affirmed making disciples from all nations, first to the Jew, then to the gentile (Rom 1:16). He did not say to convert their national identity.

In summer of 1996, Marty Waldman, rabbi of Baruch HaShem Messianic Congregation, was seeking the Lord in preparation for a sermon he was to deliver at the Union of Messianic Jewish Congregations. The Lord responded with a compelling message about Acts 15 when the first council of Jerusalem came together to determine that gentiles should be grafted into the great promise of Jesus with "no greater burden than these necessary things." It freed many gentiles to believe, because they were not told to become someone they were not created to be.

The first council in Jerusalem was entirely Jewish, and they debated whether or not to invite in the gentiles, based around the subjects of circumcision and the law. In the rabbi's vision, there would be a second council, a gathering of both Jews and gentiles, fully accepting of one another within the body of Jesus. The gentile leaders would recognize the Jewish believers as a part of the church who remained members of the Jewish community and as the elder brother who had been given the first place (Rom 1:16).

After conferring with colleagues, Marty gathered a group of leaders from both Jewish and gentile communities, and the twelve-member Toward Jerusalem Council II (TJCII) was formed with equal representation from both groups.

"It was time for the Church to welcome back the Jewish believers just as the Jewish apostles had welcomed the Gentiles in the first century," Don Finto said.[8] A member of TJCII's International Leadership Council, Don's call is "to embrace God's prophetic call for Israel and the Jewish people, and

---

8. Toward Jerusalem Council II, "Vision, Origin and Documents," 21.

thus the Israel key that unlocks world revival, in preparation for the return of the King."[9]

He continues: "When the biblical Ruth covenanted together with the biblical Boaz, they brought forth the house of David. When today's Ruth (the church from the nations) makes covenant with today's Boaz (the resurrected Jewish believing community), we will herald the return of David's Greater Son—Yeshua (Jesus)."[10]

The model of messianic reconciliation differs from other initiatives striving to apologize to the people of cultures that have been decimated by the historic church. It goes to the root of divisiveness, where it began with contempt of the Jews.

Rabbi Daniel Juster, a council member of the TJCII initiative, has been a leader in the Messianic Jewish Movement since 1972. Daniel said, "We envisioned a meeting of many Church leaders who would enter into a process of mutual repentance and reconciliation and would affirm or declare themselves in alignment with the Messianic Jewish community and its calling."[11] In 1979, Rabbi Daniel became the first president and later General Secretary of the Union of Messianic Jewish Congregations. He oversees a network of congregations in the United States and helps with the work of networks in Israel. Director of Tikkun International, Rabbi Daniel is the author of twenty books on theology.

Another TJCII leader, John Dawson, said, "We agreed that a reconciliation initiative was needed between Jewish and Gentile believers that paralleled the growing number of initiatives addressing historic of[sic] grievances, such as the memory of indigenous peoples relating to some of their experiences with Christian civilization and its institutions."[12] A native of New Zealand, John serves as International President for Youth With A Mission, giving direction to seventeen thousand staff in more than two hundred nations. In 1990, John founded the International Reconciliation Coalition, a network of Christian leaders dedicated to healing wounds between people groups, beginning with Native American and African American issues that were afflicted by the violence from a church eradicating their identity.

The council faced the deepest of spiritual strongholds that, for nearly two thousand years, kept the church in faulty thinking by presenting God as rejecting the Jews. By 1997, the leadership was traveling to England, France, the Czech Republic, Slovakia, Austria, Switzerland, Spain, Rome, Turkey,

---

9. See Don Finto's staff page at www.beltway.org.
10. Toward Jerusalem Council II, "Vision, Origin and Documents," 22.
11. Toward Jerusalem Council II, "Vision, Origin and Documents," 14.
12. Toward Jerusalem Council II, "Vision, Origin and Documents," 10.

Jerusalem, Ethiopia, North America, Vienna, Latin America, Romania, the Netherlands, and Israel, forming groups at many levels which prayed about the ongoing direction of the Holy Spirit.

As the walls between the separated peoples came down, committees of Jewish and non-Jewish intercessory teams threaded through the world, moving living water through the body. The crucifixion called the Jew and gentile to worship together and support each other, facing toward the Lord's promises to Jerusalem and seeing what is hurting in the body, with the opportunity to learn from each other. Again, they are saying, "I thank my God in all my remembrance of you" (Phil 1:3).

> The peasantry ceased in Israel, they ceased until you arose,
> Deb'orah, arose as a mother in Israel. (Judg 5:7)

Deborah was a prophet in high esteem in her nation, but when she described herself, it was as a mother. She recognized that what occurs at the heart of family is a powerful influence in the world.

It will not be a political or social movement that returns the people back to their promised land. Coming out of Egypt after four hundred years, there was no political process they could turn to, no educational system that would lead their escape. No one was listening. But God heard. It was he who led the deliverance and said, "I want you to know me." To bring about the one new humanity, he established the role of motherhood to be cultivated to preserve a people's identity.

It didn't come at the expense of stifling gifts of natural leadership. The Lord's design brings many talents to create one whole in ways that are pleasing to God. The creation is composed of birds, fishes, trees, winds, waters, and celestial bodies, each doing their part to strengthen what to the Maker is one creation.

Each of the twelve tribes had gifts that together advanced the work of God. Reuben, the firstborn, was the first strength of Jacob. Simeon and Levi added knowledge to the other tribes. It was through Judah that the scepter would never depart. Zebulun, by the coast with ships, is to bless those who come in from the waters. Dan was small, but had the bite of a snake that could bring down horse and rider, waiting in confidence for God to rescue. Gad would push back those who attacked. Asher had gifts of service, yielding foods and delicacies living in the fertile part of Canaan. Naphtalie, described as a deer set free to birth beautiful fawns, speaks of beautiful words graced with gentle compassion. The tribe of Benjamin would produce many leaders, including Queen Esther and Apostle Paul. Joseph is a fruitful bough overcoming walls, remaining unshaken even when attacked, showing us how to forgive and find healing because God's plan will surpass all other efforts.

To learn God's will is to achieve the fulfillment of all life. We are not to undervalue any gift or think we are not blessed. In his parable of talents, Jesus said we are not to hide the gifts he endowed in us (Matt 25:14–30). We are not to bury the knowledge bestowed in others either, people made in the image of God who bring their talents to make the body whole.

The contributions of women from varied communities are owed to God, who blesses her with purpose. They share, they disciple to the Lord, and they protect the children's heritage, but they do not try to convert the children of other cultures. Cherishing the internal purpose that is bound by God's ordinances, a woman lights the Shabbat candles because no agenda can give the guiding power that is the Lord's alone.

Because the enemy is here to destroy the Jews and the pastors, prevent the church from unifying, and drown out the voice of Jesus, candlelight became a celebration of God preserving the people through impossible situations. Chanukah light comes in December to commemorate the rededication of the second temple mentioned in John 10, when Jesus was in the temple courts walking in Solomon's colonnade during the Feast of Dedication. The people who gathered around him wondered if Jesus was from the darkness, desiring to grab and silence him. Jesus answered them by saying that he is the Messiah (vv. 22–30). His sheep listen to his voice and follow him. They will never perish.

Some link Chanukah to Christmas, saying that Jesus was conceived at Christmas and born in autumn during the Feast of Tabernacles. Chanukah means "dedication"; it comes from the Hebrew word *hinuch*, meaning "education." The menorah carried from Jerusalem is a symbol of the fire of Scripture living on in the millions who study its words.

The Talmud teaches that the *mitzvah* of Chanukah is a "candle for each man and his household." The commandment is to kindle the Chanukah lights in one's home. The threat of annihilation to the Jews began in families redefining marriage and morality. King Antiochus took rule at a time when the people were opening gates, making themselves vulnerable to compromising practices. Greek civilization rose up, and Antiochus declared that everyone must homogenize by following Zeus and giving up their own practices. He tried to wipe out the teachings of Israel, just as Hitler attempted to destroy it. The devil believed that, if Jewish teachings could be wiped out, then the Messiah could not come and judgment would not follow.

King Antiochus went into the holy place in the temple and abolished sacrifices to God. The temple became pagan, full of immorality and promiscuity. What once was perverse spread through culture and became law. Out of this came the desire to persecute anyone who gathered for Shabbat or worshiped the living God.

From out in the hill country, Mattisyahu ben Yochanan and his five sons watched this happening to their beloved Jerusalem. The Maccabees took a stand and refused to bow to Antiochus's ways. They called for whoever was on God's side to join with them and fight. Although they were vastly outnumbered, they defeated the Greek army twice. They had fasted and prayed, and they won. Rising in the brilliant light of faith, they liberated Jerusalem from Greek control and purified the temple.

The entire country of Israel is full of Chanukah candles shining bright in the windows during the Feast of Dedication. The light remembers men and women who made no compromise. It tells how God will fight for his people in the end days. Speaking to his disciples in the Mount of Olives, Jesus told of the end times reflecting the history of Antiochus, saying, "when you see the desolating sacrilege spoken of by the prophet Daniel, standing in the holy place (let the reader understand)" (Matt 24:15).

The faithful Maccabees lit the menorah with the small amount of the pure oil found that had been sanctified by the high priest. The oil was only enough to keep the flame alive one day, but the menorah lamps burned for eight days. Jesus would repeat the thought, saying, "Abide in me, and I in you" (John 15:4). When we come into the presence of his light, his light comes into us. The eight nights of Chanukah bring centuries of light into each candle. The shamash candle is lit first, and is used to light the first candle on the far right of the menorah; an additional candle is lit on each subsequent night by both men and women. The shamash candle represents the shining faith that the ancestors passed on to restore wonder in the Lord appearing them, his arrow flashing like lightning (Zech 9:14).

On the first night of Chanukah, the blessing is spoken:

> Blessed are you, Adonai our God, who rules the universe, accomplishing miracles for our ancestors from ancient days until our time.

The candles attest to God rolling away darkness and bringing light.

Chosen People Ministries, a Messianic Jewish nonprofit organization based in New York, describes celebrating Chanukah (or Hanukkah, as quoted here) as the celebration of Jesus bringing light to the world and to our souls:

> Hanukkah is a powerful story of God interceding on behalf of His people and showing His faithful loving kindness. When Antiochus Epiphanes, also known in Jewish history as "Antiochus

the Madman," persecuted the Jewish people and desired that they worship the Greek gods and give up their Jewish identity, the Jews revolted. As they were rededicating the Temple after an un-kosher sacrifice was made, the oil, which was only enough for one day[,] lasted for eight.

Jewish followers of Jesus see Hanukkah as time to celebrate another gift of God to our people (and the whole world!)—Jesus the Jewish Messiah. During Hanukkah we celebrate how God provided light in the Temple for eight nights. However, how appropriate it is to also remember the Light of the World, through whom we have the Light of Life (Jn. 8:12). If God had not intervened during the first Hanukkah, a Jewish virgin would not have given birth to a child who would be raised as a Jew to fulfill God's will for His life – to be the atonement for our sins. Hanukkah is a demonstration of God's unfolding plan of redemption, which Christians and some Jews celebrate at Christmas.[13]

The oil used to light lamps had to be in its pure, pristine state. A cultural environment that pressures a person to accept defiled oil was met with refusal because of the long years spent learning to depend on God and the knowledge of his ability to create miracles to save them.

During the first century, Jerusalem was the holy place and the temple the center of life. After the Jews were scattered, teachers like Yokkanen Ben Zakai adapted the teachings to say that holiness can be found in time set aside. Longing to be refreshed by the memory of all the Lord had done, the lighting of candles continued. The children grew with the prayers of Moses and the laws that are a light for the path to find God's Son.

Time itself is the place to meet with God. Shabbat covets this time to touch the eternal.

Before Jesus opened the gate for non-Jews, they were strangers, without God, having no hope (Eph 2:12–13). Through him both Jews and gentiles have access to the Father by one Spirit. Consequently, you are no longer foreigners and aliens, but fellow citizens with Israel and members of God's household.

All of the gatherings center around the invitation into the family at the Lord's table. The gentiles have freedom to participate in Jewish ways, if they desire, including the Shabbat and the feasts. Paul addressing gentiles in Colossae tells them, "Therefore let no one pass judgement on you in questions of food and drink or with regard to a festival or a new moon or a sabbath. These are only a shadow of what is to come; but the substance belongs to

---

13. Chosen People Ministries, "Did Jesus Celebrate Christmas," paras. 7–8.

Christ" (Col 2:16–17). Jesus is our Shabbat rest. "So then, there remains a sabbath rest for the people of God; for whoever enters God's rest also ceases from his labors as God did from his. Let us therefore strive to enter that rest" (Heb 4:9–11).

When Jesus rose from the dead, he met with his disciples on the first day of the week, Sunday, the day all of creation became busy doing their jobs. Gentile believers made it a day of worship. There is evidence from early Christian writings, such as Dianch in 70 AD, of gentiles meeting on both Shabbat and Sunday. At Troas, it was Saturday night when Paul raised Eutychus from the dead, considered the beginning of the first day of the week. Paul had talked until midnight after Shabbat ended, leaving after daylight (Acts 20:7–11).

The Shabbat is made for man (Mark 2:27). Future worship continues Shabbat, when life emerges from the world's influence. "From new moon to new moon, and from sabbath to sabbath, all flesh shall come to worship before me, says the Lord" (Isa 66:23). Further,

> Not many of you were wise according to worldly standards, not many were powerful, not many were of noble birth; but God chose what is foolish in the world to shame the wise, God chose what is weak in the world to shame the strong, God chose what is low and despised in the world, even things that are not, to bring to nothing things that are, so that no human being might boast in the presence of God. (1 Cor 1:26–29).

It has nothing to do with life's circumstance. It is about a call. "It was not because you were more in number than any other people that the Lord set his love upon you and chose you, for you were the fewest of all peoples; but it is because the Lord loves you, and is keeping the oath which he swore to your fathers" (Deut 7:7–8).

After such long years of being scattered across the world, under the weight of prejudice, being misunderstood and misrepresented, to "become the laughingstock of all peoples . . . made my teeth grind on gravel, and made me cower in ashes; my soul is bereft of peace" (Lam 3:14–17), the Lord reveals the vision to a Jewish man in exile, the apostle John, to assure his people of the wonderful news. "I saw a new Jerusalem coming down from heaven and God will dwell with his people forever" (Rev 21:2).

The Lord saw the people Israel, how on the day they were born no one cared about them; "[their] navel string was not cut, nor were [they] washed with water to cleanse [them], nor rubbed with salt, nor swathed with bands" (Ezek 16:4). Further, the Lord promises this to Israel: "I will make of you a great nation, and I will bless you, and make your name great, so that you will be a blessing (Gen 12:2). He called servants of the covenant from a small people so it would be the power of the message that would be reflected, not the might of a nation. The people were to daily echo the angels answering each other as they sing, "holy, holy, holy is the Lord of hosts." The whole earth is full of his glory, blessed from his high heaven. The glory is whole and undivided: "Hear O Israel: The Lord our God is one Lord" (Deut 6:4); "For behold, darkness shall cover the earth, and thick darkness the peoples; but the Lord will arise upon you, and his glory will be seen upon you. And nations shall come to your light, and kings to the brightness of your rising" (Isa 60:2–3); "That my salvation may reach to the end of the earth" (Isa 49:6); "In days to come Jacob shall take root, Israel shall blossom and put forth shoots, and fill the whole world with fruit" (Isa 27:6).

Even of Egypt and Assyria, oppressive enemies of Israel, God speaks promise.

> In that day Israel will be the third with Egypt and Assyria, a blessing in the midst of the earth, whom the Lord of hosts has blessed, saying, "Blessed be Egypt my people, and Assyria the work of my hands, and Israel my heritage. (Isa 19:24–25).

The Zohar states that God created the world so that we may know him. *Mitzvah*s weave the physical creation with heaven every time they are kept. God is at home in the kitchen, in the workplace, on long walks when the beauty of his creation is acknowledged and on death beds when his name is softly spoken because the *mitzvah* permeate the world with the presence of God lighting our path.

The sages of old call this basking in the ray of the Shekhinah, an experience of godliness unequaled to any moment on earth. The Lord achieves this moment in a person through the soul's longing for its source, growing stronger and more urgent as it descends into the shattered world. The experience sheds thoughts of the world as it did during the forty-year wandering after Egypt, and results in an unbreakable bond with heaven's fire.

I am the light of the world, Jesus said, speaking in the temple court near the menorah where the seven lights would come to mind in seven churches that comprise one body of Jesus.

After giving the commandments at Sinai, God instructed the people to build a tabernacle with its entrance facing east, a holy place where he would dwell among them (Exod 25:8). This was a sanctuary bringing God's presence into the world. The Shabbat candle lit in the home extends this presence.

The menorah that Moses made for the tabernacle in the desert and the ones in the temple had seven branches, three on each side and the middle a shamish candle, as instructed in Exodus 25. The lampstand held seven candles, a number unfolding in the creation being made in seven days, the instructions about the tabernacle with seven speeches to complete the task (Exod 25–27, Gen 1) and Aaron's seven priestly vestments.

The Chanukah menorah has eight branches, and a ninth is used as the shamash to commemorate the eight-day miracle.

The organization One For Israel states that "the items in the desert tabernacle spoke of what was to come in the New Covenant—one bride of Messiah: Jew and Gentile called together, brought purified and clean before God to dwell with him."[14]

One For Israel was established in 2009. With facilities based in Netanya, Israel, One For Israel has both a media center to broadcast the good news and the only Hebrew-speaking Bible College in Israel where pastors, ministers, leaders, Arab Israelis, Palestinians, and Messianic Jews, study and serve the Lord together along with students from all over the world, all under one roof.

One For Israel teaches that the menorah was God's idea. It first appears in Exodus 25:31–37, as God instructs the people to hammer it out of gold as one piece, weighing nearly one hundred pounds and standing about five feet high. It was a highly decorative work that had seven branches with seven lamps, nine flower blooms, eleven fruits, and twenty-two cups. The lamps gave bright light inside the dark tent of the tabernacle, a powerful symbol of God's holiness in the midst of a dark world.

The lamp was kept burning daily from sunset until morning, lighting the candles from right to left, beginning with the shamish candle (Exod 27:21). It is called the Lamp of God (1 Sam 3:3). God is light (1 John 1:5). In your light we see light (Ps 36:9).

A home where the candles are lit is a place of returning to the source of light that united Adam and Eve to ignite new life and vision. It's a time of teshuva, with thoughts reflecting on whether the week has led us closer to knowing the Lord, or away into darkness. When a woman is a bearer of this light, she steps into God's eternal unity, and draws down the light to those around her, drawing them together. A belief in a way of life is shared, an identity preserved that stretches back into the beginning of nations and forward into eternity. The women light the candle of an entire nation.

> I will make him a helper fit for him (Gen 2:18)

In the series of blessings a Jewish man speaks every morning, he gives thanks for God granting him another day, and he says, "Blessed are you

---

14. One for Israel, "Meaning Behind the Menorah," para. 11.

Hashem for not making me a non-Jew," "for not making me a slave," and "for not having made me a woman." These are expressions of gratitude for being entrusted with the responsibilities given to men to carry.

Non-Jews have the seven Noahide *mitzvah*s to follow, far fewer than the Jewish men were given through God's word. Under the Torah's compassionate laws, servants were given rest on Shabbat with the Israelites, so had more *mitzvah*s than the non-Jews (Deut 5:14).

A Jewish woman has been entrusted to do more *mitzvah*s than non-Jews and slaves. Her responsibility toward her children is a high priority, so she is exempt from the many *mitzvah*s required of men. Many have mistakenly thought that her exemption is a prohibition that ranks her as less valuable. Women are permitted to perform other *mitzvah*s, but not at the expense of the more private acts that are the foundation of how a home is lit within by God's light.

A woman expresses her gratitude for being given *mitzvah*s with the blessing, "for making me according to your will." Being made a woman reflects the creation after Adam, when God said it is not good for him to be alone. He was incomplete. This was not God's desire so he brought woman to fulfill his will and complete his creation.

Daughters of Sarah discern the people who belong to the Lord, chosen for the covenant, and make choices together with the Lord. God asks us to bring more than the brief spark of word, but to stay long enough with a shivering soul until their flame ignites to stand by itself and we see the glow of faith in their eyes as the embers blaze again. Each soul must sustain its flame.

As Jesus sat on the Mount of Olives, he spoke with his disciples about God's kingdom being like ten bridesmaids who were called out to wait for the bridegroom. They brought their lamps with them. Five were foolish and didn't bring the extra oil needed for the lamps. The five wise women brought enough oil to keep the lamps burning through his delay.

The companions are listening for the groom's voice with longing to hear him (Song 8:13). They serve as witnesses and walk with the bride to the wedding feast in the house of the groom. The groom's arrival was announced with a shofar and with his own voice, calling to the bride and her maidens.

The bridesmaids grew sleepy waiting for him. At midnight someone suddenly announced, "The bridegroom is coming! Come and meet him!" All the bridesmaids woke and made their lamps ready to be torchbearers for the procession.

The maidens who were unprepared had to run to find extra oil to buy. The celebration begins, but when they return and knock on the door, they are forbidden entry. "I never knew you," the groom says (see Matt 25:1–13). Jesus says the kingdom is like these ten women. He is speaking of a wedding process that has two stages, according to tradition. *Kiddushin* is the sanctification, the betrothal, and commitment. *Nissuin* means "marriage," and it is when the couple begins life together.

Friends of the bridegroom such as John the Baptist, the groom, and the bride and her people go out to meet each other. When they come together, the wedding takes place. Then a procession goes to the home of the groom where a feast takes place which may last for days and completes the ritual of marriage.

Realizing their lamps were empty, the foolish bridesmaids asked the others to give them their oil. The wise bridesmaids answered, "No! The oil we have might not be enough for all of us. But go to those who sell oil and buy some for yourselves." Oil represents the presence of the Holy Spirit, bringing the light of wisdom and the anointing power of Jesus. The oil in the tabernacle was olive oil for light and for anointing kings and sanctifying priests (Exod 25:6).

In giving us the Word, who is light, God is saying to get knowledge. Don't settle for belief, but come into the intimate knowledge of him. Bring questions, because he wants conversation with us so that we can acquire confidence in what we understand. He wants both the mind and the heart to be embedded in action.

The Lord said, "Know therefore this day, and lay it to your heart, that the Lord is God in heaven above and on the earth beneath; there is no other" (Deut 4:39). To help us internalize his knowledge, the Lord appointed a calendar, the hours of the day and of the night serving to sustain creation and the generations of people while earth remains (Gen 8:22).

Every word shared at the Lord's table moves us nearer to knowing God. The oil needed to illuminate a flame through the darkness can only accumulate in each individual who walks with the Lord. Everyone who is thirsty must drink for themselves. Coming to his table as a family in all our differences and shared concerns, the one new humanity overcomes divisions through their testimonies, each a flame adding to the light.

The flame requires the oil, the wick, and the vessel. When the wick is saturated, the oil will burn. Together they enable the flame to flare steadily. Man is a wick, soaking up God's word and Holy Spirit to express the divine truths for himself and others. Without that oil, desire for God flashes and burns out.

The wick releases the flame to be a light at the same time as holding the flame in the physical realm. Its yearning is to converge with God's holy fire above, yet fulfill the kindness, knowledge, and guidance on earth with the purpose of refining individuals in their specific tasks.

The Word left the palaces of his Father in heaven and came seeking his bride. Offering to serve her, cleanse her, and make a covenant with her forever, he returned to his Father's house to prepare a place for her. "In my Father's house are many abiding places," he said. "I'm coming back for you" (see John 14). The bride is to prepare, lilies among thorns waiting for the shout of his voice. The bride is brought into the presence of God's Son just as Eve was brought to Adam.

Always be ready for his return, Jesus said. There will come a moment that it is too late to prepare, the moment the Shabbat candle is lit and the Lord of the Shabbat appears. There is no more time to work. The warning addresses those who are called out, the ekklesia, who are not to assume that they can ever stop nurturing the flame to remain aligned with its source of fire in heaven.

Jesus went on to explain it in the parable of the lamp under a bush. In Luke, Jesus says that no one lights a lamp to put it in a cellar or under a basket, but on a stand so that those who come in will see it. It is not to be buried beneath the world's skewed thinking, but should be welcoming, like the table at Shabbat. Vanquishing shadows to reveal the path, the light reassures us, reminding us that we are never alone. The power never diminishes.

The ekklesia, the "called out," were called by Jews (Jesus and his disciples). The faith goes "first to the Jew" but also ensures "trouble and distress for every human being who does evil: first for the Jew, then for the Gentile" (Rom 2:9–10). Israel was set as an example of the times of exile and redemption ebbing and flowing throughout a lifetime and the persecution that would fall on Christians believing in the Messiah. The miracle through the Maccabees is that the light of the lamps kept burning longer than it should have with the lack of support they found in the world around them. He gives grace to those mourning the wrongs, coming in meekness to the Lord, brought to the table to see God's ways, and they become peacemakers between the people of all nations (Matt 5:3–9).

4

FIRE

> For behold, the Lord will come in fire. (Isa 66:15)

FIRE PURIFIES, AND SCRIPTURE has much to say about the subject. "In this you rejoice, though now for a little while you may have to suffer various trials, so that the genuineness of your faith, more precious than gold which though perishable is tested by fire, may redound to praise and glory and honor at the revelation of Jesus Christ" (1 Pet 1:6–7). Moses saw the Lord as a consuming fire, holy flames that destroy everything that is not his fire. Isaiah said to his people, "When you walk through fire you shall not be burned, and the flame shall not consume you" (43:2); "Fire goes before him, and burns up his adversaries round about" (Ps 97:3); "If any man's work is burned up, he will suffer loss, though he himself will be saved, but only as through fire" (1 Cor 3:15).

Like the miracle of the menorah on Chanukah, when the oil burned but was not consumed, as well as that of the presence of God in a burning bush that spoke out of the fire to Moses, his holy light sustains what holds his holy flame. As God refined his chosen souls to flame with his desire, the brightness grew in the nation of Israel, enlightening the communities around them, shining from Jerusalem. "I have set you to be a light for the Gentiles, that you may bring salvation to the uttermost parts of the earth" (Acts 13:47; Isa 49:6); "He will sit as a refiner and purifier of silver, and he will purify the sons of Levi and refine them like gold and silver" (Mal 3:3);

"I came to cast fire upon the earth, and would that it were already kindled!" (Luke 12:49).

The flame yearns for the mystery to be fulfilled. Rabbi Aryeh Kaplan observes:

> Just as the unborn child has many endowments which are of no use to it in the womb, but demonstrate that it will be born into a world where they will be used, so does a human being have many endowments which are of little value in this life, which indicate that man will be reborn into a higher dimension after death.[1]

Spiritual fire prepares a soul to be given a place to move among the angels in the courts of the Lord (Zech 3:7). Things never imagined are being kept for those who follow the Lord through the fiery trials. "No eye has seen, nor ear heard, nor the heart of man conceived, what God has prepared for those who love him" (1 Cor 2:9); "From of old no one has heard or perceived by the ear, no eye has seen a God besides thee, who works for those who wait for him" (Isa 64:4).

Paul says to encourage one another with these thoughts. Kindle the flame in others so the light grows strong. Paul writes to people under tremendous suffering and temptations to leave the faith in favor of being safe, reminding at every opportunity to pray continually. The Lord's consuming fire leaves alive only the flame that moves us from one glory to the next. By a spirit of burning and judgement, the Lord will cleanse Jerusalem and the daughters of Zion (Isa 4:4). Isaiah ends his message with God saying, "come and gather the people of all nations and languages, and they will come and see my glory." Set affections on these things to come, Paul said in Colossians 3:2.

Parts of the body of the church strayed into the legacy in Genesis 11, when man said, "Let's build ourselves a city, and a tower with its top in the heavens, and let us make a name for ourselves" (11:4). God had told them to populate the earth and form communities everywhere. But instead, their obsession busied with their own agenda, aiming to glorify themselves.

Martha, in the dilemma of someone overwhelmed by work, is accusing toward her sister Mary, who sat at the feet of Jesus. She is so frazzled that she disrupts Jesus speaking to the guests, asking "don't you care that I am left alone with this work? Tell her to help me!" Martha had invited him in and now she's full of her own agenda and wants the Lord to make others be what she wants them to be. Her heart is hardening. But the Lord softly answered,

---

1. Kaplan, "Soul," para. 3.

"Martha, Martha, you are anxious and troubled about many things" (Luke 10:41). Anxious, drawn in different directions by the many things that can take on importance, she'd forgotten. Jesus reminded her that "one thing is needful" (v. 42). Mary, seen often at the feet of Jesus listening to the words of God, had chosen that which protects communion with God. Seek him first.

The notion of self-importance fostered thoughts of loving Jesus in independent, self-empowering ways that are not inclusive of the ekklesia. According to the Barna Group, 61 percent of women not attending church identify themselves as believers, but found no place for themselves in the local church.[2]

The female presence is decreasing in church as other traditions disappear. There is less of a tie to place and community as job seekers pack and move with each opportunity for more education and career choices. A sense of fulfillment comes more from contributing at work than inside the walls of a church. Coming into the sanctuary with gifts and expertise, many women find their skills unneeded as they're asked to volunteer only for nursery or in the kitchen. They sit in pews quietly hoping to be known. They seek intelligent discussion about the Lord's presence in world affairs, environmental health, cultural studies, or justice issues, and don't hear how our everyday concerns tie with the Bible.[3]

Among the reasons that Jamie Bowman cites in her article "Why Women are Leaving the Church" is a consumerist mentality that has taken hold in many women. Some feel that after years of Bible studies and church services, growth was limited and they no longer need to gather with others as part of one body. By virtue of technology making communicating online easier, personal time together is replaced. Ultimately, it results in feelings of loneliness, and maintaining relationship with those speaking genuinely and transparently about their journey of faith becomes lost to the next generation.[4]

Can these women grow in the Lord's teachings if they're not participating in talking with the body? In a culture obsessed with validating emotions, the feeling of believing in a savior as an emotional belief does not bring sanctification. There can also be so much intellectualizing of Scripture and pressure to fill agendas of programs that living in personal intimacy with God is left in drought. The Barna Group found that 72 percent of women feel stressed out, 58 percent are tired, and 48 percent are overcommitted.[5]

2. Barna Group, "Those Who 'Love Jesus,'" para. 4.
3. Williamson, "Working Women."
4. Bowman, "Why Women are Leaving."
5. Barna Group, "Tired & Stressed," fig. 1.

If a woman works all week, she's seeking rest, a break from the agendas of others in longing for quiet enjoyment of family and home. She is not leaving her faith. She's prioritizing her deepest concerns, thirsting for a sense of blessing in the heart of her home and within the stillness and privacy of her heart.

Eve led Adam into the dark night when she chose the wrong fruit, and fire was given to help the first couple when they left the garden. Women take the fire and light Shabbat candles to draw people back to God where they live, in families and homes. As the Lord brings the wild branches with the olive tree to gather at his table, the core gift of Shabbat cherishing family is being renewed in the church. Salvation is more than words remembering that he died to save us. It means coming to him, wearied and overladen, and basking in his presence, which supports our origins. His forgiveness washes over us, and healing from the past joins his family together the moment the celebratory flame is lit.

As she greets the Shabbat lights, the woman guards the way in both internal private prayer and collective prayer, charged with the incredibly difficult task of raising children to inherit God's values. Mothers intuitively encourage children to walk into their fullness, valuing their ancestry within the covenant of God. In turn seeing the richness of identity that comes from heritage, other people groups are provoked to explore their own gifts, restore their original language, and through sharing recipes and traditional knowledge bring health to the land and people.

The inheritance comes through faith (Heb 11:23). Gentiles have a goal to remind Israel of their awesome God. They are here to support Israel, to shop at their stores when they are ostracized, to stand with them when they are persecuted, to tell their children they love the God of Israel because the Savior of the entire world came through their people. We've received the sword of the Spiritpirit and the shield of faith because a Jew died for us.

The boundaries that the Lord designed to guard and remember fracture more deeply with every anti-Semitic harassment on social media against Israel. The Anti-Defamation League documented more than 2.5 million tweets containing anti-Semitic language during the first half of 2016. ADL recorded that incidents of anti-Semitism in America increased 36 percent since 2015, including assaults and vandalism. On November 28, 2017, Canada's government released a report on a more than 20 percent rise in anti-Semitic hate crimes since the year before.

In Australia, anti-Semitic abuse is up nearly 10 percent since 2016, reported by the Executive Council of Australian Jewry in November 2017. On college campuses in Melbourne, Sydney, and Brisbane, a neo-Nazi group whose motto is "we are the Hitler you've been waiting for" distributed posters calling to "legalize the execution of the Jews."

In 2017, the Community Securities Trust in Britain tracked the increase of anti-Semitism rising nearly one third in the number of attacks in the first half of the year, compared with the same months in 2016. Many soccer teams now have groups of fans who identify with neo-Nazism and extreme forms of anti-Semitism and racism. Dozens of incidents of neo-Nazi fans are reported every year by Kick It Out, a watchdog organization that monitors anti-Semitic and racist abuse in British soccer.[6] Fans of Amsterdam's soccer team Ajax support the Jewish community in the city, waving Israeli flags at games and singing Jewish songs. Fans of opposing teams taunted this practice by using a picture of Jewish children who were murdered by the Nazis. Images of Avram and Emanuel Rosenthal, just five and two years old when they were killed in 1944, were sent to rival fans on social media.[7]

In 2015, the game between Ajax and Utrecht continued as dozens of Utrecht supporters sang, "My father was in the commandos, my mother was in the SS, together they burned Jews 'cause Jews burn the best" and "Hamas, Hamas, Jews to the gas." In Poland a rival team from the city of Lodz, home to a thriving Jewish community before the Holocaust, shouted "Move on, Jews! Your home is at Auschwitz! Send you to the gas!" from the stands. At the Bologna match, five hundred Lazio supporters outside the stadium gave Nazi salutes and sang Nazi songs.[8]

Repairing fallen walls means taking a stand for justice, making strangers feel welcomed, and opposing racism and neo-Nazi ideology, however risky it may be. It may bring boycotts, sanctions, mockery, and isolation, yet it restores the foundations laid long ago, and the lanes for living (Isa 58:12). It is the work of peacemakers, coming after repenting, blessed after being excluded, reviled, cast out and rewarded by heaven (Luke 6:22–23).

The result is blessing for the entire world.

As we witness the world moving toward becoming the antichrist's one world system, the Lord is joining Israelite and gentile believers into a bright flame, which has not happened since the book of Acts. The olive tree in its fullness symbolizes victory sanctified in the light of God. Late in the season, the small fruits mature, containing enough oil for the menorah lit by the Maccabees displaying the prophetic message of the times to come. During those days, the king wrote to his whole kingdom that all should be one

---

6. Miller, "Anne Frank," para. 6.
7. Miller, "Anne Frank," paras. 3–4.
8. Miller, "Anne Frank," paras. 5, 7.

people (1 Macc 1:41). Prayer was illegal. Observing God's laws resulted in punishment.

Believers were marginalized, as good was called evil and evil became the acceptable standard. The king called for everyone to worship Zeus, a god of the Greeks. Mythology portrays Zeus as infamous for his erotic behaviors—as a bull he abducts Europa, a Greek goddess for whom Europe was named. The image of her riding a monstrous bull is elicited in Revelation 17 when an angel describes the mother of harlots and abominations of the earth as "a woman sitting on a scarlet-colored beast which was full of blasphemous names . . . The woman was . . . holding in her hand a golden cup full of abominations and the impurities of her fornication" (vv. 3–5).

The seven additional days the menorah burned when there had been only oil enough for the first day bring to mind Revelation's opening act, with Jesus standing amid seven lamp stands. The Maccabees went to the temple and, seeing it defiled, re-consecrated everything to its place. They found the menorah and lit the lamps, bringing back the light of God. It was a light hidden, not seen from outside the tabernacle, but only inside the holy chamber after sacrificial atonement. After the death and resurrection of Jesus, the veil in the temple was torn, the temple destroyed within a generation, and the menorah fire released throughout all the world. We are the temple. Lit from within, we are to bring into balance any system that attempts the imposter form of becoming one body.

Forty years before Columbus's voyage to North America, in 1452 Pope Nicholas V issued the bull Romanus Pontifex to the king of Portugal, declaring that all non-Christians throughout earth are to be conquered, colonized, and their territories taken. Anyone not of the Catholic faith was considered less than human. The bull directed the king to "capture, vanquish, and subdue the Saracens, pagans, and other enemies of Christ" and to "put them into perpetual slavery" and "take all their possessions and property." The bull sanctified Portugal to continue trafficking in African slavery and take land along Africa's western coast.

The papal bull Inter caetera, issued in May of 1493, granted Spain the right to lands discovered by Columbus. In North America, the Native Americans were also divided into tribes, counted times and festivals of giving thanks by the lunar year, had fasts and laws of cleanliness, cities of refuge and festivals, and (like the Jews) were considered inferior because they were not Caucasian church members.

In the document, Pope Alexander declared that the discovered people be subjugated to the church. The Doctrine of Discovery was adopted into United States law in 1823 in the Supreme Court case Johnson v. McIntosh when Chief Justice John Marshal noted that Christian European nations assumed "ultimate dominion" over land of America and Native people lost "their rights to complete sovereignty as independent nations."

Jesus internalized the tenth commandment, "You shall not covet anything that belongs to your neighbor" (Exod 20:17), in the Sermon on the Mount to purify the heart of the greed and restlessness that come when no blessing comes from selfish desire. He applies the tenth commandment when speaking with a rich, righteous man who he asked to sell all and follow him (Matt 19:16–22). Beyond actions of other commandments, this is about a life maturing to wholly take on the concerns of the Lord beyond our own lives.

Friday evening closes the door on the empty place of grasping jealousies. God fills each heart to overflowing with grace that cannot be stolen, bestowed as royal gifts given by the king. The passage is from slavery to freedom, from the descent into the cry for the grace of God to ascending the mountain of God. Wanting more of this fire, this life of God among us, more of his purity, more of his power to unite flame and wick to release fragrance upward to heaven, the apostles wanted to see it kindled among each people group as they traveled between churches to connect them to each other.

Paul speaks of what to pursue so that the flame remains strong. He did this one thing, forgetting what was behind and straining forward in pursuit of the upward calling that took hold of him, ascending as he was refined. "One thing have I asked of the Lord, that will I seek after; that I may dwell in the house of the Lord all the days of my life, to behold the beauty of the Lord, and to inquire in his temple" (Ps 27:4). At the end of his letter to the Thessalonians, Paul admonishes believers not to put out the Spirit's fire. God had ignited something wonderful, a flame from the fire of heaven to unify as it purifies. As long as the flame keeps burning, its influence will spread.

> We went through fire and water, but you brought us to a place of abundance. (Ps 66:12)

The people who became Israel were delivered from their past and led to a wilderness. There needed to be a time of transition because Israel's hearts were the hearts of slaves. There were divisions among God's people even then. Some vied to be in leadership. Others failed to turn to knowing God and died. They saw his works, but did not understand his ways as Moses understood and aligned with God's greater purpose.

Just because someone is delivered does not mean their mind is not still in the thinking of that enslavement. Because they've come to love Jesus does not mean they yet care about what is of concern to him. The experience of wandering through wilderness cleanses years of entrenched culture. God intends a very real change.

Although he had stumbled many times, the man of God's own heart, David, was considered a great man of Israel and man of God because of his honest confession seeking to return to his God. Have mercy on me O God. Wash me, cleanse me. I acknowledge my transgressions. Examine my heart. Purge me. Restore to me the joy of your salvation (Ps 51). David, a man who continually turned toward the Lord, multiplied priests among his people, who continued the light after he died.

"He delivered us from so deadly a peril, and he will deliver us; on him we have set our hope that he will deliver us again" (2 Cor 1:10). The Lord brings us out, not merely to be free, like a bird flying from a cage. His holy fire burns up the cages so we will become a community, safely brought to the tree of life. With Pharaoh's horses closing in, the shouts of his men pursued them. Israel ran, trampling, stumbling, running down to the beach, hearts pounding. Then Moses spoke and God was present; the waters parted into a path, and the people sing. They are delivered and unified by being set apart.

At this time, Israel had a heart hardened by oppression, not by rejecting the Lord. Despondent and deeply discouraged, buried under years of slavery, they could not hear, short of breath and overwhelmed (Exod 6:9). They were unable to experience moments of entering quietness, where the higher purpose connected with their minds. When deliverance came, the situation worsened before it became better. Their flames were small, yet an ember flickered, full of hope, seeking the path where the shofar is heard.

Jeremiah called them prisoners of hope. Although they could not yet see the end in sight, it was there in the flame of their soul, which had been lit by heaven. "I will bring you out," the Lord says. The enemy steps in, whispering that the grievous things of the past are not repairable. There have been too many wrong choices. We will never be whole again.

Paul's message says, don't feed the flames of the wrong fire by returning to what has passed. Let all bitterness, anger, and wrath be put away because of the great vision before us. The enemy embitters the waters, but from heaven the Holy Spirit inspired Ezekiel to see Satan's fall in the king of Tyre. He is described as once perfect in beauty, present in the garden of Eden. Every precious stone was his in an array of beautiful colors: carnelian, chrysolite, moonstone, beryl, onyx, jasper, sapphire, turquoise, and emerald, all wrought in gold settings and engravings. They were prepared the day Satan was created. He walked among the stones of fire.

However, he abounded with pride in his own splendor. God cast him as a profane thing from the mountain of God. The guardian cherub drove him out from among the stones of fire. "I cast you to the ground," God said, and brought out fire from within him to consume him, turning him to ashes on the earth in the sight of all who saw (Ezek 28:12–19).

The first day of Rosh Hashanah, leading to Yom Kippur, begins with a candle lit with prayer for God to guard the ways in the new season. All the strange fire must be fanned out through every circumstance so that the wicks are dismantled and truth prevails among the people. After Aaron sacrificed the sin offering, the burnt offering, and the fellowship offering, Moses and Aaron blessed the people and the glory of God appeared to them all. Fire from the presence of God consumed the burnt offering on the altar. The sight filled the people with joy and praise. But Aaron's two eldest sons, Nadav and Avihu, put fire and incense in their censers and offered it before God. Fire came out from the presence of God this time and killed them.

They offered unholy fire (*ash zarah*) before the Lord, such as he had not commanded them (Lev 10:1). The descriptors "unholy" or "strange" when referring to the fire contain the same significance as its use in the sentence "to preserve you from the loose [*ashah zarah*] woman" with her seductive words (Prov 7:5). There could be no outside influence allowed in the families of God's kingdom.

Moses instructed relatives to take care of their bodies. Aaron had just seen his two eldest sons die. He was silent. Moses directed Aaron and the priests not to mourn, but because the Lord's anointing was on them, to continue into the tent of meeting and focus on completing the work of God. It is a redefined healing. When closed in by pain, he opens a window of bright purpose.

The *haftarah* (reading from the prophets) on the first day of Yom Kippur recites the story of Hannah, the mother of the prophet Samuel. Her story reinforces knowing that everything is dependent on the will of God and everything can change in a moment.

On November 15, 1941, no one knew what was happening as the steady march of Nazi boots pounded sorrow into the hearts of a community. Children woke to the sounds of their mothers' familiar voices, husbands hearing the clamor of wives preparing food in the kitchen, sounds of birds chirping and loved ones that surrounded them as they began their day. Then came starvation and random gunshots that killed both young and old, grandmother and shopkeeper. Artists painting portraits were burned to ash with musicians performing melodies and scholars who taught knowledge. The sun continued rising and setting. The moon remained faithful in its cycles of light as half a million people became dust scattered by the wind.

The Warsaw Ghetto uprising is remembered for the heroism that displayed the largest act of Jewish resistance during the Holocaust. On 14th Nisan (April 19th, 1943) the Jewish people sealed in the ghetto resisted, struggled to survive, protect their children, believe in a future, and they decided to fight. Over four hundred thousand people, unable to leave, without provisions, weakened and starving, stood against the soldiers for four long weeks before being killed, burnt alive, suffocated, or shipped to camps.[9]

Only 1 percent escaped their predators, leaving the story as the last act of their lives, burying their words to hide them or slipping them to gentile friends for those who still lived. Their cries became strong flames still burning in the rubble, years beyond the dark days. The country of Israel was reborn in 1948 from the ashes of the Holocaust like dry bones coming back to life.

The only constant in this life is the open gate of prayer. We learn from Hannah that accepting this and coming to the Lord to make our needs known uncovers the divine light in our souls. Hannah was the wife of Elkanah. She was childless, and when they traveled to Shiloh, she prayed for a child. She wept with passion, vowing to the Lord that if he would bless her with a child, she would dedicate him to God all the days of his life. Eli, the high priest at Shiloh, watched as she prayed so excessively. Her lips moved silently as she spoke in the intimacy of her solitude with the Lord. Eli thought she must be drunk, an offense in this holy place. He confronted her and accused, "How long will you be drunken? Put away your wine from you" (1 Sam 1:14).

Hannah replied, "No my lord, I am a woman sorely troubled; I have drunk neither wine nor strong drink, but I have been pouring out my soul before the Lord" (1:15). *Tefillah*, a Hebrew word for prayer, means "attachment." Prayer endeavors to rise and connect with God, the source of life, and attach with his will for us. Hannah knew that the gates of prayer are never closed to a genuine heart. She knew prayer can transform what seems unchangeable. This continued to be her mindset even after she received her baby to dedicate to serve the temple.

After they left Samuel at the temple, Hannah stood with her husband, Elkanah. He was Samuel's father, so before he left, Hannah lifted her voice to reaffirm her decision and allay any doubt as her husband listened. "My heart exults in the Lord; my strength is exalted in the Lord. My mouth derides my enemies, because I rejoice in thy salvation" (1 Sam 2:1). There is no one besides God, she said. The Lord knows who is speaking arrogantly and their deeds are weighed. The very foundations of the earth are the Lord's. He will guard the feet of faithful servants. Those who oppose the Lord will be broken.

---

9. One for Israel, "Holocaust Remembrance," paras. 2–3.

She reminds her husband (and us) that God brings death and gives life. He raises the needy from the dust, for it is not through strength that man prevails. Hannah reaffirms for her husband and herself as man and wife that this act of obedience is in the hands of God. Realities can entirely change, and no matter what, her heart rejoices in the Lord. There is no one holy like the Lord (1 Sam 2:1–11).

After her prayer, her husband went home to Ramah. Every year he went with Hannah to the temple where they offered the annual sacrifice, visited their son, and brought him a linen ephod Hannah made for him to wear. Eli blessed Elkanah and his wife, and to ease the pain of leaving Samuel, he prayed, "May the Lord give you children by this woman to take the place of the one she prayed for and gave to the Lord." The Lord graciously gave them three sons and two daughters.

As the days move into Rosh Hashanah, thoughts turn serious as the candle is lit. Awareness of falling short of being righteous is lifted by confidence in the Lord's advocacy to bring us out of judgment, wholly restored. Solemn repentance becomes joy overflowing in his mercy, because exalting him brings strength.

Rejoice. Your name is written in heaven.

There can be no joy if there is no one to light the candle, so the Lord did the work of sending the soul into the body. Kindling a light requires a vessel to hold the wick, the body that is made to hold the soul. The candle creates a dwelling place for God to illuminate the surroundings.

When the light flickers and weakens because God is not exalted, the Lord says, "Where are their gods, the rock in which they took refuge, who ate the fat of their sacrifices, and drank the wine of their drink offering? Let them rise up and help you, let them be your protection!" Then they will see that there is no god besides God and no one can deliver out of his hand (Deut 32:36–39).

He leads us through the desert, wanting us to realize that he alone is the source of living water because it is God's will that we have a way to return. "Woman, where are they? Has no one condemned you?" Jesus asked the woman who the public condemned for adultery (John 8:10). His words doused the flames around her and left her knowing who she was intended to be.

He referred to the crippled woman on the day of Shabbat as the "daughter of Abraham" (Luke 13:10–117). The title identified her as an Israelite, descended from the tents of Sarah and Abraham, a woman of faith in the Lord's house, a child of the King of kings. His eyes of mercy went right to her in the synagogue. It didn't matter to him how long a person was in bondage or diseased. His compassion called the woman to his side, knowing the innermost wish of her heart: to be relieved from the pain. "You are freed from your infirmity," he said (13:12). He called her, he touched her, and immediately a deformed woman was made straight. All at once she was a lovely woman, standing straight, glowing with gratitude for the Lord. She glorified God, and the people rejoiced.

> From heaven fought the stars. (Judg 5:20)

One of God's names is Adonai Tzavaot, the "Lord of Hosts," meaning the Lord of armies. Hannah called God by this name. God is Lord of the entire host organized into one multitude to advance his cause.

Elisha too saw that those that were with him were more than those against. When his servant woke in an early morning, he saw that the city was surrounded by an army of horses and chariots (2 Kgs 6:15). "What shall we do?" he asked the prophet. Elisha prayed for his servant's eyes to be opened so that he would see. The Lord opened the servant's eyes, and when he looked, he saw that the hills were full of the flames of God's horses and chariots.

In this age of the spiritual battle of the church, beginning its aliyah in excitement of the Messiah, growing discouraged and tired through ravines and over hills, becoming more marginalized—an army is moving into position, consisting of an uncountable number of angels, waiting by the throne for the signal of the time of the final battle.

Sight is the problem. The servant needed to be shown the truth because all he could see was the power of the Syrian army and his own smallness. They needed to know it is the Lord who defines victory.

Joshua neared Jericho and looked up to see a man standing before him, holding a sword. "Are you for us or for our adversaries?" Joshua asked.

"No," the man replied. "But as commander of the army of the Lord I have now come."

Joshua fell facedown in awe of the presence of God coming to him. He asked, "What message does my lord bid his servant?" The commander of the Lord's army replied, "Put off your shoes from your feet; for the place where you stand is holy" (Josh 5:13–15).

The Lord is on the side of redeeming his creations into wholeness. He is Lord of all creation and will not be drawn into choosing sides. Instead, he draws all eyes to him.

> O Lord, remember not only the men and women of good will,
> but also those of ill will. But do not remember all the suffering
> they have inflicted on us; remember the fruits we bought, thanks
> to this suffering—our comradeship, our loyalty, our humility,

our courage, our generosity, the greatness of heart which has grown out of all this, and when they come to judgment let all the fruits that we have borne be their forgiveness.

—Prayer found on a piece of wrapping paper in the Ravensbruck concentration camp, where ninety-two thousand women and children died.

When the Lord draws near, even those serving him stagger, saying with Isaiah, "Woe, I am lost." The smoke filled the temple with God's presence, and Isaiah was unable to live there without God's hand sustaining him. Aware of his own need, Isaiah stood before the Lord, poor in spirit, and an angel was sent to purify his lips and reassure him that his guilt had been taken away. It was from these lips that the Holy Spirit spoke of what the Messiah would accomplish. "Therefore the Lord waits to be gracious to you . . . for the Lord is a God of justice," Isaiah said. "Blessed are all those who wait for him" (Isa 30:18).

Hannah knew that the heavens and the earth were completed and all the host of them (Gen 2:1). She called upon her Creator, crying out to the one who made everything from nothing, who is Lord of all the host of creation, all the armies of angels, moving and sustaining purposes according to his command.

Christianity began in this seed. Jesus endowed the apostles with the authority of these ancient promises. The transfer of this knowledge to the gentile world was disrupted when the cultural understanding of the Old Testament disappeared from the pulpit.

For two thousand years it appeared that God may have broken his pledge to Israel. Notes from the Warsaw Ghetto are housed in the Jewish Historical Institute in Warsaw, chronicling the deportation of Jews from their hometown of Zbąszyń. In September 1946, ten clay-covered tin boxes were found under a greenhouse. Containing underground newspapers, a description of the deportations, public notices from the council of Jewish leaders, and documentations of ordinary life such as milk coupons, concert invitations, and chocolate wrappers, the treasures bring insight into the daily life and struggles of the suffering Polish Jews during the Holocaust.

The group who preserved them, comprised of historians, writers, rabbis, and social workers, were called *Oyneg Shabbos* (Shabbat Gathering), led by the Dr. Emanuel Ringelblum. They documented the history, collecting testimonies, reports, essays, drawings, diaries, and wall posters from September 1939 to January 1943.

All but three members of the *Oyneg Shabbos* were murdered in the genocide. Dr. Ringelblum escaped the ghetto and continued to return to work on the archives. He and his family were executed in 1944. He was forty-four years old. They did not seem to be a blessing to the nation where they lived. Is this what God promised Abraham?

The Lord says he blessed Abraham in all things (Gen 24:1). From Abraham's life experience, his home was torn apart when he sent Hagar and Ishmael away. His sons would not grow up together. He never saw the numbers of stars who would be his progeny, but he had to nearly sacrifice Isaac on the altar. He was supposed to be a blessing to other nations, but curses came down on Egypt because Abraham said Sarah was his sister. Sodom and Gomorrah were destroyed. He owned no land that God had promised, except the cave where he buried Sarah.

The first use of *aish* in Scripture, the Hebrew word for fire, was on the day God made a covenant with Abraham, binding his descendants and the land. When the sun had set and darkness had fallen, a smoking firepot with a blazing torch appeared and passed between Abraham's offerings (Gen 15:17). Abraham walked the length of the land. The promise placed limits around the land. But the inheritance of Shabbat, flaming light in all directions, is without bounds with its promise of the world to come.

The heroes who called their gathering *Oyneg Shabbos* held to their death the longing for the Messiah whose coming will mean that all will be Shabbat. Shabbat marks the knowledge that work will one day be completed. Under insurmountable odds, they still gathered in the delight of Shabbat light and left words testifying that the work to repair the world will succeed and be boundless in its glory.

The hearts of the people were intense with waiting for their Messiah when Jesus entered Israel during Roman rule. He heard the negative language being spoken in first-century Nazareth and the mean-spirited relationships—he saw the tears of women; the malady of loneliness in a child; the grief when the white sheet is pulled over a body; betrayal of friendships; the hopelessness in an elderly widow, looking at a future so dark for her people it is unthinkable. He entered a place of parched and thirsting people. Inflamed with compassion, he overthrew the tables and seats at the temple court and drove out those who were buying and selling.

He reminded them of Isaiah's words: "It is written, 'My house shall be called a house of prayer'; but you make it a den of robbers" (Matt 21:13). Jesus was echoing Isaiah's call of salvation seven hundred years before. "Every one who thirsts, come to the waters; and he who has no money, come, buy and eat! Come, buy wine and milk without money and without price" (Isa 55:1). As historic wrongs are acknowledged and the Lord calls the Jews and gentiles together in him, and "'will take you, one from a city and two from a family, and I will bring you to Zion.' And I will give you shepherds after my own heart, who will feed you with knowledge and understanding" (Jer 3:14–15).

The fate of the Jews and gentiles is inseparable as the Spirit pours into us to move in one ascension. All eyes are raised to the Savior, lifted to see his head crowned with thorns, his hands and feet bound to the rough wood, hearing his last breath. They come recognizing their need to be led by the mighty hand of God so that he will be exalted in them. Wanting the power that resurrects from the dead, the kingdom can come to them. They are the beauty he brings from the ashes.

Just as a sonata returns to the notes that it first began, God establishes what he first promised with the return of the Jews and with the church, returning to relationship within nations. Imploring his children not to forget God's teachings and to keep his commands in their hearts, Solomon wrote, "It will be healing to your flesh and refreshment to your bones . . . The Lord by wisdom founded the earth; by understanding he established the heavens; by his knowledge the deeps broke forth, and the clouds drop down the dew . . . keep sound wisdom and discretion; let them not escape from your sight" (Prov 3:8, 19–21).

When Jeremiah became overwhelmed by the tragedies coming onto his people, and their lack of conscience and failure to return to God, his spirit fainted. He was giving up. God said to him, "speak what is right and your spirit will be strengthened." Keep speaking the words that are true. The fire's light of the Shabbat is not bounded by time and circumstance. "The people who sat in darkness have seen a great light, and for those who sat in the region and the shadow of death light has dawned" (Matt 4:16); "While you have the light, believe in the light, that you may become sons of light" (John 12:36).

Jesus said, "Everything written about me in the law of Moses and the prophets and the psalms must be fulfilled" (Luke 24:44). When he encountered the debate about whether divorce should be allowed for any reason, Jesus referenced Genesis 1:27, establishing that God made man male and female, intending marriage between a man and woman to be a lifelong bond. The relationship transcends all others, being the first bond God established between humans.

The apostles spoke to gentiles who had no background in Scripture. They explained the beginning of creation as a foundation for the gospel (Acts 14:15–17; 17:24–31). Luke's genealogy refers back to Adam, who is called a son of God. When they preached to other Jews, they pointed to the promises to Abraham and David (Acts 2:14–41; 7:2–14). Paul explained how the sacrifice of one man who obeyed God made many righteous in the whole of humanity by referencing Genesis and the reason death came to all through the sin of a man disobeying God (Rom 5:12–21).

Peter showed his deep-rooted knowledge of the Torah by affirming the eight people who were saved in the ark, the sinning angels that were sent to Tartarus in context of the flood of judgment that comes to those who don't believe God (2 Pet 2:4–5). He restates that the earth was formed out of water (3:5). The chapter of Jude also references the fallen angels and connects this to the perversions of Sodom and Gomorrah (Jude 6–7). Jude is learned in the geneaology of Genesis 5, explaining that Enoch was the seventh generation from Adam (Jude 14).

In the complexities of interpreting Revelation, the New Jerusalem comes in images filled with the garden of Eden, the tree of life, the river that draws all believers to it. In the days when John appeared in the wilderness of Judea, proclaiming that the kingdom of heaven has come near (Matt 3:1–2), he fulfilled Isaiah's vision centuries earlier: "A voice cries: 'In the wilderness prepare the way of the Lord'" (Isa 40:3). The people of Jerusalem, all of Judea, and the region along the Jordan went out to John to be immersed in the river. His clothing of camel's hair tied with a belt resembled the prophet Elijah (2 Kgs 1:8). He stood in the desert wilderness, reminiscent of the exile. "Bear fruit worthy of repentance," he said (Matt 3:8). Judgment to purify comes before restoration.

John told the people he was immersing them in the water of creation, but the one coming after him would immerse them with the Holy Spirit and the fire of heaven (3:11). The Lord needs us to stand in that fire. The fiery trial transforms and refines by consuming the dross. Water brings rebirth, and divine flame kindles the desire to accomplish the will of God. "Jerusalem [would] be trodden down by the Gentiles, until the times of the Gentiles are fulfilled" (Luke 21:24). The Jews would be scattered but it would not be the end of the story.

> For I will take you from the nations, and gather you from all the countries, and bring you into your own land. I will sprinkle clean water upon you, and you shall be clean from all your uncleannesses, and from all your idols I will cleanse you. A new heart I will give you, and a new spirit I will put within you; and I will take out of your flesh the heart of stone and give you a heart of flesh. And I will put my spirit within you, and cause you to walk in my statutes and be careful to observe my ordinances. You shall dwell in the land which I gave to your fathers; and you shall be my people, and I will be your God. (Ezek 36:24–28)

King David had purchased the land where, fourteen generations before, the patriarch Abraham went after and defeated four kings (1 Chr 21:22, 25; 2 Chr 3:1). David said to Ornan, "Grant me the place of this threshing floor, that I may build an altar on it to the Lord. You shall grant it to me at the full price." David gave Ornan six hundred shekels of gold by weight for the place. Fire was sent from heaven when David built an altar on the site and sacrificed burnt and fellowship offerings. He called on God, and God answered him with fire on the altar.

Solomon began to build the temple on Mount Moriah at the place where David had prepared the threshing floor of Ornan. When construction was completed, Solomon prayed and fire again came from God's presence, down from heaven to consume the burnt offering and sacrifices. His glory filled the temple (2 Chr 7:1–3).

The fire from heaven burned for centuries, preserving the righteous hope and destroying enemies. When anti-Semitism rose against Shadrach, Meshach, and Abednego in their exile, Nebuchadnezzar ordered a furnace heated seven times hotter than usual. The blaze was so hot that the fire killed the soldiers who took the young Jewish men, firmly tied, to the furnace. They fell into the blazing furnace and the king leapt to his feet when he saw four men standing unburned in the flames. Quickly he called to them, "servants of the Most High God, come forth and come here!"

Leadership gathered around them and saw that the fire had not harmed them. Witnessing this, Nebuchadnezzar said, "Blessed be the God of Shadrach, Meshach, and Abed'nego, who has sent his angel and delivered his servants, who trusted in him." He decreed that "any people, nation, or language that speaks anything against the God of [the Israelite men would be] laid in ruins, for there is no other god who is able to deliver in this way (Dan 3:19–30).

Restoration begins with acknowledging wrongdoing. God told Ezekiel to raise his eyes and look at the problem. "And he said to me, 'Son of man, do you see what they are doing, the great abominations that the house of Israel are committing here, to drive me far from my sanctuary? But you will see still greater abominations'" (Ezek 8:6).

After Ezekiel fully knows the desecrations, the Lord tells him to look further at what he is now doing: "Son of man, have you seen this?" (Ezek 47:6). Ezekiel is brought to the entrance of the temple to see water coming from beneath the threshold of the temple toward the east, trickling down, getting deeper and deeper as the Spirit of God spreads through the world (see Ezek 47).

The centuries of historic problems within the church are being brought to light, and the grief of it is comforted with the great power of the joy in the

Lord emerging his true church. The Spirit says, "Look! Do you see what I am doing?" Blessed because they mourn, having seen its inadequacy to achieve serving the Lord's plan, the heart of the church turns to the Lord.

The years the locust ate will be restored because of God's love for his land and people. He will give back harvests in abundance, each seed will produce a crop, and the threshing floor will be full of grain, vats overflowing with wine and oil—and they shall be satisfied.

Locust years are the wasted years that we cannot get back; all the work that went into the fields to cultivate crops, laboring week after week, only to see the green sprouts eaten by the locusts. The years can be laden with regrets of lost opportunities, when a person follows their own desires, whether related to relationships or career. When we are suddenly awakened to seek God's will, he is then full of sorrow because those years are gone. These are the generations that tried to annihilate the Jewishness of God's plan, thinking that if they could push Israel aside, then they would inherit the promises. Instead they lost the fullness of the message.

The remarkable promise of God in Joel 2 is that these years the locust took will be restored. This promise came in response to the people in the book of Joel asking God to spare them, and to not let his heritage be a reproach. They brought their need for mercy to God because they had become aware that they were under discipline for walking away from him, and required his power to bring them back. The people had nothing, and now the harvest came to fill the years that the locust had eaten. The embrace of relationships between the Jewish part of the body and the gentile is releasing believers from the years of the locust that divided them. Disciples of the Lord are to bear fruit that will last, in the parable of the sower, thirty, sixty, a hundredfold more than crops in the past.

God says in Joel that we are to lament when we see war sweeping across the land, when we see anti-Semitism, when we see God's gift of the female being swarmed with desecrated attitudes. The people in Joel called the priests to lament, the elders to fast, and reached to gather the community to the house of God.

Years before the Toward Jerusalem Council II established, Rabbi Jonathan Bernis, president of Jewish Voice Ministries International, called Martin Waldman, saying that the Lord had put it on his heart to hold a minyan (ten Jewish men from around the world coming together and fast and pray) for a breakthrough in the Messianic Jewish Movement. They hosted a retreat in Dallas, Texas, staying together for three days of fasting and praying. Then the door opened in Russia for Jonathan to share the message of Jesus through concerts and music. Thousands of Jewish people came to faith in the former Soviet Union.

A short while afterward, the Lord spoke to Marty with a vision that became Toward Jerusalem Council II. Another door opened with the nearby Shady Grove Church when Dr. Wayne Wilks, an elder at the church in Grand Prairie, invited Marty to come and share the TJCII vision. As Wayne listened, the Lord put a burden on him to spend the rest of his life prioritizing the biblical message "to the Jew first." From this, a vision grew to form the Messianic Jewish Bible Institute in 1996. Wayne was appointed president of the MJBI, training a new generation of emerging leaders.

Rabbi Jonathan says that Israel is the key to unlocking the gate of God so loving the world that he gave his son. Daniel prophesied that many will be purged, purified, and refined, and those who have insight will understand (Dan 12:10).

The fire consumes and restores. Angels rejoice because the fire that baptized on Pentecost unified what the tower of Babel had splintered. To do that, the fire must burn off the wrong teachings that stood sentry, keeping the people apart.

Reclaiming the body of the Messiah requires undoing the confusion introduced in past generations, examining traditional theological language that shaped the rejection of Israel and to expose one-sided thinking. This is especially true of the Ephraimite movement that spread in the United States, Europe, and Israel, which said that people who become Christians are descendants of the lost tribes of Israel. Dual covenant theology became a belief that the Old Testament covenants are for Israel and that the New Covenant is for the church, giving two covenants as alternative ways to salvation for two separate groups. One law theology teaches that gentiles have the same relationship as Jews to the Mosaic law and are to apply it the same way, ignoring the "many languages and nations" that is a wealth of heritage and diverse knowledge appointed by God.

In a song of ascent, David wrote, "How good and pleasant it is when brothers dwell in unity!" (Ps 133:1). We are to walk with Israel, our worship following one beat of music from heaven, each with our instruments, dancing in one joy, each living to enter the Shabbat rest in the Lord in their own heritage, but still anticipating the Lord's return to Jerusalem.

Now thousands gather round to find the words reaching the shores of the soul, the flame growing brighter as the crew multiplies through troubled waters in continents, regions, and countries that by 2017 included Africa, Canada, the United States, Mexico, South America, Middle East, Europe, South Korea, and Indonesia. Each connection strives to eliminate misunderstandings that impede relationship in the preparation for the coming of the Lord in glory and the fullness of his kingdom. "By this all men will know that you are my disciples, if you have love for one another" (John 13:35).

Rabbi Daniel Juster is an acclaimed leader of the Messianic Jewish Movement, including the Union of Messianic Jewish Congregations, the Messianic Jewish Bible Institute, and the Messianic Jewish Studies program at The King's University. The rabbi serves as founding director of Tikkun International based in Frederick, Maryland, a network of congregations and ministries internationally committed to the restoration of Israel and the church. He's also a founding board member of Toward Jerusalem Council II.

Rabbi Daniel speaks of the New Covenant empowering us to fulfill the teachings of the Old Testament. The Jewish feasts have eschatological meaning pointing to what Jesus did for us, the sacrificed lamb, first fruits when he rose from the dead, and he's coming again, the blowing of the shofar at the Feast of Trumpets. Sukkot will remain to be a worldwide celebration of the king appointed by God.

The apostles did not exhort keeping the feasts, but left it open to invitation for gentiles, Rabbi Daniel explains. The apostles focused on behaviors, loving one another, not committing adultery, stealing or murdering; all summed up in knowing that God's love guides them.

"There are some matters in which correction is needed," Rabbi Daniel writes. As director of Tikkun International, he said, "One is replacement theology whereby the church is robbed of its own role in the salvation of Israel and the fulfillment of God's promises to Israel and the nations. Others include: misunderstanding on issues of law and grace, abstract concepts of God which depersonalize him, and not understanding Scripture in its original Jewish context."[10]

The law guides love. When God's word is opened, it rolls back the darkness and illuminates the path of life. The apostles emphasized the universal dimensions of the Torah through the Sermon on the Mount, repenting and returning to God, the discipline of studying the word, going before God and asking for his power to fulfill our destiny.

"In Ephesians 2, Paul speaks of God making of the Jews and Gentiles one new man. To some, this means the homogenization of Jew and Gentile so they are no longer distinct. This is most certainly the wrong interpretation," the rabbi says. "We must see that both communities have developed wonderful traditions by creative gifts in the Holy Spirit that meet the Romans 12:2 standard of that which is good. The completion of one new

---

10. Juster, "Is the Church Pagan?", para. 8.

man is only found in the mutual appreciation of the Jewish and the Gentile together."[11]

Those who have embraced this, including Cardinal Christoph Schönborn in Vienna and the Pentecostal Holiness under Doug Beacham, are seeing a movement of people embracing the importance of Israel and its destiny and the importance of Messianic Jews in this destiny. The definition of the church as those from all nations through faith in Jesus has been joined to Israel for the sake of the world's redemption. "It has to happen before the return of the Lord," Rabbi Daniel said. "To see the church come back from anti-semitism and colonialism . . . we are trying to see the whole world mobilized into this alignment."

All creations in the heavenly realm and on the earthly realm are to praise God (Ps 148). "Let everything that breathes praise the Lord" (Ps 150:6). Scripture tells humanity to extol the Lord with the whole heart, sing praises with all the languages and instruments cultures use, lift up hands, and dance to him. Who does not praise the Lord? The dead who go down in silence (Ps 115).

Fr. Peter Hocken walked with TJCII for more than twenty years, passing away in summer 2017. In a spring 2010 TJCII Communique article, he wrote about the one new humanity Paul speaks of in Ephesians 2. "This teaching, first in Romans and then in Ephesians, was made possible by the decision of the apostles and elders of Jerusalem, described in Acts 15," he wrote.[12]

In Antioch, where the faith was being taught to pagans, some men were teaching that unless you are circumcised, according to the custom of Moses, you cannot be saved. This brought Peter, Barnabas, Paul, and James into discussion. The apostles stood with God in his will. "We see here that the unity of the Jewish believers in Yeshua is foundational for the unity of the whole body of Jew and Gentile," Fr. Peter wrote. "In some way, the devil knows that the full reconciliation of Jew and Gentile in the one body will open the door for the coming of the Lord Yeshua in glory."[13] All those working for the one new humanity need to recognize that it will be a big battle all the way and be on guard against all that divides, he said. We need prayer protection, especially for the Messianic Jews, because their calling is foundational to the unity realized in the One New Man.

The first Jerusalem council discerned that God is taking for himself people from among the gentiles—each are called, not as a nation, but

---

11. Juster, "Is the Church Pagan?", para. 10.
12. Hocken, "Church," para. 3.
13. Hocken, "Church," para. 5.

individually by name. Israel knows that people of other nations will come to their God, and there will be a reconciliation of peoples. "Neither shall they learn war any more" (Isa 2:2–4); "All the ends of the earth shall remember and turn to the Lord; and all the families of the nations shall worship before him" (Ps 22:27).

Paul carried it forward to believers in Corinth, saying, "What we pray for is your improvement" (2 Cor 13:9). Corinth is a four-mile-wide stretch of land between the Mediterranean Sea and the Aegean Sea. A wealthy port of trade between Europe and Asia, it supported a large population of Greeks, Jews, and Romans when Paul arrived. The temple of Aphrodite stood atop the mountain overlooking Corinth, attracting hundreds of residents devoted to serving the goddess and permitting prostitution. The cult of Isis had taken root from Egypt's reverence of knowledge. The Mithras cult required initiates to undergo graduated tests to enter its mysteries.

Paul spoke to those coming to Jesus from a multiplicity of cultures who brought in their pagan influences, such as eating meat offered to idols, promiscuity, and glorifying the body and mind. His approach amid such diverse beliefs was to center focus on Jesus as he spoke of the oneness of the flame of God.

Additionally, Paul taught on the equality of spiritual gifts among men and women, Jew and gentile. But when Paul said "there is neither Jew nor Greek . . . slave nor free . . . male nor female" (Gal 3:28), members of the church misinterpreted his words, blurring the lines between male and female roles. He meant that we are all called to service, as Jew or non-Jew, a man or a woman, each in our nationalities. He addressed women who should be listening and learning to be silent, not talking disruptively while others are instructing (1 Cor 14:34). Restrictions are not opposing women holding positions in the body, but against them pushing themselves in ways that usurp those God ordained as authorities or cause the purity of home to be neglected.

Among Paul's people, women were significant in the survival of the life of Israel and the early community of believers in Jesus—Miriam, Deborah, Huldah, Esther, Junia (Rom 16:7), and Phoebe (Rom 16:1), to name a few who held community positions of judges, prophets, deacons, and apostles. It is not the gender of women Paul addresses, but the attitude of fulfilling faith. Salted with fire to melt the frozen walls between people, in order to be spiritually clean and in covenant with God, the fire Jesus yearns to see kindled urges the mind to be silent and listen for him, as Abraham and Sarah did.

Hineni means "here I am, I'm listening." God called to Moses out of a bush and Moses said, "*Hineni*" (Exod 3:4). It is this same response that Abraham gives when God called him to sacrifice his son Isaac (Gen 22:1).

Samuel did not yet know the Lord when he was with Eli, but when the Lord called he said, "Speak, for thy servant hears" (1 Sam 3:10). When God spoke to Jacob in a vision at night, Jacob replied, "Here I am" (Gen 31:11). Isaiah responded, "Here am I! Send me." (Isa 6:8).

The call from God entirely changes a life. This is the voice that entered the darkness of a universe with its brilliant light, stilled the winds of oceans, raised Jesus from the grave, and hung each star in the heavens. It now came to live in the gentiles.

The letter the Jerusalem council wrote to Antioch and other congregations brings rejoicing to the gentiles. It did not mean that the authority of the Torah would be ignored. The law instructs how to live, keep justice, and direct a family, and leads to recognizing the Messiah to illuminate his work in us.

"Is not my word like fire?" (Jer 23:29). The Lord appeared as fire descending on Mount Sinai. The smoke billowed like smoke from a furnace and the whole mountain trembled (Exod 19:14–18). His divine presence was known by fire over the tent of meeting, giving them light in the cloud during their travels (Exod 40:34–38). He crossed the Jordan ahead of Israel like a devouring fire destroying the enemies (Deut 9:1–5).

A fiery law comes from his right hand (Deut 33:2). The Midrash states that commandments were given to refine mankind. 2 Timothy 3:16–17 states that all Scripture is inspired by God, and therefore have purpose. Maimonides maintains that "Every commandment of the 613 commandments either imparts to us a true philosophy, eradicates a false philosophy, enforces a rule of social justice, nullifies injustice, bestows noble character traits, or warns against evil traits" (*Guide for the Perplexed* 3:31).

God, the Great Mystery, is Creator of all systems and balances. If he forbids, he has reason. If he asks our trust, although we don't yet see where he's taking us, the flame of our soul should not be dimmed.

5

CHALLAH

While Israel dwelt in the Holy Land and was faithful and true in its worship of the Holy One, the Shekhinah as a virtuous woman, in her own house remained with them and never left them and was the great inspirer of all the distinguished prophets who lived during the existence of the first temple.
—*The Zohar*

ABRAHAM'S TENT WAS OPEN on all sides, welcoming to everyone. With a heart of hospitality he ran to meet his guests (Gen 18:2). He hurried to the tent to tell Sarah to quickly measure the best flour and bake bread for the three holy ones who visited (v. 6). The Midrash tells us that for as long as Sarah lived there was a blessing in the dough, a lamp burning from one Shabbat evening to the next, and a cloud of the Lord's presence hovered over her tent.

Sarah brought into her home the tradition of the Shabbat candle, signifying the welcoming spirit of God and representing the presence of the holy power in the people's lives. The cloud symbolized a home where the laws of family purity are observed, and alludes to the cloud of the Shekhinah displaying the feminine aspect of God's glory. The blessing in the dough represents the commandment that would be given, "And the first of all the first fruits of all kinds, and every offering of all kinds from all your offerings, shall belong to the priests; you shall also give to the priests the first of your coarse meal, that a blessing may rest on your house" (Ezek 44:30).

When Sarah died, the miracles disappeared until Rebekah came. When Isaac brought Rebekah home, the candle burned again, the dough was blessed, and the cloud returned. Isaac, grieved by the death of his mother, was comforted by the continuance of the presence of God's honor (Gen 24:67).

The women bring purity (*niddah*), light (*nerot*), and blessing (*challah*) to their family when they embrace these *mitzvot*. Family is stabilized. "A man should always be careful to respect his wife, because the blessing in the home is not there but for her" (Bava Metzia 59a).

All the tribes inherited land in Canaan except for the tribe of Levi, who were to be priests protecting the holy name of YHVH with the precision of God's commandments. The priests separated from the community so they could be ritually pure in order to serve in the temple, trusting that God would support them through the offerings of the people. *Challah* was one of the gifts due them.

After the destruction of the temple, the rabbis knew they would one day return to their land, and valued the giving of *challah* so much that the people kept the commandment wherever they lived. One twenty-fourth is separated from the dough and set aside from bread served at the beginning of the Shabbat meal.

In the past two thousand years alone, the Jews have had their property confiscated, books burned, and synagogues demolished, been expelled under edicts of eviction, forced to convert and deny their heritage, massacred and burned alive, denied their practice of worshiping God as well as employment, attacked by mobs, publicly tortured, ostracized, forced to wear horned hats, and/or forbidden to speak blessings in more than two hundred countries. Jerusalem has been destroyed twice, besieged, attacked, and captured dozens of times, and yet the people and land remain testimony to God's words, "Why do the nations conspire, and the peoples plot in vain? The kings of the earth set themselves, and the rulers take counsel together, against the Lord and his anointed" (Ps 2:1–2).

Finding their way to Jerusalem's wailing wall, the Jewish people come from across the world just to touch the stone where, in the ruins, the words of the priests still speak. The tears run down the wall like a river of prayers, the weeping of the prophets longing for the daughter of Zion, a sweet scent rising to the heaven.

Survivors find each other, wordlessly recognizing. "We have survived." "God has preserved his remnant." Homes long ago darkened hold in the scream of shattered windows when the enemy came for them. Unspoken hope filled those rooms, begging families not to leave as they were dragged away. The broken candlesticks of Shabbat were left behind as they scattered among the nations, petals of light from a flower of flame. The stones of the Kotel make it all fade away; all the malicious taunts and cruelties disappear as prayer receives promise. The wall stands defiant, scarred by the chisels of the Romans trying to destroy it in 70 AD, testifying to its wait for the Lord's return.

Ezekiel's vision of the angels with the spinning wheels revealed the glory coming to hover over Jerusalem during the Israelite exile. As Ezekiel watched, the glory departed, moving to the door of the temple, going up from the city and stopping over the mountain in the east where it hovered over the region of River Chebar. More than ten thousand exiles were brought to that region. Ezekiel was among the first to be taken captive, brought to live in a place called Tel-abib, which was by the River Chebar. The Lord had shown the prophet that wherever the people went, whatever they endured, he would be with them if they followed his glory.

David sang about how the Lord turns our darkness into light. He called out to God when he was in distress. God reached down from on high to rescue David, and "the earth reeled and rocked; the foundations of the heavens trembled and quaked, because he was angry." He thundered and parted the heavens and came down, soaring on the wings of the wind (2 Sam 22). His rescue shakes lives as he changes the direction of his people.

"Remember the Shabbat," the Lord told them after gathering them. He provided a space in the lives of his people to always draw near to him wherever they made their homes. On Shabbat, people welcome God's presence and reaffirm that he is king. The truth is a flame, a fortress of heaven's fire; they carried it into nations. Being at home in the sacred Scripture with the faith of Abraham and Sarah, they traveled into unknown lands, yet were always moving toward the rebuilding of Jerusalem. The Messianic Jewish Movement took root in the diaspora, anticipating the fulfillment of God's promise of his glory (Ps 122:6). They continued Shabbat, the only ritual listed in the ten commandments.

Preparing bread for Shabbat demonstrates awareness of God's participation in each facet of the day. Taking *challah* continues a dependence on manual labor in the fields, no matter where the people live. God sends the rains and the sun. He made the soil and the seeds. The farmer plants, waters, weeds, and harvests. Trucks carry the bounty to storehouses to be ground and packaged, so they can be sent to stores. All the elements of God's will that go into making bread possible to bake in the kitchen are brought into thanksgiving when the two *challahs* are lifted and God is blessed as the provider of bread.

Among the mixing bowls, salt, eggs, and flour, is the thought of the matriarch of a nation, Sarah, keeping the tasks before the Lord. Sarah's home was elevated to the realm of God, and life transcended that of being a nomad.

It has been said that one braid represents the command *zachor* ("remember"), another represents *shamor* ("guard") and the third braid is for *b'Dibbur Echad* ("God spoke," "remember," and "guard" as a single interdependent thought). Shabbat bread also represents the unity of weaving together all the diversity of the north, south, west, east, up above to heaven, and down below on earth, as we strive to live outwardly with his inward light.

Challah recipes can be creative, using whole wheat, barley, rye, oat, spelt, or a combination of these—or it can be gluten-free, with honey, sesame seeds, or even chocolate chips. The geographical span of baking evolved its own traditions. *Challah* made in Tripoli often uses caraway seeds. Moroccans favor raisins, nuts, and anise, which are symbols of sweetness and fertility. Though *challah* is made in different ways in different languages, all are united in the heritage of remembering how the worlds were framed by the word of God.

When the dough is kneaded, it is placed in a bowl, covered, and left to rise for a few hours. Before separating the *challah*, the following blessing is spoken:

> *Baruch atah Adonoi Eloheinu melech ha olam asher kidesha-nu b'mitz-votav v'tzi-vanu lehaf-rish challah*
>
> Blessed are You, Lord our God, King of the universe, who has sanctified us with His commandments and commanded us to separate challah.

Accepting the sanctity of her role upon herself, the woman prepares the food, asking God to observe every detail. She asks that God's abundant mercy enable her to observe the holiness of the Shabbat and festivals with her family.

The *challah* is an offering that the priest once offered on the altar, which God accepted. The custom now is to burn it in the oven by itself, then wrap and discard it in a respectful way. The aroma of bread baking fills the house with the union that comes when God oversees every detail of a home, refining the family with an infinitely higher awareness that the Lord has made life possible.

In his parables to show that the kingdom of God begins in the small ways that we keep, Jesus told of men working out in the fields, one losing a sheep, and a man planting a mustard seed. Then he told of a woman baking bread: "To what shall I compare the kingdom of God? It is like leaven which a woman took and hid in three measures of flour, till it was all leavened" (Luke 13:20–21).

> [Jesus] asks people—male or female, privileged or peasant, it does not matter—to enter the domain of a first-century woman and household cook in order to gain perspective on the domain of God.[1]

When women carry out the *mitzvah* of *challah*, they express recognition that there can be no blessing in the home without the Lord participating. The cycle of housework, jobs, shopping, cleaning, washing dishes, and preparing dinners can become empty and tiresome if there is no meaningful understanding of how she is part of the growth of God's plan, there in her kitchen, in her home, at the dinner table, as she lights the Shabbat candles.

The flame gathers those in loneliness. Some come to the table so shy that they feel unworthy to be cared about, or carry a hurt so deep no one can possibly understand. Some isolate themselves by turning inward so their shame won't show. With no one looking into their eyes, they seek connection on the internet, or find a psychiatrist, or turn to alcohol, overeating, under-eating, sleeplessness, oversleep, or loss of concentration on long-term life because they feel that it doesn't matter.

Shabbat reflects the Lord welcoming all to a place at his table. It was not good for man to be alone. The Shekhinah is exquisitely feminine in its language, flowing over borders to relationship with others, vanishing the chasms inside time, which allows rebirth that needs spiritual, emotional, intellectual, and physical nourishing. Shabbat is a day of relationship bringing the desire of all nations together under the canopy of the Lord of the Shabbat.

Jesus kept the practice. "And he came to Nazareth, where he had been brought up; and he went into the synagogue, as his custom was, on the sabbath day. And he stood up to read" (Luke 4:16). The Lord spent Shabbat helping people in their relationship with their Creator. The apostles followed his example. "Then Paul went in, as was his custom, and for three weeks he argued with them from the scriptures" (Acts 17:2); "And he argued in the synagogue every sabbath, and persuaded Jews and Greeks" (Acts 18:4). The apostles observed the day, emphasizing the newly birthed person God is in the process of creating: "by which he has granted to us his precious and very great promises, that through these you may escape from the corruption

---

1. Green, *Gospel of Luke*, 527.

that is in the world because of passion, and become partakers of the divine nature" (2 Pet 1:4).

God wants there to be a time for us to grow closer to him from week to week. He blessed the Shabbat because he rested from all the works he had made, and sanctified the day as holy time (Gen 2:1–3). "And let us consider how to stir up one another to love and good works, not neglecting to meet together, as is the habit of some, but encouraging one another, and all the more as you see the Day drawing near" (Heb 10:24–25).

Relationship takes time. God wants us to have the time. "Open to me the gates of righteousness, that I may enter through them and give thanks to the Lord" (Ps 118:19); "I am the door; if anyone enters by me, he will be saved" (John 10:9); "Blessed be he who enters in the name of the Lord!" (Ps 118:26).

Despised, rejected, a man of sorrows, Jesus knew the loneliness of coming to his own, though his own did not receive him. On the cross, even his beloved Father could not look on him. The crowd taunted. His disciples abandoned him. He was "like a lonely bird on the housetop" (Ps 102:7).

The experience is not about circumstance, but about relationship with God, our inside refuge who is with us always. The prophets and disciples suffered those lonely moments, but they knew the ending because the eternal Lord was their Shabbat. Seeing the glorious victory shielded the certainty that protected their strength. God hears the song of the bird singing alone on the rooftop. Not one falls without him.

Paul, facing a horrible death, passes onto Timothy the message to guard the treasure and remember the accurate teaching of God. The word will become distorted, so you must continue to carry the torch high. Speak the truth, even when those around you reject the doctrine.

The Amidah, the central prayer of the Shabbat, means "to stand." Written by men of the great assembly returning from Babylon to rebuild the temple, the eighteen blessings of the Amidah open with blessing the God of Abraham, Isaac, and Jacob, who were all given his supreme promise of homeland and a redeemer of humanity. Composed long before Jesus was born on earth, the Amidah affirms the Lord's holiness. Because the future is held by the children, in order to help kindle their flames to be strong enough to stand burning alone, the people stand in his presence and recite the blessings on Shabbat. The words become embedded in the minds of those who don't yet know how to pray. They tell God that they are his followers, a privileged people to be called by his name. The covenant is reaffirmed. He is praised for his power to restore the dead to life, sustain the living, heal the sick, free the captive, and raise the fallen. His great mercy is acknowledged, and his holiness is proclaimed.

In the last three blessings, God is asked to accept prayers and is thanked for his past, present, and future kindnesses. Prayer draws nearer to him, asking for his presence to be restored to Zion and bringing him words that express his own will to redeem his people. On Shabbat, God is brought praise and gratitude. Being unthankful means treading against others and God. Shabbat teaches how to sustain the power of peace.

The Shekhinah appears when the Lord sets apart, as he did when he separated Eve from Adam, when he separated Noah's family, and when he led Abraham to separate from Lot (who decided to return to another way of life). Moses was led to separate his people into a new nation.

The home on Shabbat is separated from the world. The woman of the Hebrew home is referred to as the *akeret habayit*, or "the foundation of the home." Woman was separated out from man, a thought that comes when *challah* is separated from the dough, because new life comes only from lives joined together. The women in question are akin to Proverbs 31; as the mother of Jesus said to the servants, "Do whatever he tells you" (John 2:5). She recognized a need, turned to the source of life, and the wine of celebration poured into the lives around her.

The Word prepared a banquet to welcome all who would come to his table and hear of the divine spark in our soul necessary for goodness in this world. In his wisdom, the Lord structured each life with cause and effect to provide each soul their way to connect with heaven above. Every soul is born facing a challenge, whether it is greed for money and fame, or addictions that destroy entire families. It may be reluctance to accomplish the unknowable. It may be illness or loneliness. In a world of bondage and redemption, Egypt and Exodus, humanity would climb cliffs, descend into pits, trace the edge of deserts, and scale the snow-topped mountains.

With each step comes the opportunity to come into his rest and work with him. At the Lord's table, he gives the choice to perform a divine mission of his compassion. Knowing this takes away the excuse that we were too poor, too alone, too angry, or too weak to accomplish what was laid in our path. Challenges are the will of God presenting an opportunity to come nearer to him. When the prodigal turned to face his father's home, the father ran to welcome him in. Welcoming those who want to return to the table emulates an attribute of God. His kindness fed the people of Israel with the grain of heaven when they wandered in wilderness.

Jesus was a visitor to homes that kept Shabbat. While sitting at the table of a prominent Pharisee, Jesus looked around at the people and observed guests choosing seats of honor for themselves. He told the parable of those who exalt themselves being humbled, and those who humble themselves being exalted. He advised that when someone invites you to a wedding, don't take the place of honor, because someone else may come and the host will have to ask you to move to a lower place. Take the lowest place, he said. If the host moves you to a higher place, you will be honored. It is the host who determines where each person belongs (Luke 14:7–14).

The church must go where the glory leads, as in Ezekiel's vision of the Shekinah moving under God's direction, and should not cling to the empty ruins of traditions, or they will be outside the glory. They must continue to grow up, maturing at each step as we see a wider view of the Lord's movement bringing about his one new humanity. If we don't come together to give the Lord thanks, how can we come into the oneness that is God.

> Let the favor of the Lord our God be upon us, and establish thou the work of our hands upon us, yea, the work of our hands establish thou it (Ps 90:17).

Apostles encouraged hospitality and sharing with each other in personal ways (Rom 12:13; 1 Pet 4:9). Jesus had girded himself with the towel of a servant to cleanse the feet of his disciples. Serving became the belt of righteousness and faithfulness in his glory.

Shabbat reminds of our responsibility to invite those who are troubled to come rest with us. The soft glow of candlelight invites the soul to a quiet place as people gather to break bread. The blessing being spoken lifts the veil bringing relief, a breeze of strength as the candle flares its light. The Lord is present. Through Jewish history, the Hebrew word *keruv* has directed tradition to bring close all who feel far from the community. *Keruv* means to draw near and welcome. Tradition tells of the kindness of Aaron, the high priest and brother of Moses, toward all of God's creatures, and of bringing others close to the Torah. King David's devotion brought the nation of Israel and all gentile believers near to God.

Moabite women had been used to seduce men away from God's ways (Num 25). However, the Moabite Ruth was accepted into Israel. Her words spoke upon the heart of Boaz, and she was invited into community to share a meal. Boaz invited her to have bread. As a foreigner, she sat down with the family and he offered her a generous portion of roasted grain. She had all she wanted, and there was much left over, which she brought home to Naomi. "The name of the man I worked with today is Boaz," Ruth told her. She worked with (not for) him, and Naomi, possibly referring to the Lord, said, "He has not stopped showing his kindness to the living and the dead," to the memory of and promises to those who came before (Ruth 2:19–20). The redemption for both women began when Ruth vowed on the road to Bethlehem to trust in the Lord of Israel.

Welcoming non-Jews who wanted to worship God and know his ways had no other requirement than what Ruth said: "Your God will be my God." "The Lord recompense you for what you have done, and a full reward be given you by the Lord, the God of Israel, under whose wings you have come to take refuge!" (Ruth 2:12).

After coming through generations of enemies, surviving the worst against humanity, and still having the ability to utter song to the Lord, the people were then told by churches to give up who they are and become gentile believers. Jews became a people who are hated for refusing to leave their heritage and be converted into other ways of worshiping. But even those who converted were not safe. Race cannot be changed, and Europe justified the extermination of the Jews. The word "anti-Semitism" was coined by a German journalist in 1879 to describe the emergence of the prejudice.

Yet even after Holocaust education, interfaith meetings, and antiracist legislation fervently pledging "never again," anti-Semitism continues its relentless dialogue to douse the candle of the laws of God's oneness that fulfills Jerusalem's destiny and accomplishes the union of one new man. Only two years after representatives of forty-four governments met in Stockholm in January of 2000 to fight anti-Semitism, synagogues and Jewish schools in France and Belgium were firebombed and Jews were attacked in the streets.

They came to be viewed as victims, identifying the word "Jew" only with words like "Holocaust." But God said that "all who are incensed against you shall be put to shame and confounded; those who strive against you shall be as nothing and shall perish. . . . those who war against you shall be as nothing at all" (Isa 41:11–12); "For I am the Lord your God, the Holy One of Israel, your Savior" (Isa 43:3).

It was a mistake to think that giving up Jewish identity and assimilating would ever stop the enemy's hatred. Both because they kept to themselves and because they settled everywhere, anti-Zionism opposed Jews as a nation wanting to exist with self-governance and self-defense. To the Lord, they are known with an identity of bringing light as repairers of the world, entrusted with God's message through a struggle spanning thousands of years to bring the world back to God.

Sharing the customs of the home has been a cornerstone in building relationship between nations, denominations, and cultures around the world. As a woman, Eve saw that the fruit of the forbidden tree looked good, was sustenance, and would bring wisdom. She he responded to an innate desire to share provision with others. In its balance, God instituted communion to appeal to the senses of delight, sharing food, and growing wiser.

In October 2015, TJCII leadership journeyed to Bohemia, now the Czech Republic, to lead the Bohemia Prayer Journey, recognizing and repenting for abuses of the Lord's Supper perpetrated over centuries. Participants traveled to Terezin, where tens of people died in a concentration camp. More than 150,000 others, including many children, were held there for months or years before being boarded onto trains and sent to die at concentration camps, including Treblinka and Auschwitz. The leadership shared a Shabbat dinner together, which was hosted by Benjamin Berger and Avi Mizrachi, both leaders in TJCII. The dinner was held in the city of Tabor, the center of the Hussite rebellion that sparked the Bohemian wars between the Orthodox Catholic Church and Christian Hussites that lasted from 1413 to 1434.

Donna Ballard serves as the TJCII Director of Outreach, International in Dallas, Texas, wrote in TJCII's spring 2016 newsletter:

> Sitting around the Shabbat table on the same ground where wars led to years of division, TJCII participants rejoiced in the life-affirming unity of the Shabbat and considered it an extraordinary and humbling opportunity to express the heart of Yeshua's prayer, "... that all of them may be one, Father, just as you are in me and I am in You. May they al-so be in Us so that the world may believe that You have sent Me.[2]

As political correctness infiltrated society, Jewish believers were considered another ethnic group to have freedom to worship their faith in their own cultural practices. Yet they are the people of God's covenant—he is their glory, and it was through them that the Messiah and the gospels came to the world. As membership declines in mainline denominations, the fullness of the olive tree restores the wealth of blessing to congregations.

Donna says that clarity is needed. The Messianic community being the resurrection from the dead is the Jewish side of the olive tree. There is a great need for the gentile side to come into unity, enabling reconciliation to fulfill the phrase "Jews and Gentiles united for the Messiah's return." Reconciliation will only be complete with the presence of both sides of the olive tree deeply rooted in one source.

The prodigal church had tried to blot out the Torah, thinking that the church would inherit the blessings; instead, they lost the full value. Jesus intended every people to be blessed by sharing in the God-graced gifts of other nations. He said, "And if you salute only your brethren, what more are you doing than others?" (Matt 5:47). The Jewish rejection of Jesus as Messiah opened up the riches for the gentiles. Scripture says, "How much more will their full inclusion mean!" (Rom 11:12).

---

2. Ballard, "Messianic Jewish Leadership," 6.

Spending time with God is covered by the last prayer of Jesus before he was crucified. Having finished his Father's work, his hour had come. He would soon return to the glory he had in his Father's presence before the world was made. Jesus lifted his eyes to heaven, saying, "I do not pray for these only, but also for those who believe in me through their word, that they may all be one" (John 17:20–21). Out of Jerusalem, the call spread throughout earth to come into the oneness through his peace. "For you have been born again, not of perishable seed, but of imperishable" (1 Pet 1:22).

Each soul is a candle lit by God. He breathes into us as he did into the first man and woman, into Israel, and into the church. God blows out the flame at the end of a life. A candle lit on the anniversary of a death is a remembrance of the soul of the departed. It shines with faith for the resurrected life to the One who knows all mysteries. The mourner's Kaddish recited on each anniversary of the death is not about death, but about lifting the greatness of God and remembering our mission is from him:

> Glorified and sanctified be God's great name throughout the world which He has created according to His will. May He establish His kingdom in your lifetime and during your days, and within the life of the entire House of Israel, speedily and soon; and say, Amen.
>
> May His great name be blessed forever and to all eternity.
>
> Blessed and praised, glorified and exalted, extolled and honored, adored and lauded be the name of the Holy One, blessed be He, beyond all the blessings and hymns, praises and consolations that are ever spoken in the world; and say, Amen.
>
> May there be abundant peace from heaven, and life, for us and for all Israel; and say, Amen.
>
> He who creates peace in His celestial heights, may He create peace for us and for all Israel; and say, Amen.

On Yom Kippur, candles are lit at home in honor of deceased parents, and they burn the entire holiday. This candle is a *ner neshama* ("soul light") in Hebrew. As King Solomon wrote in Proverbs, the spirit of man, the life breath of man (*neshama*) is the lamp or candle (*ner*) of the Lord (20:27). The flame that gave light during their lifetime continues to glow after their passing. Everyone is to light a candle or lamp on Yom Kippur to acknowledge and ask forgiveness of past wrongs of our own and those who went before us because the effect is still with us.

There is a history of hurt that must be carried into shared understanding. The difficulty of sharing beyond intellectual knowledge of God to begin a new way of being in relationship that we've never experienced takes time and intention to recognize these barriers. Personal unresolved bitterness in the body of Jesus needs to be brought to God privately first before peacemaking is enabled. Resolving preoccupation for self and what we want others to be is covered by God. "Love does not insist on its own way; it is not irritable or resentful" (1 Cor 13:5). Reaching out to safeguard others with the beauty of God's laws is an obligation, from "love your neighbor" to "give proper rebuke." In the process of sanctification to become sons of the God of peace, the Lord of the dove—the grower of the olive tree—moves the ekklesia away from its own agenda and toward him.

Give thanks in all circumstances; for this is the will of God in Christ Jesus for you (1 Thess 5:18). Remembering the desert experience, how fiery snakes appeared on the landscape when they began to complain and didn't give thanks for all the Lord had done, *keruv* became central in preparing the table of Shabbat. People died when the fiery snakes bit them until Moses was asked to intercede. He made a bronze snake to hold high up on a pole. Anyone who was bitten looked at it and was healed. The people had been brought out to be separate, but it was thankfulness for deliverance that silenced complaints and brought the people into fellowship (Num 21:4–9).

It was a Jewish believer who took these lessons to the gentiles, grafting thousands into the olive tree. The tree grew quickly in its message of restoration. The first Jerusalem council (Acts 15) honored the roles of each group, and the prayer of Jesus was being fulfilled. The council realized that gentiles did not have to convert to become Jews in order to have salvation. But by the fourth century, the gentiles decided that Jews needed to convert to be gentiles in order to have salvation. Both the church and synagogue fell into this thinking: to believe in Jesus, you could not be Jewish.

The original design of the church included all nations; instead, historically the church crushed indigenous identities and left out the Jews. However, in our day, we are seeing renewed relationships come together, fostering attitudes of respect and understanding regarding the value of heritage, all held in God's plan for "every nation and tongue" (Rev 5:9). This movement has flourished.

God's favor with the leadership began with gentiles from the United States and Europe, as well as Jewish leaders from Israel and the United States. In September of 2006, Jewish and gentile people who know God from thirty-six countries convened for a prayer conference in Jerusalem. Rabbi Daniel Juster, member of TJCII International, visited Korea, Japan, and Singapore for Passover in April 2017. His visit to Korea to work with TJCII coordinator Jeong Jacob Lee brought together leaders from the Korea House of Prayer, the Presbyterian Baekseok University, and a vibrant Messianic Jewish Conference.

With long meals sitting at a table together, Dan said the result was a restored confidence in God's end-time purposes for Israel. In Singapore, a meeting for leaders was sponsored that opened the door to return again for talk among people from all nations and how they are joined together.

In Christendom, replacement theology eventually took the form of the European Holocaust. In the Islamic world, it continues to take the form of hatred and hostility toward Israel.

Reverend Brian Cox, another member of the TJCII International Leadership Committee, is an Episcopal priest serving in Washington DC as director of an academic program devoted to faith-based diplomacy. In 2012, Reverend Cox and other TJCII members went on a mission to Kenya, Uganda, and Ghana. A Pentecostal bishop spoke during a meeting at the Evangelical Alliance in Nairobi to tell of a vision he had seven years earlier in a prayer meeting at the top of a nearby mountain. He saw the nation of Kenya coming to the mountain's peak, and all the nations of Africa and the Jews from Israel followed. The bishop saw the nations reconciling with Israel and understood that this would release God's blessing on the entire continent of Africa.

The turn to the Messiah is central to the message foretold in chapters 36 and 37 of Ezekiel, the focus of the restoration of both Israel and the humanity of other nations. In chapter 37, Ezekiel sees a valley full of dry bones. He is instructed to call them forth, and they are assembled. The men and women of Israel stand before Ezekiel. The Lord tells him to prophesy to the four winds, all directions, to come breathe the Spirit into the assembled house of Israel. Ezekiel speaks, and the winds come from the north, the west, the south, and the east. The people come alive, like the gathering in the upper room when the wind of the Holy Spirit came on them.

Rabbi Ari Waldman, Martin's son, sees the movement of Messianic Jewish believers around the world as the fringe of the house of Israel. The Spirit reached them first, but he moves breath from all four directions into the center. Messianic Jews are the first fruits of coming into one body.

Jeremiah states God's promise that Israel will never cease to be a nation before him. Just after being declared a state in May 1948, five armies gathered against Israel to destroy her. With few weapons, Israel won. In 1967 and 1973, war again came against the land and, remarkably, Israel survived. Words in Hebrew are being brought back to life, and Scripture is being spoken as the early body of believers understood it.

The first aliyah took place in the late 1800s, with immigrants coming from Russia and Yemen. A second aliyah of Russian Jews moved because of pogroms and anti-Semitism. After World War I and until 1923, a new group from Russia came and began creating a sustainable agricultural economy.

The next aliyah took place from 1924 to 1929, with Jews seeking to escape anti-Semitism in Poland and Hungary.

The rise of Nazism in Germany and across eastern Europe led nearly a quarter of a million Jews to enter Israel by the beginning of World War II. They included professionals, doctors, lawyers, and artists, who created a thriving economy. When war broke out between Israel and the Arab states in 1948, many of the Jews living in Arab countries abandoned their homes and belongings and fled to Israel under threat of persecution. Ethiopian Jews began moving to Israel in multitudes by the late 1970s. After being allowed to immigrate in the 1990s, nearly one million Russian Jews moved to the homeland.

The number of Messianic congregations in Israel rapidly tripled since the 1990s, now numbering more than three hundred . In the United States, there are hundreds of Messianic congregations associated with the Messianic Jewish Alliance of America, the Union of Messianic Congregations, and the Association of Messianic Jewish Congregations, with worldwide membership surpassing half a million. There is growth in England, France, Belgium, the Netherlands, Australia, Ireland, New Zealand, Australia, Latin America, Brazil, Argentina, and New Mexico. The growth is rooted in prayer together, as living stones, his temple. "If a house is divided against itself, that house will not be able to stand" (Mark 3:25); "By wisdom a house is built, and by understanding it is established" (Prov 24:3).

TJCII's "A Cry to the Church" states:

> Please hear our cry that one day a Second Council of Jerusalem at which the leadership of the Church from the Nations (Gentiles) will recognize and enter into full communion with the resurrected Church from the Circumcision (Judaeis) annulling all the decrees and legislation against the Jewish expression of the Church.

Since TJCII began, Pope John Paul II took initiative in an expression of sorrow for the sins of Catholics against Jews through the ages. The Jewish ghetto of Rome was established in 1555 when the Pope segregated the Jews in a walled quarter with three gates that were locked at night. Conditions were deplorable and frequently flooded by the nearby river. The Jews were under various restrictions and degradations, including having to wear yellow clothing to identify themselves as Jews, attend compulsory Catholic sermons on Shabbat, and run along the main street during Rome's annual carnival as the crowd mocked them, threw trash, and fell on them with often fatal heavy blows. An angry mob attempted to torch the Jewish ghetto in

1798, but rains put out the fire. Ten years later, the ghetto was abolished and the walls torn down, but history remembers.

When visiting Yad Vashem and praying at the Western Wall in Jerusalem in March 2000, the pope signaled change. In September 2006, Archbishop Rowan Williams of the Anglican Church, and Chief Rabbi Shlomo Amar and Chief Rabbi Yonah Metzger of Israel, signed an historic declaration establishing a framework for relationship to develop between them. It is written, "Know therefore that the Lord your God is God, the faithful God who keeps covenant and steadfast love with those who love him and keep his commandments" (Deut 7:9); as Paul said, "forgetting what lies behind and . . . pressing on toward the goal for the prize of the upward call" (Phil 3:13–14). The blood of Jesus cleanses all sin.

God's holiness will never reconcile to the divisions. The bitterness has already poured onto the cross of execution when Jesus cried in agony, "It is finished" (John 19:30). His holy response to division that began in the garden of Eden with a man and woman is the only sacrifice that can bring those he called from among the nations into one wholeness. The prophet Micah said, "Who is a God like thee . . . He does not retain his anger for ever because he delights in steadfast love" (Mic 7:18).

They were to be a nation of priests in a world that is without hope. *Challah* represents being separated into hope, brought to the temple for the priests who offered sacrifice for the sins of word, thought, and deed. Once placed on the altar, the smoke from the sacrifice ascended high to God in a decree of gratitude. Flames flashed as fire joined with the flames in the Shabbat candles and flames of heaven's holy and perfect light when "the fire of the Lord fell, and consumed the burnt offering" (1 Kgs 18:38).

The first fruits are the believers who offered their entire lives at his altar. Not a percentage of tithe or tax, but the whole self given to whatever work the Lord chose for them. Jesus sought those who would forsake all others and take on the yoke of his kingdom. He searched for lowly and heartbroken disciples who thirsted for God's way and would welcome his call with open heart. His fire purified the dross in their lives so that he could lead them.

Those who understood the Torah were given the mission to carry his message. Every Jewish male knew what the phrase "take on my yoke" meant. They were being called to carry the words of God. They would take up the cross and follow him. Jesus took it further, saying, "Take my yoke upon you . . . You will find rest for your souls. For my yoke is easy and my burden is light" (Matt 11:29–30). Declaring himself Lord of the Shabbat, discipleship no longer was about following a single teacher or teaching, but each follower, male and female, would be taught to be a *talmidim* ("disciple") of Jesus. Each is called to be a flame of heaven.

Paul quotes the covenant, as God said, "I will live in them and move among them, and I will be their God, and they shall be my people. Therefore come out from them, and be separate from them" (2 Cor 6:16–17). In affection for the New Covenant, this Jewish man said we are being open and giving with you; our hearts are wide to you, so why are you making restrictions between us? Anyone in Jesus is a new creation, honoring God's work to destroy divisions through his Son. The new has come. Calling the church coworkers, Paul implored, "We beseech you on behalf of Christ, be reconciled to God . . . so that in him we might become the righteousness of God" (2 Cor 5:11–21).

In Bethany, a dinner was held in honor of Jesus. Those who gathered were once outcasts, condemned, and apart from community, echoing Psalm 23:5: "Thou preparest a table before me in the presence of my enemies." Mary was there, who Jesus had delivered. Her sister Martha was there and their brother Lazarus reclined at the table who Jesus restored from the dead. The gathering was at the home of Simon, a man who Jesus had healed from leprosy. As she looked around at the faces around the table, Mary was filled with gratitude for the Lord and, wanting to express her heart, came to him with an alabaster jar of expensive perfume to anoint him (Matt 26:6–13, John 12:1–8). These are people who knew the meaning of *challah*, whose hearts understood the idea of being separated to support the high priest who could enter the holy of holies and reconcile them to God. The result avails the Lord to mediate between the two worlds, heaven and earth, and the two peoples, Jew and gentile.

The law of *challah* recalls God's presence in the temple, the experience someone chosen by God, the Scriptures being given, and the promise of the Messiah. Removing a token amount of dough and throwing it into the fire of the oven while reciting the blessing is an offering to God from the bounty of creation and the depths of trust in him to separate them and take away the pain.

Embedded in the cycles of nature needed for bread is the knowledge that we are vulnerable. We suffer loss and we weather storms, yet we are given strength and are renewed. Birth and death, youth and age, and the passing seasons each tell of an ancestor's history and of a child's future, internalizing the flowing rhythm of God's design. God's faithfulness is our shield (Ps 91:4).

As per Ruth's example in 1:16–17, every gentile who enters into the covenant is considered a true proselyte as they become a child of Abraham and Sarah. "Look toward heaven, and number the stars, if you are able to number them . . . So shall your descendants be," the Lord told them (Gen 15:5). They will shine brightly, glorifying God in the dark world. "Praise him, all you shining stars!" (Ps 148:3).

> The major problem in terms of Jewish/Gentile cleavage came with the Christians, but not in the early period. That Jesus himself was a Jew and never thought of himself as outside the fold of Judaism is beyond doubt and debate. He was at home in synagogue and Temple: he "went into the synagogue as his custom was." He learnt the Jewish tradition, though it is anachronistic to apply the technical term "rabbi" to him. He observed the Sabbath and dietary laws, though he echoed the Pharisees in urging the wider philosophy of Jewish observance to be understood. He used midrashic method and was an effective parabolist.[3]

The Pharisees, or the separated ones, came together to uphold the law of God. Jesus did not stand against the Pharisees. The many aspects guiding each day all are under *halakha*, Jewish law, translated literally as "the way of walking." Jesus came to fulfill the walk, not abolish it. As a Pharisee, Paul rejoiced in the Torah, finding in every word how God guides his people, defining life beyond the margins of laws and practices. However, as history descended, pulling gentile believers into thinking that the temple was destroyed because Jesus rejected his people and replaced them with the church, the Judeo-Christians diminished in numbers or were absorbed into gentile groups who understood nothing of the traditions and promises.

> Could you be a Jew without the Sabbath, festivals, circumcision and dietary laws? The answer was no—but you could become a Christian. Could you be a Jew without saying *Sh'ma Yisra'el*— "Hear, O Israel" and proclaiming the absolute invisibility and indivisibility of God?—again no: but you could become a Christian if you accepted the re-worked status of Jesus.[4]

The blood shed over which church practices to follow was influenced not only by interpreting the Lord's teachings, but from an innate desire to hold onto what parents did who did what their grandparents did. Yet Jesus said to be willing to let go of the ways of a mother, father, sister, and brother for his sake. "He who loves father or mother more than me is not worthy of me; and he who loves son or daughter more than me is not worthy of me;

---

3. Apple, "Jewish Attitudes," para. 16.
4. Apple, "Jewish Attitudes," para. 21.

and he who does not take his cross and follow me is not worthy of me" (Matt 10:35–38). Go where the glory goes.

Before the church left the table, the meaning in how God delivered from every stumbling place was shared with the gentiles. Long-held biblical traditions were honored as the early church grew in numbers. The people retained the fear of God. They had seen the two who instantly died when they withheld money for themselves. They knew the story of God consuming Aaron's sons when they offered unauthorized fire in the presence of the Lord, and had heard about Uzzah, who took hold of the ark when the ox stumbled and died for touching its holiness. These episodes all occurred so that the community would walk in rightness.

Holding the seven stars in his right hand and walking among the seven lampstands, Jesus speaks to the church in Pergamum, commending them for remaining true to his name in a place where Satan had set up his throne. But he held a few things against them that he wanted cleansed. "You have some there who hold the teaching of Balaam, who taught Balak to put a stumbling block before the sons of Israel, that they might eat food sacrificed to idols and practice immorality" (Rev 2:12–16). As in the days just before they were to cross the Jordan and enter the promised land, the enemy was trying to compromise God's teachings. Paul witnessed this happening, and said that "they all look after their own interests, not those of Jesus Christ" (Phil 2:21).

The church separating itself by keeping the teachings of the Word is the mark of a pure church. Then, like Simeon at the temple when the newly Jesus arrived, there is the same sense of seeing what has been promised: "for mine eyes have seen thy salvation which thou hast prepared in the presence of all peoples, a light for revelation to the Gentiles, and for glory to thy people Israel" (Luke 2:30–32).

> And those who are wise shall shine like the brightness of the firmament; and those who turn many to righteousness, like the stars forever and ever. (Dan 12:3)

The Shabbat meal serves two *challah* on Friday evening in remembrance of Exodus. For forty years, three million people were given twice as much manna on Friday so they would have it for the day of rest. A commandment was given that all of it had to be consumed on the day it was given, and none of it could be left over for the next day. Each day, the world is given the Lord's strength. "Therefore, do not be anxious about tomorrow, for tomorrow will be anxious for itself. Let the day's own trouble be sufficient for the day" (Matt 6:19–20).

The Exodus revealed God's involvement in the needs of each person. This bedrock formed a nation who for more than three thousand years laid a tablecloth each Friday, thinking of the dew that covered the ground before the bread of angels came down. Since her inception, Israel prayed for the other nations of the world. David foresaw that the "nations will fear the name of the Lord, and all the kings of earth thy glory" (Ps 102:15). David asked that his words be recorded for the coming unborn generations "that men may declare in Zion the name of the Lord, and in Jerusalem his praise, when people gather together, and kingdoms, to worship the Lord (102:21)"

The closing prayer of Shabbat is the Aleinu, meaning, "It is our duty to praise." Many believe that the prophet Joshua wrote these words after leading the people across the Jordan River, expressing the struggle of being made a people of God and ascribing greatness to the One who brings his knowledge into our hearts. The prayer then asks for the world to come into God's oneness and for Israel to fulfill being a blessing to all nations.

During the Reform movement, the verse "for God has not made us like the nations of the land" was extracted by some congregations in the diaspora, not wanting to be singled out for being Jewish.

Aleinu translation:

It is our duty to praise the Master of all,
to acclaim the greatness of the One
who forms all creation.
For God did not make us like the nations of other lands,
and did not make us the same as other families of the Earth.
God did not place us in the same situations as others, and
our destiny is not the same as anyone else's.
And we bend our knees, and bow down,
and give thanks, before the Ruler,
the Ruler of Rulers, the Holy One, Blessed is God.
The One who spread out the heavens,
and made the foundations of the Earth,
and whose precious dwelling is in the heavens above,
and whose powerful Presence is in the highest heights.
Adonai is our God, there is none else.
Our God is truth, and nothing else compares.
As it is written in Your Torah:
"And you shall know today, and take to heart,
that Adonai is the only God,
In the heavens above and on Earth below.
There is no other."

Therefore we put our hope in You, Adonai our God,
to soon see the glory of Your strength,
to remove all idols from the Earth,
and to completely cut off all false gods;
to repair the world, Your holy empire.
And for all living flesh to call Your name,
and for all the wicked of the Earth to turn to You.
May all the world's inhabitants recognize and know that to
You ever knee must bend and every tongue must swear loyalty.
Before You, Adonai, our God,
may all bow down, and give honor to Your precious name,
and may all take upon themselves the yoke of Your rule.
And may You reign over them soon and forever and always.
Because all rule is Yours alone,
and you will rule in honor forever and ever.
As it is written in Your Torah:
"Adonai will reign forever and ever."
And as it is said: "Adonai will be Ruler over the whole Earth,
and on that day,
God will be One, and God's name will be One."[5]

There is nothing that compares to God—he is one Father to all, moving through lives in one harmony, unseen. No image can be made, and we cannot limit him; he is without the boundaries of form, revealed to us through words. His attributes are known through the prophets, and his anointed issue the invitation into the boundless place of his Shabbat rest. He is the God who wants to repair and bring kindness, desiring everyone to be restored to his image.

There is a narrow path that now leads between the unbalances of the church on one side and the people it has hurt on the other; it passes between boundaries that press the past in on both sides. Messianic Jews stand in the gap between the two. "And your ancient ruins shall be rebuilt; you shall raise up the foundations of many generations; you shall be called the repairer of the breach, the restorer of streets to dwell in" (Isa 58:12). To repair the fallen walls is to bring the boundaries of God's ways around others, restoring the foundations laid long ago for the process of understanding each other in God's book.

Messianic Jews, seeing union begin between denominations that had long ago had wedges pushed between them, have been visiting indigenous nations who for so long suffered from colonization trying to force them into being a people they are not, erasing their God-given heritage as their

---

5. Jewish Virtual Library, "Jewish Prayers: Aleinu," para. 6.

homelands and resources were taken. Apologies have been made, but as Messianic Jews step in, a broader meeting place cascades into understanding the value Jesus places on heritage, clans, and families. Sons and daughters of the land of Israel believing in the Messiah create a space for other nations to be healed.

Donna Ballard wrote in the May 2017 newsletter that TJCII Ireland has a love for Israel that is led by team member Paddy Monaghan. In February of 2016, the TJCII International Leadership Council member Benjamin Berger spoke at a conference called "Church Unity God's Way: the One New Man" at a Catholic parish hall in Jerusalem, at St. Mark's Pentecostal Church, and at a seminar at All Nations Church. TJCII Ireland's Catholic and Protestant participants move to support the Jewish people and the principle of unity among the body of Christ "that they may become perfectly one, so that the world may know that thou hast sent me and hast loved them even as thou hast loved me" (John 17:23).

For example, the Vineyard Church, with five churches in Northern Ireland and one in Dublin, has heard the call toward unity. Pastors Alan and Kathryn Scot lead a congregation of more than a thousand, and pastors Seán and Debbie Byrne lead a three-hundred-member congregation in Dublin.

About one thousand members of the Catholic Charismatic Renewal Ireland gathered for their annual conference in June of 2017, reaching out in new relationships with Protestant and Pentecostal leaders. About eighty leaders attended the conference in Rome in June when Pope Francis requested its leaders to include a seminar on messianic belief. Sister Mary Paul Friemel, an intercessor and member of TJCII's NOW generation in Europe, reported their meetings in the May 2017 newsletter. In Krakow, Poland, the gatherings were intense, she said. Worship, sharing, and prayer formed in groups in Budapest, Hungary and another in Vienna for the momentum in the Spirit to lead them. In Germany in March of 2017, they met with the German TJCII leadership team for a weekend of deepening fellowship. Trips were planned to build fellowship in Romania and a weekend in Kiev.

In every corner of the earth, there has been injury to the church's relationship with Israel and misguided ideas about Jesus, places where the Lord's voice is now heard. In 1391, the church incited a terrible pogrom against the Jews in Seville, who had lived there for centuries. The pogrom spread through Spain and Portugal, murdering fifty thousand Jews and destroying their communities. For twenty years, the massacre continued to decimate the Israelite people. In despair, two hundred thousand Jews succumbed to forced conversion to Christianity just to stay alive. Hundreds of thousands of Jews remained steadfast in their heritage as they were forced to leave the land that had been home for generations. They immigrated to other countries, such a Italy, Turkey, Germany, Poland, and Lithuania.

Fleeing the Czar's pogroms in the early 1900s, Jews came to America, bringing their creative arts, theater, science, dance, and literature, and resisting attempts at assimilation into the gentile world. But by the Roaring Twenties, the desire to get ahead swept many of the 4.5 million American Jews to hide their Jewishness—until now, when the church is beginning to embrace their identity.

If we are to comprehend the words of Jesus, we need understanding of how the Old Testament flows into the New Covenant. "If you believed Moses, you would believe me, for he wrote of me. But if you do not believe his writings, how will you believe my words?" (John 5:46–47). Like Abraham and Sarah, whose tent was welcoming, Jesus set the example of receiving all people who come to him. Preparing his people for the redemption of all nations, as he taught he said, "Is it not written, 'My house shall be called a house of prayer for all the nations'?" (Mark 11:17). He was noted for his inclusion.

The first-century church understood that this grafting was to be offered to the ends of the earth. From the Torah's teaching of Genesis, they held onto common knowledge that all are God's offspring, descended to multiply into boundaries of nations. All were called to be reconciled with the Creator.

The church shared fellowship that defined their daily lives, their possessions, overcoming their differences by coming together to sit in the light and break *challah* together. They were told not to offend each other, so they observed Old Testament teachings of ritual purity and the laws forbidding bringing pagan practices into worship. Jonah's story carried to the apostles, telling them of the man who God sent to the gentiles, the Assyrians, with a message to repent. Jonah had also been raised in faith founded on remaining separate from other nations, yet the Lord extended his hand through Jonah to what he knew to be a wicked people. The Holy Spirit was poured out also on the gentiles, reaffirming God's will to the apostles that the Lord wished to cleanse all hearts; they responded to society and organized to help the widows, the poor, the orphans, and the isolated. The Jew would share the teachings of the God of Israel with the gentiles, but to keep respect between them, people of other heritage were free to continue in their own language and customs of giving thanks. Removing the prejudice was a priority to Jesus.

Paul speaks to the distinction between Jew and gentile when he reminds us that Jesus' death on the cross shattered the wall that had divided ever since God gave the commandments that made Israel a separate and holy nation. He broke down prejudice for the second commandment to be fulfilled: "You shall love your neighbor as yourself" (Matt 22:39). James also addressed prejudice, telling the people not to have personal favoritism as they hold their faith in Jesus (Jas 2:1).

The one new humanity is the church's glory, separated from the world and dedicated to the high priest, seeing how every blessing comes through the Father, the Son, and the Holy Spirit. He made the mystery known to us so we could learn his ways and bring unity to all things in heaven and on earth. We were chosen to be separate with the same power that raised Jesus from the dead and seated him in the heavenly realms, far above all rule and authority, power and dominion, and every name that is invoked. God placed all things under his feet and appointed him to be head over everything for the church, which is his body, the fullness of him who fills everything in every way (Eph 1:9–23).

The Shabbat morning prayer service is especially beautiful in enhancing the holiness of God's plan. The blessing of the Shema is spoken. The emotion of the whole of their history is heard when someone says *Shema Yisrael, Adonai eloheinu, Adonai echad* ("Hear O Israel: The Lord our God is one Lord") (Deut 6:4). When Jesus was asked by a scribe which commandment is the most important, Jesus quoted Moses by reciting the Shema. "The first is, 'Hear, O Israel: The Lord our God, the Lord is one; and you shall love the Lord your God with all your heart, and with all your soul, and with all your mind, and with all your strength'" (Mark 12:28–29).

Shema Yisrael is a call for Israel to gather, and for the entire world to know that God is One. It is said that the people gathered at Mount Sinai like one man with one heart, witnessing the world of heaven come down to reconnect with earth. When God spoke, they saw God's meaning with the clarity his presence brought. They saw the truth of what they were hearing, understanding that the Lord is sovereign over every detail of creation. They saw that he opened their discernment, and they were able to know that the entire creation was generated by his words. The prayer remained so vital that it was spoken at Auschwitz in secret, in long lines of prisoners, one by one, guarding each other to fulfill the *mitzvah* of *tefillin*. Proclaiming "Hear O Israel, God is our Lord, God is One" is a cry to unify in God's oneness. He has made each creation as a comment on the inner mystery of heaven's power, though we see his light through a prism, refracting into separate events.

Israel gathered to God, knowing he is One, as Adam and Eve knew before they ate from the tree of knowledge of good and evil, causing only the surface of the physical world to be seen. Creation no longer shone with being contained within the Word. It became fragmented, and one of the fragments was a split into denominations of followers of God's Son. Jesus determined to unify the Jews and gentiles so that the world will emerge in God's presence and again see that everything is bound by him.

On Shabbat, God is blessed for creating the universe. He is thanked for remaining involved in every moment of his creation. He is blessed for making it possible to live in accord with the angels who honor him, for being the Creator of lights and for choosing his people with love. God is asked to help hearts be able to understand, listen, learn, remember, teach, guard, and fulfill his words.

The search of the mind strives beyond just knowing that there is one God. It is a hope yearning for the messianic age when our knowledge is complete again, his wisdom satiating the entire earth like the Great Flood of Noah's time, when the wellsprings of the great deep and the windows of heaven were opened. "For the earth will be filled with the knowledge of the glory of the Lord, as the waters cover the sea" (Hab 2:14); "All the earth shall be filled with the glory of the Lord" (Num 14:21).

Humanity, the splendor of the image of God, will emerge from baptism as the express image of God. The flames unite in such power that "at the name of Jesus every knee should bow, in heaven and on earth and under the earth, and every tongue confess that Jesus Christ is Lord, to the glory of God the Father" (Phil 2:10–11).

Shabbat helps us remember this glimpse into our future. When the Shabbat comes, the Holy One descends from his throne of glory to meet with the people, and angels sing their hymns of praise. "Lift up your heads, O gates! And be lifted up, O ancient doors! that the King of glory may come in" (Ps 24:9).

6

HAMAN

She went to inquire of the Lord. (Gen 25:22)

THE BIBLE'S REPRESENTATION OF womanhood is in the courage described in the poem, "Ode to a Capable Wife." Her character is noble, her hands work for her family, and she reaches out to the poor. She is creative, an astute business woman, and able to discern the needs of others (Prov 31:10–31).

Paul carried this cherished Jewish tradition into his message when he told women to be keepers at home who guard the ways of God (Titus 2:4–5). The enduring words of Paul advance the kingdom, encouraging younger women to be radiant in their personal lives, keeping the laws of purity and kindness. Be busy at home with the *mitzvot* of women.

Women lighting the candles for Shabbat and the festivals create a space inside time for the most secret heart to come aside and be in the presence of God. Notes from Moses' life emphasize the importance of this, telling of Moses, Aaron, and the seventy elders of Israel going up the mountain after the giving of the ten commandments. Needing time to separate and have fellowship with each other, they retreated from the crowd, walking up the mountain to eat and drink in the gracious presence of God (Exod 24:9–11). The tradition sustains the people because the enemy has not changed his ploy to cause division in relationships.

When modern feminism thirsted for honor, it gained salaries for women, corporate power, more divorces, and children left alone to find their way. Their search to contribute resulted in conflict because they mistakenly thought that if their gifts were not like those of men, they were not as valuable. Roles were valued pertaining to what had been a man's job, including smoking cigarettes, drinking in bars, and increasing their numbers in prisons.

Rebelling against the image that she should be always smiling in a spotless well-ordered household, the movement tragically forgot the spiritual dimension. Without it, women are left restless, trying to live up to a distorted image. The youth coming up behind them lost their spiritual presence as the bondage of working for the bank account took time away from trusting God with the Shabbat rest. The definition of rights did not include being a wife and daughter who honors their heritage.

Male attributes generally mark the measurable goals of life, while those of the female are the relationship itself. God breathed an eternal soul into the body, but the world's materialism pressed the physical needs to be fed, beautified, adorned, and skilled. Focusing solely on agendas of moving forward with jobs, education, and houses marginalized families basking in a relationship that is growing stronger with God. Society told women to seek their own gratification. Narcissism became a norm. Valued for what they do, not for who they are, society has taken on the characteristics of Sodom and Gomorrah, leaving them feeling more lonely than ever, desolate in their desecration of relationship with God.

In all this, the Jewish woman held the wonderful gift of God, which linked her to a long and deep heritage that made every older woman a grandmother, sharing her traditions. Daughters could "aspire to live quietly, to mind [their] own affairs . . . as [the apostles] charged [them]" (1 Thess 4:11). They are distinguished, with prayers for God to grant them the blessings of all who went before them, showing that sufficiency is in God.

> May God bless you
> with the strength and vision of Sarah,
> with the wisdom and foresight of Rebekah,
> with the courage and compassion of Rachel,
> with the gentleness and graciousness of Leah,
> and their faith in the promise of our people's heritage.

Solomon's woman of valor affirmed God's desire for her heritage. Even when the sky crushes with the weight of oppressions, the table is laid, the candle lit, and, like pilgrims, her people build homes around faith wherever they settle. The thirst of the restless mind is calmed. The search for purpose is satisfied in an identity serving the Creator. Why spend money for what does not satisfy? (Isa 55:2). Why spend a life on what does not answer the spirit's poverty? "Every one who drinks of this water will thirst again" (John

4:13–14); "The poor and needy seek water, and there is none, and their tongue is parched with thirst, I the Lord will answer them, I the God of Israel will not forsake them" (Isa 41:17).

It was enough reason to sing, knowing the Lord still holds life in his hands as he did on the first day he breathed into creation. "Blessed is the [woman] who trusts in the Lord . . . [she] is like a tree planted by the water, that send out its roots by the stream, and does not fear when heat comes, for its leaves remain green, and is not anxious in the year of drought, for it does not cease to yield fruit" (Jer 17:7–8).

Distressed days when God's presence feels far distant are retrieved by collective memory reciting the way the sea could not drown the people the Lord had chosen to carry his words into the world. Giants could not slay them. Haman could not exterminate them. Nations of the world could not kill them. The waters would rise in deep floods, but the water belongs to the Lord. The fire used at the burning stakes is fire the Lord will use to judge. His holy word spoke. "I will not lie to David. His line shall endure for ever, his throne as long as the sun before me, like the moon it shall be established for ever; it shall stand firm while the skies endure" (Ps 89:35–37).

The Messiah's birth was first proclaimed "to all who were looking for the redemption of Jerusalem" by Anna, an eighty-four-year-old woman, when Mary and Joseph brought infant Jesus to the temple to present him to God (Luke 2:38).

As the Lord fulfills the redemption of Jewish believers to their destined place in the body of Messiah, the accomplishment of his work reveals the great price Jesus gave of himself to bring Jew and gentile into one new humanity (Eph 2:15). He saw us all there in the numbers of stars in the constellations above, shining just as God promised. "The Gentiles are fellow heirs, members of the same body, and partakers of the promise in Christ Jesus through the gospel" (Eph 3:6). It brought shared persecution that, between 30 AD and 2000 AD killed seventy million people for knowing Jesus.[1] By 2011, a believer was being killed somewhere every five minutes.[2]

John wrote to believers as a Jewish man in exile. He said that he was their brother in tribulation. When the presence of the Lord was revealed, he fell down before him as if dead in the sight of the one who holds the keys of death and hell. John looked into the eyes of the friend he'd walked the dusty roads with and saw his eyes now flamed with fire, revealing what is within us, seeing through all that covers us. He cannot be disputed. John saw his feet like fine brass, feet of judgment like the altar of the temple burnished

---

1. De Groote, "Christian Killed Every 5 Minutes," para. 7.
2. De Groote, "Christian Killed Every 5 Minutes," paras. 1–2.

in fire. He is coming to trample out his enemies (Rev 1:9–20). Regal, unchallenged in his authority, the voice of the Lord of all creation is among many waters, full of majesty, cascading with power, unstoppable. We'll stand silenced before the sound of a thundering waterfall (Ps 29:3–4). He holds seven stars in his hand, holding all the universes in his hand, holding the angels of the seven churches (Rev 1:20). The entire ministry is in his hand, regulating the times and seasons. "He has put on garments of vengeance for clothing, and wrapped himself in fury as a mantle" (Isa 59:17).

God has warned that as time moves, Earth further unravels from the garden of Eden. Each generation will let go of another prohibition and accept the profane. In recent society, there have been women giving expression to Lilith by portraying her as a role model for women who are empowered against male domination. In the Talmud and rabbinical teachings, however, Lilith is a female demon who seduces men, threatens the lives of babies, and endangers women in childbirth. Her name comes from the Hebrew word for night, *laila*, as she pursued men in darkness to defile his soul, possibly based on the pagan demon Lilu in Gilgamesh and Babylonian legends. The darkness is called Lilith. This is how far women have wandered in their thinking, as the early church wandered from its beginnings. This is how far the serpent in the garden has encroached to bring down entire nations by clouding the identity of female in creation.

What we call adult entertainment the Lord says is lust and adultery that rips apart the fabric of homes. Society calls sodomy an alternative lifestyle. The need for food becomes glutton. The desire for sex becomes abuse. The treason against heaven refuses to see its need of the power of light that brings us into balance by giving us sight.

The names of those who grieve with the Lord are recorded, glimpsed when the glory of God called to "the man clothed in linen, who had a writing case at his side." The Lord's Spirit moved him to "go through the city, through Jerusalem, and put a mark upon the foreheads of the men who sigh and groan over all the abominations that are committed in it" (Ezek 9:3–4). The tears are recorded in God's book (Ps 56:8). He keeps track of sorrows, knowing us before we were born, numbering our days, coming near to collect our tears to wipe them away in his throne room as he reconciles every wrong in each person (Rev 21:4). We want our pain to matter to God. We need him to care about our struggle, whether it is having to pay an overdue bill, the tossing of a restless night, or the death of a son in battle. We are in dread if he disregards the place of our homes.

He says that he will guard us and keep the flame of our soul lit through this wilderness journey. He has come to heal our wounds if we will come to him and speak honestly with him. "The Spirit of the Lord is upon me, because he has anointed me to preach good news to the poor" (Luke 4:18). The darkness was sifted, and the fire and spirit were sifted. God's voice spoke into the void and guided it. "The voice of God is upon the waters" (Ps 29:3).

> But the path of the righteous is like the light of dawn, that shines brighter and brighter until the full day. (Prov 4:18)

Conscious of dependence on the Lord's voice, the people have eaten matzah (called the "bread of faith" because it has no leaven) every Passover for thousands of years. The home and the food have been scrupulously inspected for their presence at Passover as a reminder of the virtue of giving God the glory and not esteeming self-importance. By eating matzah, thought focuses on the power of God, who alone breaks bondage. The virtue extends to holding the body as a vessel in the beauty that comes in the quietly private acts done for the benefit of home and those in our care.

Woman's role both supports and influences man's will, not as a controlling person, but as a guide that helps him choose God's way, or stands in his way when he is about to oppose God's instructions. For example, Abigail was married to Nabel, a harsh and rude man. No one could reason with him. She woke one day and a servant brought her a message that her husband had insulted David by rejecting his request to share provisions for festival food. Abigail heard that David was going to have his band of men take up the sword and strike back, and she was told that the presence of David had been good, acting as a wall of protection around them and their sheep, so she gathered loaves of bread, grain, raisins, lamb, fig cakes, and wine, preparing a banquet for them. She didn't tell her husband, but she was doing it for his good.

Abigail slipped away to ride into the mountain ravine to have a private conversation with David. She bowed before him, acknowledging her husband's unkindness. Full of humility and yet boldness, her words honored him and helped him see that the choice he was about to make was not his destiny. It was not God's will. She spoke to his heart (1 Sam 25:2–35). The ways of the Lord enlighten the eyes and make the heart feel its joy (Ps 19:8). David responded by praising the God of Israel, who sent out Abigail to meet him that day, stopping him from carrying out vengeance with his own hands.

True feminine beauty is poised in the way a woman carries herself with sensitivity to affect another life. The women drawn to be around Jesus just to know the bright light from heaven are women receiving the truths and providing for God's servants—as some examples, the Levites, priests, Elijah (provided for by a widow), and Elisha (his providor was a wealthy woman). The great role of women is to minister to the work being done among us. In Luke 23, the women came to care for Jesus in death, and when he rose in chapter 24 they were the first to be aware. In the process, their own relationships healed, and it can be guessed that their children followed, as families often convert together in the New Testament. They loved the message, listening and absorbing. The mighty God who parted the powerful sea is believed. His work is known.

Yet it takes only one heartbreak to cause doubt.

Young women who have nothing that marks the transition to womanhood want to be known. They want to be close to someone and have someone close to them, but the offer of culture is the sexual identity without knowledge of the spiritual and emotional effect on their womanhood. Society does not support her knowing for herself what feels best, but an entire host of angels is with her if she says no to that culture.

Being spared the pain of failed relationship means saving intercourse for the right person. It is a force used to comfort or to steer in a wrong direction. It can bring true intimacy or create the illusion that gives only loneliness. Scripture teaches that, before a person enters the physical relationship, developing a relationship that burns in God like two independent flames will brighten the world around them when they come together.

God wants relationship to be unique. He wants his men and women sensitive to messages between them, undiluted by regrets or thoughts of others. He wants relationship kept whole, protecting us from a descent into ourselves. Love is not about falling in but ascending up, deliberately protecting a space for listening to self, the other person, and the Lord.

In Romans 1:18–32, our merciful high priest reveals that his wrath is toward ungodliness that suppresses the truth God wants for every person. Because of the tenderness of God's mercy, Jesus said, "your faith has made you well" (Matt 9:22). Our behavior does not flow from psychology, but from the degree of intimacy with our Creator. In Revelation, Jesus speaks to his church: "Behold I stand at the door and knock, waiting to come in and share the meal with you" (Rev 3:20); "In returning and rest you shall be saved; in quietness and in trust shall be your strength" (Isa 30:15).

The rest that Jesus offers is extended to homes in every neighborhood, but inside homes where people are not giving thanks, families are separated from each other. Inside their homes, they are fractured; children hear other voices telling them to be independent from their parents, that they do not need the bond of love they give; or, they are left knowing that the only way to be well is to be separate from their family's way of living. They wonder for long years, "Where do I belong? Where do I fit?" They did not hear their part in the story of God.

This is God sharing his story. If you seek wisdom as silver, and search for her as for hidden treasures, she will enter your heart. Discretion will protect you. Wisdom will save you from the ways of wicked men and from adulterous women and their seductive words (Prov 2:4–17).

Esther was a young Jewish woman living in exile in the Persian diaspora. Her Jewish heritage was hidden, and she was purified with myrrh and oils to became a queen. Being a beautiful woman gained her position in the empire, but it was her reverence for the Lord that won the praise of her people. When the dark night of genocide fell on her people, her light of faith burned undimmed.

Her story unfolded about four hundred years before Jesus was born during her people's exile in Persia. Many Jews were in despair of their national future, both in the land and in exile, because of cultural assimilation. Esther's cousin Mordecai refused to bow before Haman the Agagite, a descendant of an Amalekite king who was an enemy of Israel during the time of King Saul (1 Sam 15:32). Haman conspired a plan to slaughter all of the Jewish people. When Mordecai learned of Haman's plan, he went to the palace, weeping and clothed in sackcloth to tell Esther, who he had raised after her parents had died. He had counseled her not to tell the king her nationality. Now he says that it is time.

Esther feels completely insufficient. She cannot approach the king without being summoned. The penalty would be death. But Mordecai stands firm. The lineage of the Messiah is being carried by the people of Israel. The knowledge of his coming and of God's words had been entrusted to them. Mordecai tells Esther, "Think not that in the king's palace you will escape any more than all the other Jews. For if you keep silence at such a time as this, relief and deliverance will rise for the Jews from another quarter, but you and your father's house will perish. And who knows whether you have not come to the kingdom for such a time as this?" (Esth 4:13–14).

His words ignite Esther, and she resolves to risk execution and see the king. She calls for all the Jews to gather for a three-day fast as they prayed to the Lord to make a way for them. God prepared the king's heart. Esther appeared before the king and found favor. She invited him to a dinner party, accompanied by Haman. At a second dinner party, Esther revealed that she is Jewish and unmasks Haman's plan to kill her people. The king, who has come to care for Esther, is angered, and had Haman executed. The Jews received permission to defend themselves against their enemies. Mordecai was elevated to the office of grand vizier.

Like Daniel, surrounded by a dominant culture at odds with God's instructions, the book of Esther demonstrates how a life in exile can still glorify God's will. She was marginalized, and survived by not revealing she was a child of God. Her prayer was received in the throne room, the flashing thunder and dancing flames of light, the mercy seat, where the angels stand ready to do God's will.

Mordecai recorded the events and sent letters to all the Jews in the king's provinces to have them celebrate a festival called Purim every year, early in spring, when the moon waxes full. It is a time to remember how God delivered his people and turned their mourning into joy. Purim means "lots," the method that Haman used to decide the date to wipe out the Jewish people in Persia.

The days of feasting and joy are to be kept by descendants through every generation (Esth 9:17–22, 28). There is a fast the day before Purim from dawn until dusk because Esther fasted before she went before the king, and she asked her people to fast with her. The next day celebrates God's deliverance. There are Purim *spiels* (meaning "plays"). Children and adults dress as characters to reenact the story with the façade of masks. Esther and Mordecai's names are mentioned to cheers of "hurray!" and shouts of "boo!" drown out the name of Haman being uttered. This symbolically fulfills the verse, "You shall blot out the remembrance of Am'alek from under heaven" (Deut 25:19).

These are days of gladness, for sending great food to one another and gifts to the poor (Esth 9:22). The Megillah—the scroll of Esther—is read on the eve of Purim and again during Purim day.

Esther's Jewish name was Hadassah, meaning "myrtle tree," which is a tree that will grow back again and again after it is cut down. Esther was her Persian name, meaning "star." Because her name is identified with the bright morning star, she is connected to Psalm 22, which is meant to be sung to the tune of the same name. The first line was spoken by Jesus to his Father in heaven: "My God, my God, why have you forsaken me?" Esther may have meditated on these lines, which praise God the savior of Israel.

> Yet thou art holy, enthroned on the praises of Israel. In thee our fathers trusted; they trusted, and thou didst deliver them. To thee they cried, and were saved; in thee they trusted, and were not disappointed (Ps 22:3–5).

The bold burning light of Esther is reflected in Proverbs 31. "Charm is deceitful, and beauty is vain, but a woman who fears the Lord is to be praised." Her fast aligned with examining herself in her relationship with God and showing God that she desired his will. Jesus extended the fast to all believers, individually and collectively, for personal needs and for the ingathering of Israel and the church. Being able to come near to God is an awesome mercy when the decree for sin in the land is eternal death (Ezek 18:4).

The enemy spirit of Haman is unrelenting in its intent to destroy the people God chooses. It dwells in inexplicable hatred throughout generations and in political battles over dividing the land of Israel. Even among people who say they believe Scripture, there is a disconnect with Israel and an unprecedented breakdown of family as God designed.

But there is always a remnant that God keeps among his nations. Isaiah saw the stump of a tree that had been cut down. He saw the shoot of new growth. A small group of Israelites survived the invasion of the Assyrian army. God's word brings them back to the promised land (Isa 10:20–22). There has always been a remnant of Jewish people who believe Jesus, even in the most difficult times. Even at the present time there is a remnant chosen by grace (Rom 11:5). The dragon makes war with the remnant of seed who keep the commandments of God (Rev 12:17). As Isaiah said, "If the Lord of hosts had not left us a few survivors, we should have been like Sodom, and become like Gomor'rah" (Isa 1:9; Rom 9:29).

Like Esther, we face the intimidation of what may happen if we speak God's will. For some it will mean risking their life. For others it will mean scoffing and mockery. The fast to seek God is prayer, asking him what role we will play to take a stand. It is a prayer that awakens the soul. "Unite my heart to fear thy name" (Ps 86:11).

It takes a gentle hand to patiently graft in branches, helping it attach to the root and grow. The word of God flowing from the fountain of blessing through the branches quenches thirst. Restlessness is subdued, no longer pushing opinions onto others. Disagreements are presented to the Father's presence, secured by the root.

With dignity and courage, not knowing how deeply the days may darken, as a woman of Proverbs 31 lights the candles, her family hears God say "do not be afraid." An epic history forms Israel's festivals because at every vicious persecution, "do not despair" is what has been passed down. *Zachor* and *shamor*. Remember and guard. God promised, "I will return you to your own land" (Ezek 36:22–28). We are incomplete and inconsolable until we lift eyes to give thanks for the future that has been assured.

> As for me, I disregard my own honor and stand upon the honor of Heaven. (Midr. Sam. 25:6)

As Jesus walked by at some distance, the afflicted called out, "Master! Have mercy on us!" Others Jesus laid his hand on and touched or spoke, and they were cleansed, but when healing was needed he told them to go show themselves to the priests. It was the priest who diagnosed leprosy and could free them from isolation when he determined a healing. Jesus was saying to go be pronounced clean so they could return to community. Otherwise the only people to fellowship with would be others with leprosy or miserable human beings, with no day-to-day interaction with healthy people or with people gathering in thanks each week.

Esther would have been cut off from her people had she not stood in her faith. In the parable of the wedding feast, Jesus spoke of being cut off and left in outer darkness (Matt 22:13). A gate crasher at a wedding was discovered to have no right to attend, and the master of the feast commanded him to be cast into the outer darkness. This darkness describes a place of great sorrow, unspeakable loss in eternal regret, away from the brightly lit celebrations of God's victory. It is called the nether gloom of darkness (Jude 13), a place reserved for those who did not accept the invitation to be cleansed to have a seat at his Shabbat feast. However, Jesus is the light (John 8:12). "When thou hidest thy face, they are dismayed" (Ps 104:29). His purity, his glory, and his holiness are joy. Darkness symbolizes depravity and affliction (Ps 82:5).

The first reference to someone being cut off from their people is in the instruction for Israel to be circumcised according to God's covenant. Any male who is not circumcised is to be cut off (Gen 17:14). In the book of Numbers, anyone who sins deliberately is to be cut off because he has despised the word of the Lord (Num 15:30). Breaking the fast on the Day of Atonement, sexual violations, and ritual impurities resulted in being cut off.

Many laws in Leviticus draw distinctions between those deemed acceptable and those considered unclean and untouchable. The laws exclude lepers, women who are bleeding, and those who are blind or with physical defects, all of whom must stay outside the camp because of their uncleanliness. Those violating the Shabbat were in the same category as those who betrayed their people and resulted in being cut off (Exod 31:14). One by one, Jesus cleansed them all, healing lepers, healing the woman with an issue of blood, restoring sight to the blind, healing the lame and disfigured, and restoring the voice of the mute. They were no longer cut off, but were welcomed back into community.

Isaiah prophesied that when the Messiah appeared, "the eyes of the blind shall be opened, and the ears of the deaf will unstopped; then shall the lame man leap like a hart, and the tongue of the dumb sing for joy" (35:5–6). When John the Baptist sent people from his prison cell for assurance that Jesus was the awaited Messiah, Jesus answered in Matthew 11:5 by reminding them of Isaiah's words. His holiness, incorruptible and all-powerful, fulfilled what John knew to be the signs for which his people had waited. The Lord of the Shabbat came to bring all into community.

So serious a commandment was it to keep clean from surrounding cultures, that inscriptions were posted warning gentiles not to come inside the temple. Anyone stepping over the marked-off boundary was responsible for their own death. Archaeological excavations begun in 1967 discovered the Soreg Inscription warning in Greek:

> No foreigner may enter within the balustrade around the sanctuary and the enclosure. Whoever is caught, on himself shall he put blame for the death which will ensue.[3]

Steeped in these teachings, Peter dreamt in Acts 10:9–16 of unclean foods that God said not to reject. As he pondered the meaning of the vision, there was a centurion in the Italian Regiment named Cornelius who prayed often to God. One day, an angel of God came to him and said, "Your prayers and gifts to the poor have come up as a memorial offering before God." The angel told Cornelius to send men to Joppa to bring back Peter, who invited the men into his house to be his guests. When he went to Caesarea, Cornelius invited Peter into his home, and he stayed for a few days. The doors between had opened. Peter said to him, "You yourselves know how unlawful it is for a Jew to associate with or to visit any one of another nation; but God has shown me that I should not call any man common or unclean" (Acts 10:28).

While Peter was preaching the good news, the Holy Spirit came on all who heard the message. The circumcised believers who had come with Peter were astonished that the gift of the Holy Spirit had been poured out even on gentiles. Peter said, "Can any one forbid water for baptizing these people who have received the Holy Spirit just as we have?" (10:47). The Lord's death and resurrection broke down the wall separating the people, affirming that we can be cleansed as the very core of the word brings healing into the body, rescuing each child of captivity, so they can enter their Shabbat.

No matter how someone has been raised to think, they've been given the responsibility to independently gain knowledge of their Creator. It is not enough to observe practices because we were raised to do things a certain way. Knowledge must be sought. The Bereans were more noble because they sought the Scriptures to see what is true (Acts 17:11). Unbelievers need to be prompted to discuss why they do not believe.

Becoming aware of being solitary, apart from community, is the prodigal's story. The prodigal son came to himself, remembering whose child he was in his father's house. Jesus said to Peter, "Who do you say that I am?" (Matt 16:15). It is divine light that awakens this truth. The prodigal realizes

---

3. Price, "Gentiles Forbidden," para. 3.

whose child he is and says, "I will go to my father," resolving to say, "I have sinned against heaven and before you" (Acts 15:18). He wanted to be home, to be with his father, even as a small servant in the household. He ached for home, coming in tattered clothes, stinking of dirt, walking a long way to get there.

The father had watched, prayed, and waited. The moment he saw his child on the horizon, he ran to gather him in his arms and walked with him all the way back. Similarly, with hands clenched, holding onto hope; palms open, asking for heaven; and hands reaching, seeking the Lord's presence, the church has walked a long way to return. Seen on the horizon, finally facing the right direction, the messianic community runs to welcome her.

Micah ached when he saw no one turning to the Father. "Woe is me!" (7:1). He was looking for fruit but found nothing. He was left thirsting. "The godly man has perished from the earth" (7:2). Not one upright man could be found. Micah was brokenhearted. He looked out at the landscape and did not find the fruit of God fulfilling his design. All around, people behaved in desecrating self-serving ways. Micah was looking for someone who remembered that they are a child of God.

Truly he is a God who hides himself (Isa 45:15). If I go to the east, the north, the west, or the south, I do not find him (Job 23:8–9). Isaiah says that no one calls on his name or tries to lay hold of him because he has hidden his face from them. It can seem that God turns away. In distress the psalmist longs for the living God, thirsting like a deer for flowing streams. "When shall I behold the face of God?" he asks (Ps 42:2). People continually say to him, "Where is your God?" (v. 3). He once led the people with songs of joy as they ascended the mountain to keep the annual festivals, but now he feels empty. He determines to remain turned toward God and wait. "For I will again praise him, my help and my God" (vv. 4–6). Even the prophets had to wait to hear from God.

Micah ultimately says, "I will look to the Lord, I will wait for the God of my salvation; my God will hear me" (7:7). It's not in our control. From the cross, Jesus spoke seven statements that reveal a pattern for the lives of those who are to recognize that God is working his plan for his people:

- "Father, forgive them" (Luke 23:34). We are to see God's will for the enemy to return to him.
- "Today you will be with me in Paradise" (23:43). From the foundation of creation, when the Spirit moved across the water Jesus prayed for people to know him. We are to honor the hearts that return.

- "Behold your son, behold your mother" (John 19:26–27). We expand to take in each other, promoting differences that bring gifts to the table.
- "My God, my God, why hast thou forsaken me?" (Matt 27:46). Our good intentions will meet with the fire of persecution, the times God seems hidden and we cannot find him near.
- "I thirst" (John 19:28). Blessed are they who thirst for righteousness, for they will be filled.
- "It is finished" (19:30). Shabbat teaches that God's will is to complete us and there will come a time the work is done.
- "Father, into thy hands I commit my spirit!" (Luke 23:46). He entered the rest that the Father appointed at the beginning of time, inviting us with him, all those who thirsted, who accepted his finished work.

He let us know that we would go through valleys descending into darkness, and experience difficult challenges; even while we ascend, we tend to question the Lord's presence as the process of reconciliation unfolds. In the Bible, waiting is the way we come to understand when we are not yet finding the fruit we search for in God. Each divine and celestial light, from the smallest lightning bug to the most brilliant star, is in the Lord's hand, placed in the creation containing his name. The light led the Israelites through the wilderness. The light gathers the Israelites back to their homeland, on eagle's wings soaring above the circumstance on earth, through baptizing waters that separate, with fire that clears a pathway. The light always leads home.

"The friendship of the Lord is for those who fear him, and he makes known to them his covenant" (Ps 25:14). The great anguish of sudden trauma can do nothing more than watch for God to act, because even when he's hidden he's working to make a heart new.

The members of David's line—which ultimately led to the birth of Christ—experienced many dark and dangerous days, such as Jacob's harrowing journey, packing his bags to flee danger at the hand of his brother Esau, alone and afraid. However, God appeared to him in a dream and promised him that the land he rested upon would be given to him and his descendants. He was told that God would protect him throughout his journey.

Like Jacob, Israel's most powerful encounters, producing beautiful psalms and prophetic visions, have been when they felt most alone and fearful, with the enemy in pursuit, only to ascend from the depths, God's word lifting them to the heights of their place in his whole.

Joseph was the hope of Jacob among his twelve sons. The eleventh son, born before Benjamin, he grew into adolescence surrounded by peers whose word could not be trusted, who were prone to violence, and who had no boundaries in terms of sexual lust.

"Sons have I reared and brought up, but they have rebelled against me," God said of his own children (Isa 1:2). Jesus came to his own and his own received him not. Joseph lived those same words. As one marked for God's work, he was born into the antagonism that resides in a world where a deep rooted nature says, "I will not bow." Yet the one despised is the one who holds out the only hope.

God's redeeming work advances in the life of Joseph's brothers because of the courage of a teenager who took a stand and didn't keep silent about the word of God spoken to him. The living God, touching unbelieving friends who may sometimes be quite cruel, wants them to have his words.

Joseph was seventeen, and no one wanted to be with him. A dream told Joseph that he would be lifted up and be the family's hope for the future. To those perishing, it is foolishness, but to us it is salvation. Betrayed and sold for silver, he was thrown into the lowest place to be exalted in the highest place as a redeemer. Joseph's is the story of how to cope when surrounded by lies, when descended to the pit of despair, when sexual advances are made, how to fully exonerate when violations have been confessed, and how to trust in God, who will lift him up.

In September 2005, TJCII held the first Latin American Consultation in Buenos Aires, Argentina, with Messianic Jews from Argentina and Brazil. Liliana Saez, member of a Bet-el Messianic Jewish congregation in Buenos Aires, wrote that, "After the Inquisition the mothers told their sons to keep silent, and they lived with the fear of death if they revealed their identity. It was like I was living all those experiences. I felt like I was being cut in pieces, as if the Body of the Messiah itself would be divided and dispersed."

Father Peter Hocken, a Catholic priest in England and member of the international TJCII leadership council, spoke a prayer and said that this long history of oppression and suffering has to be more fully addressed. It cannot be quickly handled and then dismissed. The deep wounds inflicted require time and the grace of the Lord to be healed. "We believe that the eventual healing of this massive wound will unleash unimaginable blessings for the church and for the Jewish people," Peter said.[4]

Embedded in the memory of Jewish history is a summer of violent mobs threatening death if not forcibly baptized, inflammatory anti-Semitic sermons, riots spreading, thousands beaten to death, many sold into Arab slavery, and some submitting to conversion just to survive. Between 1412 and 1415 AD, Catholic revival pushed the passage of anti-Jewish laws

---

4. Hocken, "Marranos," 7.

through coercion but by the mid-fifteenth century the Jews who were baptized, or "reconciled," faced expulsion anyway because of purity-of-blood laws.

At first, they could still consult Jewish literature and talk within the Jewish community. Then any object of Jewish identity brought persecution. The Torah continued through oral history because God had commanded the people to "teach diligently to your children" (Deut 6:6–7). Gradual tightening of the snare resulted in being burnt at the stake, imprisoned, or forced to convert, along with Protestants and anyone who disagreed with the church. The Inquisition confiscated property to support its slaughter.

"This gave a new importance to the role of women, particularly the mothers of families, in the practice and spread of crypto-Judaism," Peter said.[5]

Pressed down by insults, Israel still heard the shofar's proud tone binding them to the living God, proclaiming that they are still his. A room within the home, away from public eyes, served for gatherings of study and prayer. The Shabbat was kept, and women lit the candle, often covering windows with a dark cloth or setting the candle under a table where it could burn down. They prepared on Friday, cleaned the house, set out the best linen, wore their best clothing, secretly gathering with family and friends as the Inquisition pried informants to betray them.

"You seek to kill me, because my word finds no place in you," Jesus said (John 8:37–38). Wanting us to have the fullness of life in him, Jesus warns of the danger in being unwilling to hear his word and be changed. "Our confidence is in the Savior of the world, the Messiah of Israel, who shed his blood on the cross to bring about this reconciliation," Peter said. "The confession is a means, the reconciliation is the end . . . But forgiveness requires that the full catalogue of sin and evil be truthfully confessed and acknowledged."[6]

Father Patrick Desbois, a French Roman Catholic priest, has been searching for mass graves of Jews executed in the Ukraine, Moldava and the former Soviet Union since 2004 with his organization Yahad-In-Unum. By 2017 they had discovered 2,700 extermination sites where more than one million Jews were buried.[7]

Many of the six million murdered during the Holocaust were killed in fields and forests as a spectacle to entertain the public.[8] As lockets, rings, and necklaces with stars of David were uncovered, Fr. Patrick said he be-

---

5. Hocken, "Marranos," 19.
6. Hocken, "Marranos," 54, 55.
7. Braverman, "Father Patrick Desbois," paras. 1, 7.
8. Braverman, "Father Patrick Desbois," para. 1.

lieves these victims have waited for their graves to be discovered. "We found you," he said. "We finally found you."[9] It is his mission to make every one of their lives count.

Father Patrick says he does this work because anti-Semitism still happens. "It's not the past, unfortunately. It seems to be part of the future."[10] We will lose the battle if we don't force the enemy into the light. "If we don't study our enemies, they are under the water. If we study them, they are above the water," he said.[11]

The history of the Jews is miracle after miracle in the presence of those who must choose whether they are Hamans or allies. "At this their hearts failed them, and they turned trembling to one another, saying, 'What is this that has God done to us?'" the brothers of Joseph asked (Gen 42:28). They had been awakened to question their true self in relation to God and their brother, fully aware of their limitations. All that pride and pretense Joseph saw in them in his youth are gone, and he discerned that what his brothers meant for harm, God turned for good by sending him out ahead of them. Sarah and Abraham went out before the people. The people went out into the wilderness before other nations. "And now do not be distressed, or angry with yourselves, because you sold me here; for God sent me before you to preserve life" (Gen 45:5).

> Yet thou art holy, enthroned on the praises of Israel. (Ps 22:3)

Shabbat ends with *havdala*, which is a ceremony that distinguishes the holy from the earthly. Because the time of Shabbat was established by God at the beginning of creation, it is a day of introspection, asking how the week has brought us closer to knowing the Lord, what has been created within us to bear the fruits of his sensitive light and how can we grow more mature by the next Shabbat in the ways we deal with the world.

Separating the holy day enjoys all senses of speech, hearing, sight, smell, and taste, experiencing the gifts that God seeded in creation. The *havdala* candle joins wicks to ignite the past, present, and future into a single brighter light. Before dusk on Friday, women light two candles that lead into the world of Shabbat. On Saturday, as Shabbat ends, the *havdala* service uses one candle with at least two wicks. The two Shabbat candles have symbolically merged into one flame to shine out into the week.

The first of the four blessings is made over the wine.

---

9. Braverman, "Father Patrick Desbois," para. 4.
10. Braverman, "Father Patrick Desbois," para. 11
11. Braverman, "Father Patrick Desbois," para. 18.

Barukh atah Adonai, Eloheinu, melekh ha'olam
Blessed are you, Lord, our God, sovereign of the universe

Borei p'ri hagafen (Amein)
Who creates the fruit of the vine (Amen)

The second blessing is spoken over fragrant spices such as cloves, cinnamon, or bay leaves in a special box that represents compensation for losing the Shabbat spirit by returning to the work world. The scent revives the spirit as it faces wilting into the week.

Barukh atah Adonai, Eloheinu, melekh ha'olam
Blessed are you, Lord, our God, sovereign of the universe,

Borei minei v'samim (Amein)
Who creates varieties of spices (Amen)

The third blessing is recited over the candle's vivid flame, distinguishing the day as set apart and acknowledging that God gave Adam and Eve fire when they left the garden of Eden.

Barukh atah Adonai, Eloheinu, melekh ha'olam
Blessed are you, Lord, our God, sovereign of the universe

Borei m'orei ha'eish (Amein)
Who creates the light of the fire (Amen)

The closing is the *havdala* blessing recited over wine in honor of how God separated different elements for life to continue in balance. After the blessing, the wine is drunk. A few drops are used to extinguish the candle's flame.

Barukh atah Adonai, Eloheinu, melekh ha'olam
Blessed are you, Lord, our God, sovereign of the universe

Hamae v'dil bein kodesh l'chol
Who separates between sacred and secular

bein or l'choshekh bein Yis'ra'eil la'amim
between light and darkness, between Israel and the nations

bein yom hash'vi'i l'sheishet y'mei hama'aseh
between the seventh day and the six days of labor.

Shabbat leaves with the turning of the sky bringing stars into view, and the world returns to a new opportunity. The week will bring temptations, but growth from Shabbat to Shabbat brings determination to turn away from what once pulled us in. Our growth is revealed. Work is elevated to a more inspired purpose of the week.

Many of the most important gatherings appointed by God are held in the home, such as Passover, the Shabbat, the Chanukah menorah, and Sukkah, through practices that assure the continuation of the family knowing God. It is in the home where women are pillars, conducting the entry into the holy days by lighting the flames and preparing foods that promote conscious relationship to God. When a woman lights the candles, she is saying, "We have survived, not because of our strength, but because of God's will that our home serve the Lord." She lights the candles to expose the darkness and draw others to awaken the wonderment. She displays God, wanting others to join the multitude from every nation, standing before the throne, clothed in white robes, praising the Lord with all the angels and elders. They've come through great tribulation. They have washed their robes white in the blood of the Lamb.

The source of her standing comes from reservoirs of inner quietness, long able to speak intimately to God from the tumult pouring through her emotions. Her prayers come throughout the day, while putting food in the oven, dressing children, going to a job, or speaking with a friend, and they are for such things as her husband's place of employment or that she would be made worthy to raise children in the Lord's instructions, all in conversations with her Maker.

"Every day I will bless thee, and praise thy name for ever and ever" (Ps 145:2); "his praise shall continually be in my mouth" (Ps 34:1); "I will give thanks to the Lord with my whole heart" (Ps 111:1). Scripture tells us who should be praising the Lord: his angels and all his heavenly host; the sun, moon, and shining stars; the waters above the heavens and the sea creatures in the deep ocean; lightning, hail, snow, and clouds; winds, mountains, and trees; all animals and birds; all nations and all rulers; young men and women; and old men and children (Ps 148). Who does not praise the Lord? "The dead do not praise the Lord, nor do any that go down into silence" (Ps 115:17). The spiritually dead are without weapon and have no victory. At the Lord's table, they can come to know themselves.

As youth grow up, they gain the ability to channel a rush of deep feelings, learning to remember their ancestors through the customs and to share the joy of the promises in the world to come. They've been raised to know who they are as adults, without gender confusion (because the male and female are expressly celebrated in their unique identities). There is not the confusion that pervades when "rights" are the focus at the expense of responsibility toward God and community.

The cycles of life acknowledge God clothing the naked, feeding the hungry, guiding the steps of man, and granting kindness. On hearing of a death, God is acknowledged for the life he gave in forming the human in wisdom and creating in him a miraculous system of the heart and body, he who heals all creatures and does wonders.

On hearing thunder and seeing lightning he whose might and power fill the world and does the work of creation is blessed. A rainbow brings blessing to God, who remembers the covenant and keeps his word. He has created the great sea, and these animals and all of nature in his world. He has given his wisdom to those who revere him.

He has created the sun to rise and to set (Eccl 1:5). When Sarah's sun set, the Lord raised Rebekah to continue the light. Born before Sarah died, she was readied in the ways that Sarah illuminated the world with God's ways. Like Sarah, the dough she kneaded was blessed, the cloud was visible over her tent, and the candles burned from one Shabbat eve to the next. "Isaac thus found comfort after his mother's death" that Rebekah's deeds resembled those of Sarah (Gen 24:67). Isaac sought in a wife the traits that would uphold his home's righteousness.

Isaac prayed for his wife because they were childless, and the Lord answered. Two babies restlessly jostled within her and, wondering why, she went to inquire of the Lord, possibly meaning that she went to the judges or prophets of the day. The Lord said to her, "Two nations are in your womb, and two peoples, born of you, shall be divided; the one shall be stronger than the other, the elder shall serve the younger" (25:23).

Israel was God's choice, so Rebekah loved Jacob. Her children grew, and she made sure that her husband passed the blessing to Jacob. This naturally angered his older brother, Esau. When Rebekah became aware that he wanted to kill Jacob, she went to her husband, and they had Jacob sent to her family (27:42–43). Like Eve, if one son killed the other, she would have lost them both. She intends to protect both her sons.

The wives of Moses, Isaac, and Jacob were each found next to a well of water. Rebekah was carrying a jar of water when Jacob's servant saw her beauty. She offered him water, and rushed back and forth with her bucket for water for all his camels, which were thirsty after a long journey. The servant saw her generous kindness.

Rebekah's family asked her, "Will you go with this man?" and pressed her to stay. But her answer was, "I will." Similarly, the first action God asked of the first Jew, Abraham, was, "Go from your country and your kindred and your father's house to the land that I will show you" (Gen 12:1).

Like Abraham, Rebekah chose to place trust in God as she went into an unknown land. Independence of conscience is a trait of all born into Abraham's faith. The world teaches that happiness is deprived without material goods, physical capabilities, and children, who will be who we want them to be. But the Book of Law says that the highest obligations are to serve the Lord with joy, to give thanks in all circumstance, and to trust the Lord's plan through disappointments, because his will refines the soul to elevate a person.

It can feel very small in this vast universe to be human, unnoticed as creation continues on its way with or without us. Man's destiny is to return to the dust that originated him. He is grass that withers, a flower that fades, only a fleeting shadow like a passing cloud, a dream that vanishes. Yet the day that God made man and woman was the completion of a jewel in his creation. The Word teaches that we are here to work with God to repair the world and prepare for the return of Jesus. Judaism teaches that the phrase "for me the world was created" means that every person has a responsibility to respond to problems in the world. We're given the ability to affect what happens in it.

"Thus, each individual has to say: For me the world was created." (m. Sanh. 4:5). The phrase took on a meaning of extreme narcissism as humanity reached the twenty-first century. The youth became addicted to how many likes and followers they have on Instagram and Twitter. Friday nights are for going out for a night on the town, in fear of missing out with friends, or watching television. Saturdays are for sleeping late, going shopping, or for children to watch cartoons.

In a culture continually affirming itself with messages to believe in oneself, Jesus says, "Believe in God, believe also in me" (John 14:1). The Lord is with you. He will not fail you. In him, all things you are to do in this life are possible.

Rosh Hashanah is referred to as *Yom Harat Olam*, the birthday of creation, when we became partners with God in creating each other's lives. We are instruments in changing how a story may end. Being virtuous implies being valiant and skilled at warfare. The virtuous woman extends her hand, unafraid to speak in the face of the enemy. Echoing Moses and Jesus with the same light from heaven, she is saying, "Let my people go that they may worship."

The verse "Her husband is prominent in the gates," in the Woman of Valor poem (Prov 31:23), is attributed to Michal, David's wife, for protecting him from her father Saul's wrath. Michal and her brother Jonathan loved David. The Midrash expands on this, showing that Michal protected David from danger within the house and Jonathan from external danger. When Saul's guards prevented David from escaping, Michal let him down from the window. When guards came to her rooms, she pretended that David was ill.

She placed an idol with a net of goat's hair in his bed to make it appear he was asleep. Saul was angry when he learned of his daughter's deception, but she had stood by the will of God for her husband.

As our culture sweeps women into uncommitted relationships, many deeply yearn for the communion of marriage but are not finding the blessing. The 2017 Pew Research Center reported the marriage rite in the United States plunged from 72 percent in 1960 to 51 percent in 2010.[12] In 2012, about 20 percent over the age of twenty-five had never married, more than double since 1960.[13]

Women who, like Eve, offer a man the fruit of the tree of knowledge instead of life only encourage men to devalue relationship. All the effect of catastrophe on the mind, the descent that steadily loses the communion of the soul, reverberates into the framework of social stability. Commitment to the Lord is an undivided life that the Lord illustrates in the foundation of home. "Do you not know that your bodies are members of Christ? Shall I therefore take the members of Christ and make them members of a prostitute? Never! Do you not know that he who joins himself to a prostitute becomes one body with her? For, as it is written, 'The two shall become one flesh.' But he who is united to the Lord becomes one spirit with him" (1 Cor 6:15–17).

Rebekah, the second Jewish matriarch, is first mentioned in relation to marriage when Abraham sends a servant to find her as the wife of his son Isaac. Further, the last time she is mentioned in Genesis is in relation to marriage, instructing her son Jacob to go to Haran for a wife. Born among deceitful people, Rebekah's spirit remained clear. It is said that she grew up as a lily among thorns. She came from a dysfunctional and untrustworthy family who tried to dissuade her from marrying Isaac. She remained pure, however, a sign to her descendants of the ability to stand in light, even when surrounded by a world's wrong messages.

"I will go," she said to her family, choosing the holy wind of the Lord to lead her and support her courage. From the moment she says yes, they are betrothed within a covenant. "Set me as a seal upon your heart" (Song 8:6) continues to be recited as a marriage blessing. The man gives the woman a gift that reflects his ability to provide well, and it is something she will cherish the rest of her life. It may be a family heirloom, a ring, or a cover for her prayerbook; something not only beautiful, but which carries spiritual meaning in the couple's lives. The bride's parents give the groom a gift, such as a tallit or desk set for his professional needs. The wedding won't be held

---

12. Cohn, "Barely Half," para. 2.
13. Cohn, "Barely Half," para. 5.

on Shabbat or on festival days. These days are for the Lord. Tuesday is often chosen because, on the third day of creation, God twice said "It is good."

The wedding is full of giving thanks. "This is the day which the Lord has made; let us rejoice and be glad in it" (Ps 118:24); "Let the bridegroom leave his room, and the bride her chamber" (Joel 2:16). She has prepared and waits in readiness.

An invocation sets the marriage in the presence of God. "Blessed may you be who come in the name of the Lord; we bless you out of the house of the Lord. May he who is mighty, blessed and great above all, may he send his abounding blessings to the bridegroom and bride."

Jesus said to Jerusalem, "You will not see me again, until you say, 'Blessed is he who comes in the name of the Lord'" (Matt 23:39). This is a traditional Hebrew greeting in his culture, spoken to the Maccabees as they triumphantly entered Jerusalem on Chanukah, or welcoming someone into your home. Jesus returns, the Lion of Judah, to his firstborn when Israel looks toward him as Messiah and welcomes him back. "Let Israel say, 'His steadfast love endures for ever' . . . "Let those who fear the Lord say, 'His steadfast love endures for ever'" (Ps 118:4).

The mothers, relatives, and friends have been busy for days, preparing the flowers, which bring scent and color, and the meal to serve at the reception. The choice is unlimited, all of it to give honor to God. There may be melons and berries, poached fish, braised sweetbreads, chicken broth with matzo balls, ice cream and tea, salads and nuts, coffee, smoked salmon, stuffed mushrooms, dried fruit and knishes, and wine, "which gladdens the heart of man." It is a time to rejoice with the couple as a new family. The meal is a *se'udah mitzvah*, expressing gratitude.

It is a great honor to be asked to lead the blessings, raising a cup of wine and reciting the grace. When the grace is concluded, the cup of wine is put down, and a second cup is raised for the recital of the last of the wedding blessings. The wine in both cups is mixed in a goblet brimming with beauty, reflecting the shimmering light of soul and body.

Jesus told his chosen, "I shall not drink again of this fruit of the vine until that day when I drink it new with you in my Father's kingdom" (Matt 26:29). As a symbol of the union, the bride and groom sip from the wine. "I will betroth you to me for ever; I will betroth you to me in righteousness and in justice, in steadfast love, and in mercy" (Hos 2:19).

The wedding is the entry into a new life together. Patterns of their relationship with God are in the home, as well as in prayer books, foods, Shabbat candlesticks, the wine cups, the spice box, Passover seder plates, the menorah, a cup for Elijah, and other treasures that speak of the Messiah's promise to be used through the couple's lifetime together as the home becomes a place of shared concerns in a larger community.

Blessed before God, a union was never intended to be separated. The Lord hates divorce, "so take heed to yourselves and do not be faithless" (Mal 2:16). Jesus verified the command, saying that Moses permitted divorce because of hardened hearts, but it was never this way from the beginning (Matt 19:8). The Apostle Paul brought greater understanding: "[Nothing] will be able to separate us from the love of God in Christ Jesus our Lord" (Rom 8:38–39).

"Therefore, while the promise of entering his rest remains, let us fear lest any of you be judged to have failed to reach it . . . For we who have believed enter his rest . . . but the message which they heard did not benefit them . . . Those who formerly received the good news failed to enter because of disobedience" (Heb 4:1–13).

"See! The Lord has given you the sabbath" (Exod 16:29). The Lord's table overflows with the bounty of harvest, which was prepared when he first breathed creation into being. At the end of the Shabbat morning liturgy, a beautiful hymn, entitled "Adon Olam" ("Eternal Lord"), expresses the worlds within Jewish prayer:

> The Lord of the Universe, who reigned before anything was created.
> When all was made by his will He was acknowledged as King.
>
> And when all shall end He still all alone shall reign.
> He was, He is, and He shall be in glory.
>
> And He is one, and there's no other, to compare or join Him.
> Without beginning, without end and to Him belongs dominion and power.
>
> And He is my God, my living God, to Him I flee in time of grief, and He is my miracle and my refuge, who answers the day I shall call.
>
> To Him I commit my spirit, in the time of sleep and awakening, even if my spirit leaves, God is with me, I shall not fear.

7

NIDDAH

To bless the new moon at the proper time is like greeting the Divine Presence.
—Sanh. 42a

A LUMINOUS GLOW IN the sky, the moon was formed before Adam and Eve breathed, when God created time. He made stars and planets in patterns of motion with the rhythm of death and birth. All move in the cycle of his works—the sun brought forward from his place, the moon from her dwelling, to continue the work of bringing light to the world.

The moon wanes into darkness, trapping us in our ruins, hidden like the mysteries of God's presence. Yet even when darkness seems complete, like Israel the light waxes full again, bringing her story of God's endless love, never to be extinguished. No matter how much the people ebb and flow from mourning into celebrations, the light returns "gazing in at the windows, looking through the lattice" (Song 2:8–9). The Israelites watched for the moon to ascend with her bright hope, following the sun across the sky. The hour her sliver of light appears, the new moon is to be sanctified on earth and in heaven. Called Rosh Chodesh, it is a time appointed to meet with God.

In Jerusalem, the Sanhedrin (a rabbinical council) waited for at least two witnesses to report its appearance before sending the message in fire signals up on the hills. The herald call stirred the people to assemble and receive the light cast upon earth and all that they love. Each new month begins with asking for the gates to open to receive strength with the Lord because time makes us weaker, and the measure of our days needs to be realized at each stage. Voices join angels as song exalts God in heaven, whose glory is above all earth bringing the promise of bright beginnings.

Psalm 148 is recited to join creation in praises from the deep sea to the heights of all his heavenly hosts, for at his command the masterpiece of creation was orchestrated and established forever. In starry nights, when the people gather to keep his appointed time, God hears them say yes to all he asks. He hears them want his kingdom to come in the lives of their children, for every good and perfect gift, and to live his heartbeat.

The downpour from heaven seals God's name upon us, anointing because of the story told in the moon's light, marking the cycle of festivals from Passover to Tabernacles. Coming as the promise, as a gift opened to heaven, the doorway of light is The Way, the first name given to the teachings of Jesus, coming with descriptors and verbs such as "given," "received," "baptized," "immersed," "filled," "come upon," and "poured out upon," fluidly moving to purify and strengthen.

Isaiah told the people that a time would come when the entire world will honor the new moon and Shabbat, worshiping God in the return of Messiah. "From new moon to new moon, and from sabbath to sabbath, all flesh shall come to worship before me, says the Lord" (Isa 66:23).

Keep a close watch on the teachings, Paul wrote to Timothy (1 Tim 4:16), reflecting Solomon, who said to guard your heart above everything else, for it is the source of life (Prov 4:23). As moonlight disappears at the end of each month, we are reminded of the struggle to purify in dark times while moving toward the restoration, when the glory of God is fully on earth and the dark corners lose their shadows.

In Joshua 7 the people crossed the Jordan and came against the army of Ai. They were defeated and left fearful and despondent. Joshua dropped to his knees with his face on the ground before the Lord. The Lord told him to stand up. The Lord walked with Joshua throughout all the camp to show him where the trespass was that weakened his people. It is the prayer of David's psalms that God give him more light. Search me and know my heart. Purge me.

The sin that God brought to Joshua's attention was committed by an Israelite named Achan, who had stolen devoted items, a beautiful Babylonian robe, silver, and gold and hid them in the ground inside his tent. The Lord told Joshua to consecrate the people and prepare for the consequence. With a saddened heart, Joshua heard Achan's confession. Together with all of Israel, he obeyed the Lord and took Achan, the silver, the robe, and the gold; Achan's sons and daughters; his cattle, donkeys, and sheep; and his tent and all that he had to the Valley of Achor. Here they were stoned and then burned.

The Lord purifies by drawing up the prayer of David, changing rainstorms that drown a dream into gardens of new colors. He humbled his people and let them go hungry so that he could feed them with manna. God says, "I will make her like a wilderness, and set her like a parched land, and slay her with thirst" (Hos 2:3).

When she has found that no other source will sustain her, and all she thought she could depend on has let her down, he "will allure her, and bring her into the wilderness, and speak tenderly to her . . . and make the Valley of Achor a door of hope" (2:14–15). The wrongs buried in a life are taken away. It is here where she responds to life as she did in the days of her youth, as she did when she came up out of the bondage of Egypt in joyous triumph. In that day, God's covenant gathers in all creation, the beasts of the field, the birds in the sky, and the creatures moving along the ground, so all may lie down in safety. The people acknowledge that he is Lord, and he responds to the sky and to the earth. There will be rain to bring new wine, olive oil, and grain. The people take root in the land and he calls them his people (2:21–23).

When the Lord descended upon Mount Sinai to establish his word, fire thundered and lightning flashed as the sound of the trumpet echoed through the ascending smoke (Exod 19:18–19). The Holy Spirit went out before them to part the sea and shake the earth to guide the direction of the people toward the holy temple.

The Word speaks, and the universe trembles to shake off the past's murk, longing to be clean again. Where can I go to hide my shame? The ocean is not deep enough. The darkness does not cover it. Unbearable loneliness presides because relationship is only possible when God brings light. Shame shrinks a soul inward, unable to lift the glow of its candle because the flame illuminates the harm within us.

Tamar, the daughter of King David, felt this shame as a young woman when her half-brother Amnon tricked her into his rooms, betrayed her trust, and raped her (2 Sam 13:1–22). Descending like the surface of the ocean, diving away from the sun to hide in the deep, she had nowhere to turn. She was inconsolable and was "desolate" (v. 20), most likely meaning that she didn't marry, have children, or build a home of her own. Her capacity to have those relationships was psychologically ruined.

After she was raped, her mother and the other women may have gathered around her as flames, trying to reignite Tamar's soul. She was a daughter of Israel. Listen to her words: "No, my brother, do not force me; for such a thing is not done in Israel; do not do this wanton folly" (13:12).

She knew the teachings of God. Her identity was clear to herself. She was versed in God's participation in her ancestry's redemption. She knew the promises for her people's future. The practices of worshiping God, simple acts of relationship like lighting the festival candles, speaking the blessings, attending the reading of the word, and the immersion in water that women took for spiritual cleansing each month, were all ingrained in her life.

Beautiful Tamar refused to be silent. The very holiness of God who she once prayed to in easy words, had been defiled. Her cry is the hope of every life to be free from assaults, especially within the family that should be a safe shelter.

In the eyes of God, the poor in spirit are highly esteemed. It is in them that God, who lives in a high and holy realm, chooses as the place to build his kingdom (Isa 57:15). "The sacrifice acceptable to God is a broken spirit; a broken and contrite heart, O God, thou wilt not despise" (Ps 51:17).

Betrayed and wounded, the psalmist wrote, "My companion . . . violated his covenant. His speech was smoother than butter, yet war was in his heart" (Ps 55:20–21). The hardship is a circumstance. It presents a challenge of growth with the Lord, but it does not define who we are walking with the Lord. Seek my face, the Lord says. "Cast your burden on the Lord, and he will sustain you," the psalmist writes. "He will never permit the righteous to be moved" (55:22). For theirs is the kingdom. The vision of the new day is before us, an unchanging and certain destination.

We grieve, but not as those without hope. Emotions of anger, hurt, and fear were woven into mankind by God as signals that something is not right. It is not a sin to feel these; "be angry but do not sin" (Eph 4:26). To the church in Smyrna in their suffering, Jesus tells them that he knows all that you are experiencing. He is with us in it (Rev 2:9).

When Tamar stumbles to her mother and the women, they saw what had been taken from her. They were unable to restore her and felt heartsick at their own lack of ability. They put their arms around her and pulled her close, saying that they loved her still. Like the prodigal returning to his father, Tamar honored them by turning to them. It was acknowledged that something bad had happened.

But shame goes too far, sinking in thoughts that no one can change the past, instilling ideas like "I am unworthy; I am not good enough for anyone." Shame isolates. God's people are perceived as "over there" on the holy ground, in holy assemblies, in the holy sabbaths, a holy nation clothed in holy garments (Exod 3:5; 12:16; 16:23; 19:6; 28:2).

Jesus turned and saw the woman who reached out and touched him in faith and hope. "Take heart, daughter," he said; "your faith has made you well." (Matt 9:22). To John, he says, "I am the first and the last," reminding him that he is a citizen under a king who has been from the beginning and will be through all eternity (Rev 22:13); "Behold, I make all things new" (Rev 21:5).

Once they had sinned for the first time, Adam and Eve stood, ashamed by their nakedness. The Lord felt their discomfort separating them from him. He responded by covering them in animal skins in Genesis 3:21, commonly viewed as the first sacrifice. When Elijah perceived that Elisha was chosen by God, he cast his cloak around him (1 Kgs 19:19). Jesus now gathers his disciples by cloaking them in righteousness. He puts his robes around us, paid for in ancient beginnings, his blood washing all shame to be as white as snow. We are brought to see ourselves as he sees us. Being given sight brings us to rest in holy mercy to bring us to full glory. Releasing the past does not exonerate the person of wrongs they have not acknowledged. There can be no exoneration. But Jesus does not want the tyranny occupying the hearts of his people. His promise will wipe away the many tears from abuses and regret when he comes again.

The beautiful new world of Adam and Eve devolved as people populated the earth. The *bnei elohim* were taking daughters as they pleased. *Bnei elohim* (or nephilim) is taken to mean those who had once been at a high level of spirituality, but had fallen and were corrupted. They were in positions of authority and had fallen from their greatness, causing the world to fall and the hearts of people to despair.

God saw this wickedness on earth (Gen 6:1–5). The behavior of men taking women by force without their consent, or seducing and using them with a sense of entitlement, unleashed God's wrath. "Build an ark," he said to Noah, and he instructed people and animals to come aboard two by two, male and female, as God designed. God established his covenant with every living creature of the earth (Gen 9:8–10). All of creation has been redeemed by the Word.

The moon waxes with arms opening to invite the isolated and lonely, the ones teased and mocked for being born into a belief of Jesus, and the wounded caught in their shame. The light reaches to the hearts of the grandmothers, the mothers, and the children, none important enough to the world to hear, all stripped of their value. The mother of the thief who hung on the cross beside Jesus was weighted with shame until Jesus poured heaven's words on her son and her eyes lifted to him.

The enemy wants us to think that being brokenhearted is an end destination, but every time a believer goes through a valley of trouble there is a door of purifying hope offered. It doesn't mean the damage is undone. The wrongs have happened. We may emerge through that door as an amputee, a widow, without our children, or in the ruins of a bombed city. We may be desolate like Tamar, but we will emerge with a soul still flaming. Peter entered this very same door when he realized his own failings in denying the Lord, and his shame was removed. God has redefined healing for us beyond what we would ask. He will always carry his people out of every descent to a higher purpose.

In the morning of Shabbat, February 4, 2017, a masked vandal drove up to Chicago Loop Synagogue in the heart of Chicago's downtown business district and stuck two swastikas on the front doors, then smashed the synagogue's glass window before driving away. This was only one in a series of relentless assaults of hatred. Jewish community centers closed for the third time that winter after anonymous bomb threats. Swastikas had been found in schools, scrawled on the wall of a local library, and carved inside Chicago's Holocaust Museum.

The day after the synagogue was vandalized, a young Muslim family brought flowers and a card signed "with love," and left it at the building. Soon other letters filled the wall from the Chicago community, offering solidarity. The synagogue's president, Lee Zoldan, invited all of Chicago to a meeting later that week. A huge crowd from all around the city packed the shul to overflowing. Relationship was birthed from embers longing to give expression to the soul's flame.

God does not ask that we have the ability to stop the awful feelings the wrongs caused. Forgiveness too easily offered discounts the holiness of atonement for sin. What Jesus says is to pray for enemies. Pray for the will of God to be done. Pray for each other, so that you may be healed. Paul told us to press on for the things ahead (Phil 3:14). Leave these hard things behind, because those things that hurt will never come where we are going.

There are those among us who will be put to everlasting shame because they never saw their need for the Lord. And there are those who carry shame for past mistakes. even though the Lord has assured that they have been forgiven. Even those of faith are burdened by areas where they failed to respond well, didn't pray enough, or didn't watch for God enough. However, shame that others try to put on us when we don't deserve it is never to be accepted. Paul suffered accusations when all he was doing was honoring God. Defamed when he spoke in court, wrongly called an enemy of Israel, shame was heaped on Paul. And yet, he said, "For I am not ashamed of the gospel; it is the power of God for salvaiton to every one who has faith, to the Jew first and also to the Greek (Rom 1:16).

Shame is about where to put belief. "No one who believes in [the Lord] will be put to shame (Rom 10:11; 9:33). "Look to him, and be radiant; so your faces shall never be ashamed" (Ps 34:5).

The willingness to pardon someone of their wrong resolves shame. But forgiveness does not mean rationalizing a behavior and covering it over when it is discovered. Forgiveness honors the act of someone returning to the right way. Before Joseph forgave his brothers, at their first encounter he saw that they acknowledged they had done wrong. "In truth we are guilty concerning our brother, in that we saw the distress of his soul, when he besought us and we would not listen; therefore is this distress come upon us" (Gen 42:21). Later, in chapter 44, Joseph tests Judah, whose idea it was to sell him into slavery in the first place. Joseph has Benjamin falsely charged for stealing. Judah offers to take his place so that Benjamin can be freed, and Joseph sees that there has been remorse leading to transformation in Judah. He can be forgiven, because Joseph sees that they are being restored to the image of God, who reconciles all things.

After being lifted from imprisonment, Joseph instituted the joy of Rosh Chodesh when he was viceroy in Egypt, saying to sound the ram's horn at the new moon (Ps 81:3–5). It was celebrated with music and singing for joy to God our strength, who unfailingly brings light. The gathering was so much a happy expression of God's presence that God threatened to take away these times of joy as a consequence of disobedience (Hos 2:13).

Moses called the people to assemble on the new moon, speaking of commandments to be obeyed. Solomon said that the celebration and festivals are an ordinance forever to Israel (2 Chr 2:4). The kings of Israel held the feast of the new moon (1 Chr 23:31), and the people were encouraged to seek guidance from the prophets during the new moon (2 Kgs 4:23). Saul held the feast when he was king. When David had to flee, he sent a message to explain his absence from the king's table on the new moon (1 Sam 20:5–17, 24–29).

The church of the New Covenant continued to acknowledge the new moon for centuries. There was much to be learned about God's plan for his people through the appointed days, but it was an option for gentiles to join in, verified by the verse, "Therefore let no one pass judgment on you in questions of food and drink or with regard to a festival or a new moon or a sabbath" (Col 2:16).

However we come through the door opened by Jesus, God invites us to know ourselves as people seated around the table of the Lord of the Shabbat. "Blessed are those who are invited" (Rev 19:9). He will break bread with us and reach out his scarred hands where we are engraved. He will offer the finest of the fruits of heaven, and finally the wine that he said he would not drink again until he drinks it with us in his Father's kingdom (Matt 26:29). We will remember with joy how he kept the promise of his word.

We are tempted to turn away from stories like Tamar's. It is an awful story, violent and full of sorrow. But all around us we hear the cries of the violated who found no justice, their survival stories, and the ways their view of themselves and God has been distorted. We see the torn garment that once softly protected them, now as a symbol of distress.

Amnon had gotten Tamar alone. He isolated her. We need to stand guard, a lit candle with the presence of Jesus, and if the unthinkable does happen, we are not to leave the victim alone. King David didn't act when he learned of the incident, leaving Tamar to feel that her pain did not matter. The sights and sounds of those suffering are pressed onto our souls so that God's concerns are our concerns.

Remembering the stone that gave them water, the sandy miles following the cloud by day and the flame at night, the holy songs, the years when they escaped only by denying a Jewish name, trust is placed in the blessed judge of truth. Justice will come. Every person who knows God has lost someone to the enemy that never tires of trying to turn his people into ashes. Shaved heads, starved bodies, and the strange fire of ovens exclude, expel, berate, and kill.

God put the agony into the souls of his prophets, priests, and kings, gripping the soul, stirred by the masses who have no shepherd. A life is shaken, and the Spirit brings the words of Jesus to our remembrance, always pouring his winds from heaven, which lead the aliyah up toward Jerusalem, sitting on her mountains and waiting for her king. Her highland limestone has been endowed with tales of poverty and riches, of mourning and dancing, always a queen of warriors who proud of her, loving her because God has chosen her.

"Next year in Jerusalem" becomes the prayer as terror mounts itself against hope. Resettlement again and again in lands where blood stains will follow. Remember thy loving kindness O Lord, because we may need to flee too.

> Grasping the truth of God is the reward. No other reward could be better. This is the goodness. No greater goodness could follow. —Maimonides

The soul of every believer follows a cycle of living that descends into hardships, only to ascend to heightened relationship with the Lord. Understanding that each event is deliberately used for God to show himself faithful, there can be no fear.

Mary Magdalene's life descended into relationships that devastated her life, only for her aliyah to raise her to be a servant of the living God. Mary was a woman who found sanctuary in Jesus, a man she could trust, a man who respected her, cleansed her of her demons, understood the torment in her heart, and gave her purpose in her life. God needed her. A Jewish woman, she was the first he appeared to after rising from the dead and so the first to bring the most important message the world would ever hear. The voice of self-condemnation never stopped until Jesus spoke her name. The faint embers struggling within her roared into bright flame when she knew she was known. There is a hope that can come true, a love that will not discount her.

Springs of living water flow from the throne room of God in heaven into our hearts to refine us into peacemakers. The mother of John Mark, Mary, opened her home as a place of fellowship. This was where many gathered to pray for Peter when he was imprisoned, and where Peter went when he was released (Acts 12:12).

It was from this home that John Mark accompanied Barnabas and Paul on a mission. But as they reached the rugged coastline, he left them (Acts 13:13). Later, when Barnabas wanted to include John Mark again, Paul said no (15:37–39). Strongly disagreeing about someone who had left the path, Paul felt that John Mark was unable to stand up to the beatings, persecution, mockery, and imprisonment that these Jewish men would encounter to bring word of God's mercy to the world.

Barnabas persisted. He had been an encouragement to Paul when no one had trusted him. Paul ranked highly as a Jew and a Roman. Son of a Pharisee and well educated by a highly respected rabbi, Paul was zealous for God and knowledgeable about literature and philosophy. But not until he saw his poverty of spirit, calling himself "foremost among sinners" (1 Tim 1:15), after he encountered the resurrected Jesus and asked him who he was did he come to be part of the glorious righteousness that is God's movement among us. Paul would later write to send for John Mark because he was useful, but at the time he saw only John Mark's failures. Not until the focus emerged wholly on the concerns of Jesus was relationship restored. He shines upon us to save us (Ps 80:7; 76:4).

Crossing the cleansing water transformed three million slaves into a nation. Water is the sacred narrative of the Lord's history, who appointed the *mikveh*, the ritual immersion in a natural body of water, symbolically enacting a profound change in an individual's life. Shabbat comes down from heaven, only to be received by clean vessels. All those who have felt only the pain of life and travel the dusty valleys of sorrow are invited to come to the stream. Water was flowing before God spoke to create the world. It comes before new growth, before all the herbs and grains present at the Shabbat table, and before lives came into relationship.

Niddah

The *mikveh* is commanded in the laws of family purity for women in their role of preparing for their relationship with theri husband. Called *niddah*, the obligation of family purity elevates the relation between husband and wife, the only one of the mizvot that is exclusively a woman's. The most private of laws, the Bible requires sexual abstinence, beginning with the onset of menses and concluded by purification in the *mikveh* (Lev 15:19).

The *mikveh* is a beautiful experience, floating and wholly surrendering. Stepping across a vast expanse of time, the water invites us to learn what it means to be called on to be guardians of a trust linked through generations. Sarah, Rebekah, Rachel, Leah, and Mary the mother of Jesus, all cleansed in the water of *mikveh*. It supports identity as a woman of God, part of a people who never forgot they are to bring the gift from heaven to earth.

In the evening at the end of her time of month, women are to set aside the tumult of chores, paying bills, and worrying over children, and must seek the remedy of God. She prepares herself by bathing, shampooing, brushing her teeth, and clipping her nails before entering the *mikveh*. She steps into the water and, while standing shoulder deep with nothing between her and the water, she recites the blessing.

> *Baruch atah Adonai Eloheinu melech ha'olam asher kidshanu b'mitzvotav v'tzivanu al hatvilah.*
>
> Blessed are You, Lord our God, Ruler of the universe, Who has sanctified us with His commandments concerning the immersion.

She dips entirely under the water two or three times.

Throughout generations, the *mikveh* for family purity has drawn near to the mystery of life and the privilege of coming together in a marriage that is the union of the image of God. *Niddah* sanctifies sexual relations, guiding the union back to a conscious place with God. Intimacy between man and wife is reclaimed, closing the gap that the demands of the world cause, opening the relationship to develop communication where we are sustained by faith in God.

When she returns home, she says to her husband, "I am *tahora*." This means they now have complete access to each other. The laws governing *niddah* are laws of holiness to refine us, empowering the will to resist, persist, and believe God. God commanded the people to make themselves a holy people by accepting his instructions in mutual responsibility. The husband agrees to restrain and wait for his wife. He must also know God.

*Mikveh*s have been created in nearly every city where Jewish families abide. Constructing a *mikveh* is complex in the modern day, still requiring water to be in its natural state: rain, a lake, a river, or water gathered in a cistern. In Newton, Massachusetts, Mayyim Hayyim Living Waters Community Mikveh and the Paula Brody & Family Education Center[1] is a threshold to the ancient practice entering the twenty-first century. In tradition, they state:

> Perhaps this time of uncertainty encourages a renewed desire to connect with one's roots. Perhaps there is a collective knowledge that, just as with the flood God brought to Noah's world, with every disaster there is an opportunity to start over. Or perhaps, just as the mikveh resonates back to the water of a mother's womb, the idea of just crawling back in for a bit feels like the right thing to do.[2]

Niddah supports a woman's sense of self in relation to the world around her and gives her an opportunity to submerge into the depths of hope or into the sorrow of her mourning. It gives freedom to choose God's way for herself in a world where relationships have become disposable. *Niddah* allows marriage to have its times of emotional distance and toilsome work days by bringing them together each month on a night held in a context beyond their own needs.

She continued praying before the Lord. (1 Sam 1:12)

Miriam's life unfolded through the need for water and the wells that accompanied Israel through much of their desert journey. Her name is thought to have formed from the word *marar*, meaning "strong" or "bitter"—like myrrh, a fragrant medicine (Job 27:2; Ruth 1:20)—and *yam*, meaning "seas" or "waters" (Num 34:1–6). She served as a life-giving presence of the nation's water source.

Miriam sang the first song of Israel with her brother Moses, the song of the Torah, proclaiming the Lord's greatness. Her strength with God overflowed to lift the women into a circle dance after the nation was delivered from the army of Egypt (Exod 15). They danced in unrestricted joy; together their entire beings merged in the expression of victory coming in song.

When Miriam died, the community became aware that their water supply in the desert was disappearing (Num 20:2). With death imminent, they turned against Moses and Aaron. God instructed them to gather the people and he generously yielded water from a rock. Whether spending hours walking to rivers and carrying heavy buckets, vulnerable to violence, or the worry of toxins in piped-in systems and climate change limiting

---

1 Visit their website at www.mayyimhayyim.org.

2. Bornstein, "Mikveh," para. 7.

natural resources, women in every culture historically bring the compassion for thirst that marked Miriam's life.

Women do not have set times for prayers; their prayers are a spontaneous outpouring of heart any time of the day to seek as deeply as God's mercy. Additionally, women's prayer life does not require them to wear the tallit. God told women to "not wear anything that pertains to a man, nor shall a man put on a woman's garment" (Deut 22:5). Wearing a tallit appears to many to be feminist rebellion that went too far in demanding rights instead of valuing responsibility. People of God refrain from doing what may appear to be forbidden in the Bible. God said to avoid the appearance of evil (1 Thess 5:22). It may cause others to stumble on a wrong message.

God also said to have joy in his instructions. In this case, it is not being a woman the laws specifically address, but the minds that bring balance to the whole. When Paul told women to be quiet in church, he was telling them to listen to the teachings of those who had been educated by generations of scribes chosen by God. He was saying to the gentile women that they did not yet know the God of Israel and now had the opportunity to be silent and learn. He was telling women to be intimate with God, as he knew them to be in his culture: lighting the Shabbat candles, keeping the practice of *challah*, and making the home a place of light. He was speaking of women like Mary, found listening at the feet of Jesus, compared to Martha, who was vocal about her own agenda.

Rabbi Shlomo of Karlin (1742–1792) said, "The greatest pitfall Jews face is to forget that they are the children of the King." Three centuries later, women had become ambitious and academically well-educated, pursuing careers and tragically being portrayed everywhere as objects for physical pleasure. With genders no longer differentiated and marriage no longer held sacred, women leave behind a string of casual broken relationships. Committing to the future out of love is no longer the motivation. The result is hearts everywhere weighted with regret.

> He who has not seen the rejoicing at the place of the water-drawing has never seen rejoicing in his life (t. Sukkah 51a)

A decree for Israel, an ordinance of the God of Jacob, is to sound the ram's horn at the new moon and when the moon is full on the day of the festival (Ps 81:3). The proud blast of the shofar sounds the soul's longing, piercing with a collective plea asking God to remember us for life.

Both the Feast of Tabernacles and the Feast of Unleavened Bread begin when the moon becomes fully lit. During the Feast of Tabernacles (Sukkot) in temple days, the priests walked down to the pool of Siloam, just south of where the Western Wall is today. They filled a golden vessel with water from the pool and carried it up to the temple, the crowd of people singing songs and dancing before the Lord as they came through the Water Gate. This ceremony, called the Illumination of the Temple, refers to Isaiah 12:2–3:

> Behold, God is my salvation; I will trust, and will not be afraid;
> for the Lord God is my strength and my song, and he has become my salvation.
> With joy you will draw water from the wells of salvation.

Tall golden candelabras stood seventy-five feet high in the Court of Women, each holding up four gold bowls. The people danced in praise of God and Levites played harps, lyres, and blew the shofar as they proceeded down the steps from the water drawing ceremony. Four young men climbed ladders with jars of oil to fill the lamp stands. When they lit the bowls, all of Jerusalem was illuminated, and the people remembered the pillar of fire that guided Israel through their wilderness and the promise of a Messiah who would bring light to a lost and darkened world.

Jesus walked up the hill with the crowd to celebrate *Simchat Beit Hashoavah*, "the joy of drawing water." "On the last day of the feast, the great day, Jesus stood up and proclaimed, "If any one thirst, let him come to me and drink. He who believes in me, as the scripture has said, 'Out of his heart shall flow rivers of living water'" (John 7:37–38). He was proclaiming the wonderful victory of the people's story. "The Spirit and the Bride say, 'Come.' And let him who hears say, 'Come.' And let him who is thirsty come; let him who desires take the water of life without price" (Rev 22:17).

"Can any man forbid water?" asked Peter (Acts 10:47–48). Versed in the living water of salvation, the water of baptism, and the beauty of the water drawing ceremony, Peter caught the vision of God bringing light to the entire world in a message that came to every generation. There will be mercy for those who thirst. Matthew would say, "In his name shall the Gentiles trust" (Matt 12:21).

Jewish families continue to construct a *sukkah*, the small booth the Israelites are commanded to dwell in for the week of the feast (Lev 23:33–43). God wanted a place to meet with them in his lower realms as they journeyed through the wilderness, and in our wilderness time while we wait for the Messiah's return. The huts may be built on patios, balconies, or in forest campgrounds, decorated with fruits, ribbons, and pictures. Meals are eaten in the *sukkah*, and when weather allows, people sleep there at night. The fragrant scent of earth and branches, sheaves of corn, bunches of grapes, palms, and willows reminds them of how they once dwelt in temporary shelters during the forty-year journey to their land.

The harvest moon suspended in the sky shines through the lacey boughs, with stars peeping in glimmering brightness, like the candles that are blessed. Inside is a meeting with Abraham, with Sarah, with the past and all the promise of the world to come. A fresh breeze sways through the huts; the harvest has ripened with time, likewise ripening God's plan of holiness coming to fruition on earth. When Solomon dedicated the temple at Sukkot, he prayed for the Lord to hear the prayers of any foreigners that would come there to pray (2 Chr 6:32–33).

The holiday begins the prayers for the rainy season. Zechariah foretold of this time after the Messiah returns and the survivors from all nations that once stood against Jerusalem will now go up year after year to worship the king and celebrate the Feast of Tabernacles. Any nation that does not will not receive rain (Zech 14:16–19).

Mankind climbs steep hills, hikes long trails, and travels miles to see stunning scenes of waterfalls, oceans, lakes, and rivers. Pooling into creeks, surrounded by wildflowers, water captivates hours of mankind, wading and taking pictures. Deep in the soul, the water reminds us of origins, the high spiritual worlds raining words into the void to bring breathtaking views of God quenching the thirst of creation.

The Illumination of the Temple ceremony was utterly captivating, speaking of Torah compared to water, the gift from God descending like flowing water bestowing the future promise to the suffering.

Sukkot transforms the solemn repentance of Yom Kippur into days of dancing and singing. Seeing this, the author of the book of Hebrews said to strip off every weight that slows us down, run the race, and endure, because Jesus is now seated at the place of honor in the throne room and he has taken down the wall that once forbid other peoples to enter his temple (Heb 12:1).

He has showed you, O man, what is good. (Mic 6:8)

The power that holds the winds, blazes the stars throughout the universe, spins the earth around the sun, quakes the earth, and rules the oceans is gathering people of every nation in the story the moonlight tells. "On this rock I will build my church," Jesus said, referring to Peter (Matt 16:18). He is building his church. Nothing prevails against this.

After centuries of untruths, the darkness yields. Those who have climbed the ascent toward the temple have met each other. Peter, who forsook Jesus and walked away, denying him, was sought again at the sea where Jesus first found him. The church walked away, denying the Israelite heritage of Jesus and the mission God assigned to the Jewish people. How much more will their fruit bear now as the natural olive branches revive and flourish to absorb more light for the tree that grows? (Rom 11:12).

Under cover of night, Nicodemus, a Jewish leader and teacher, approached Jesus, recognizing that he was sent by God but aware of the criticism of his peers. "Jesus answered him, 'Truly, truly, I say to you, unless one is born anew, he cannot see the kingdom of God.' Nicode'mus said to him, 'How can a man be born when he is old? Can he enter a second time into his mother's womb and be born?' Jesus answered . . . 'Do not marvel that I said to you, "You must be born anew"'" (John 3:3–4, 7). Jesus was saying that a rabbi such as Nicodemus, who is learned in both the written Torah and oral law, should know what being "born again" means, because he experiences new birth in his culture all the time.

The practice occurs when something significant transforms a life. Within Jewish understanding, getting married is a born again experience. The previous state of being single changes to become part of something new. When they have a child, this is viewed as another born-again experience. They have gone from being a couple to becoming a family. When a man goes through the steps of training and becomes a rabbi, he has had a born-again experience. Unclean persons were required to become ceremonially clean through immersion before they could bring a sacrifice to the temple.

Converting to Judaism is also a born-again experience. This transformation for men included physical circumcision. Coming to trust in Jesus as Messiah requires a circumcision of the heart, performed by the one who created us. Jesus answered Nicodemus, "No one can enter the kingdom of God unless they are born of water and the Spirit" (John 3:5).

Born-again events require an immersion in water. When John the Baptist said, "I baptize with water; but among you stands one whom you do not know" (John 1:26), he was following the ancient teaching. John was performing the *mikveh* blessing in a natural body of flowing water, the River Jordan. The concept began in Leviticus 11:36, when the Jewish people were instructed to gather only running water that had not touched the carcass of certain creatures.

When we are baptized, we are immersed, wholly suspended under water, surrendered entirely, holding back nothing, cleansed to emerge transformed. We are acknowledging that we are ritually unclean and turning back to God to be identified as a new creation (2 Cor 5:17). Nicodemus would have understood the roots of transformation. The oral law of the Talmud teaches that the Spirit of God over the waters refers to the Spirit of the Messiah. The Spirit directs all change moving the world, his creation, back to its original state of perfection.

For Jews, baptism is a practice of their identity as people of God. When gentiles are baptized, they come into relationship with Jewish believers. The church has used baptism of Jewish people to mean they are no longer Jewish. Jesus meant it as the promise to those in darkness to be drawn out into the light from above, as he fulfills the promise of reconciliation.

The *mikveh* gathers drops of water into a pool. Solomon noted that "the beginning of strife is like letting out water; so quit before the quarrel breaks out" (Prov 17:14). Peacemakers stone up the water to create the pool for cleansing, restraining words of strife that lead to division, quick to hear, slow to speak. Bringing about this new man took all the work of the matriarchs and patriarchs of Israel, the prophets, the only Son of God, the Holy Spirit, and the many called to bring God's relentless pursuit of peace. It happens by yielding, baptized, into his death.

Before the born-again experience, there is *teshuvah*, or "turning to the Way." Jesus said "you must be born again" to Nicodemus, an upright man who already knew God. Nicodemus was learned in Scripture, a sincere and successful man. Yet Jesus said to this man that he needed rebirth. "How can this be?" Nicodemus asked (John 3:9).

The origin of *mikveh* goes back to Genesis, when earth was unformed and the Spirit of God hovered over the surface of the water. God gathered the water together and let dry land appear. God said that it was good, meaning that it was pristine and undefiled.

In the time of Noah, the earth again was submerged beneath water in order to set apart Noah's family. Life was still there, under the water, but it could not grow or offer its gifts until it emerged. Likewise, the soul is still there, beneath the sin, separated from the light, waiting to be born out of the baptizing waters. Noah waited for the rain and waited for the water to rise. He entered the ark. Then Moses journeyed down the Nile in an ark created because a debased society was killing babies. He was brought out of purifying water, appointed to bring his people through the water of the Red Sea. The great stones that built the temple were lifted from the sea as the water subsided. John the Baptist came, immersing people in water, saying, "Behold the Lamb of God who takes away our sin!"

The Lord brought the first man, Adam, out of earth that emerged from water. He breathed into him, and he was brought to life. Similarly, God brought the church out of the water of baptism and breathed life into us. We had bodies, but they weren't yet empowered to carry out God's work until the Spirit illumined. "I send the promise of my Father upon you; but stay in the city, until you are clothed with power from on high" (Luke 24:49). The Spirit teaches all truth to transform a person emerging from the waters into the image of Jesus and into the one body he prayed for us to be.

All Jews (including Nicodemus) and also the gentiles are called through the water to receive the Spirit of rebirth by turning to Jesus. Jesus is the firstborn from the dead, leading the way to purity from defilement and life from death. It is founded with the promised regathering of Israel. "Again I will build you . . . Again you will . . . go forth in the dance of the merry makers. Again you shall plant vineyards upon the mountains of Samar'ia" (Jer 31:3–5).

In recognition of God commanding Abraham to leave his country to be given the land of Israel, in 1917 British foreign secretary James Balfour penned the Balfour Declaration, committing Britain to help the Jews establish their homeland in response to the twenty-year dream of Zionism to return home. When the peace conference convened in Paris in 1919, Winston Churchill endorsed the declaration, saying, "It is manifestly right that the Jews who are scattered all over the world should have a national centre and a national home where some of them may be reunited. And where else could that be but in the land of Palestine, with which for more than 3,000 years they have been intimately and profoundly associated."[3]

However, in November 2015, the UN passed a resolution that Israel must give the Golan Heights to Syria. "The UN voted this way, I guess, so that not just the 50,000 Jews living there but also the Druze would be slaughtered by ISIS which is just on the Israel-Syrian border fighting whoever comes near them," wrote Shira Sorko-Ram, co-founder of Maoz Israel. "If this doesn't make sense, it's because it doesn't."[4]

Israel is the only UN member state whose right to exist is constantly challenged and the only one that's been targeted for annihilation by another UN member state. By a fourteen to zero vote, on December 23, 2016, the UN Security Council adopted Resolution 2334, stating that settlements of Israel's people in Palestinian territories since 1967 are a flagrant violation of international law and has no legal validity, giving Palestine the opportunity to establish the land as a Palestinian state.

> Be strong and of good courage; for you shall cause this people to inherit the land which I swore to their fathers to give them. (Josh 1:6)

---

3. Ben-David, "Winston Church's Defense," para. 6.
4. Sorko-Ram, "Trump, God and Israel," para. 45.

More than three million Jewish people have left their homes to move to the land of their mothers and fathers since the UN voted to recognize "a Jewish state in the area called Palestine" in 1947 and passed Resolution 181, which established Jerusalem as a "corpus separatum," meaning a "body of separate entity." Their heroism today defies the violent assaults on their men, women, and children every day. Shira Sorko-Ram writes that, "Hatred against Jews is actually hatred against the God of Israel and Yeshua, the King of the Jews."[5]

The Ministry of Diaspora Affairs, monitoring anti-Semitism on the Internet with new technology, found that "anti-Semitism and incitement on the Internet has increased exponentially and reaches tens of millions of people all over the world," increasing 200 percent in Germany between 2015 and 2017.[6] "The system is capable of detailing how many anti-Semitic posts and messages are currently being circulated and what countries and areas contain the highest volume of anti-Semitic traffic. So far, the system conducted a successful pilot demonstration and identified over 500 thousand anti-Semitic posts, which reached more than 40 million people."[7]

The Coordination Forum for Countering Antisemitism reported that in April 2014, the season of Passover, swastikas were drawn on Jewish property in university dormitories around America. At the University of Central Florida, eleven swastikas were carved into the walls of a young woman's apartment.[8] In the beginning of the fall semester in 2014, two students from East Carolina University sprayed a swastika on the apartment door of a Jewish student. The same day, a Jewish student at the University of North Carolina was told "to go burn in an oven." The student was told that she is being hunted because of her support for Israel. "I have been called a terrorist, baby killer, woman killer, [told that] I use blood to make matzah and other foods, Christ killer, occupier, and much more," she said.[9]

At the University of California at Santa Barbara in October of the same year, fliers were handed out accusing Israel of the 9/11 attacks. Days later, anti-Semitic graffiti was found on the Jewish fraternity house in Emory University in Atlanta, and again in Northeastern University, where swastikas were drawn on flyers for a school event. A few cars in the parking lot of the University of California at Davis campus were scratched with anti-Semitic slurs and swastikas, and the symbols were found again at Towson University

---

5. Sorko-Ram, "Anti-Semitism," para. 46.
6. Eichner, "New System," paras. 2, 13.
7. Eichner, "New System," para. 11.
8. "UCF Student Finds Swastikas," para. 2.
9. "Jewish Student," para. 7.

on a chalkboard in the center of the campus. What would the victims of the Warsaw Ghetto say to those who ignore these incidents?

In the fifth century, when Ezra and Nehemiah brought groups of Jews back to their land, enemies stood against their return. Today, Israel faces Iran's one hundred thousand missiles and the hatred of the Arab citizens in the West Bank and Gaza, who are ready to give their lives to defeat the Jewish people.

The world opposes Israel because their return signals a step toward the return of Messiah, who will judge the nations. But for the people of God, "like cold water to a thirsty soul, so is good news from a far country" (Prov 25:25). "But you, O mountains of Israel, shall shoot forth your branches, and yield your fruit to my people Israel; for they will soon come home" (Ezek 36:8).

"That a people should go into exile, be dispersed, and yet survive for 2,000 years, that they should be a nation without a national homeland and come back again, that they should re-establish that homeland and revive their ancient language is a miraculous, singular event," Sorko-Ram wrote. "No one ever did such a thing."[10]

There were only a known twenty-three Messianic Jews in Israel in May 1948, according to One for Israel's "The Messianic Jewish Movement in the Modern State of Israel."[11] Forty years later, in 1989, an estimated 1,200 Messianic Jews praised Jesus in Israel. In 1999, of the 4.8 million Jews living there, about five thousand knew Jesus. A conservative estimate in 2016 counted thirty thousand Messianic Jews in the land with continued unprecedented growth. The Messiah is being proclaimed once again from Zion.[12]

In 1995, the US Senate and House of Representatives approved the Jerusalem Embassy Act to move the US embassy to Jerusalem. The act stated that Jerusalem is to remain an undivided city and be recognized as the capital of the State of Israel. This was never put into action. Presidents Clinton, Bush, and Obama failed to implement the decision, each signing a presidential waiver. However, in a December 2017 speech, President Donald Trump announced recognition of Jerusalem as Israel's capital and his plan to move the US embassy from Tel Aviv to Jerusalem. "God proclaimed through his prophet that he "[has made] Jerusalem a heavy stone for all the peoples; all who life it shall grievously hurt themselves" (Zech 12:2–3).

In the book of Revelation, when the seals are broken, the earth trembles (Rev 6). According to Joel, "the earth quakes before them, the

---

10. Sorko-Ram, "Trump, God and Israel," para. 26.
11. One for Israel, "Findings of New Research," para. 7.
12. One for Israel, "Findings of New Research," paras. 18–20.

heavens tremble. The sun and moon are darkened, and the stars withdraw their shining," as heaven rolls back (2:10–11). Judgment comes with great quaking and clouds of dark—at the giving of law at Mount Sinai (Exod 19:16—20:20), and when Jesus died, the earth trembled, the sky darkened, and the veil to the holy of holies tore and opened on the day of Passover (Matt 27:45–54). This is the moment we glimpse as we remember to guard the Shabbat, the moment we stop and all work ceases. Out of the darkness, the Lord of heaven comes, bringing light.

The prophet Joel foresaw the days when God restores the fortunes of Judah and Jerusalem, a time God gathers all the nations and brings them down to the valley of Jehoshaphat to enter into judgment on behalf of his people, his heritage Israel, because they scattered his people and divided up his land (Joel 3:1–3). To Israel, he says, "I will bless those who bless you, and him who curses you I will curse; and by you all the families of the earth shall bless themselves" (Gen 12:3).

Rains began falling on the dry lands of Texas after a ten-year drought in May of 2015. That month, Texas governor Greg Abbot signed a bill into law to stand with Israel.[13] Saturating rain began to fall. It was Israel's sixty-ninth birthday.

In February of 2017, an event at the state capital in Austin brought a first-time rally called "The Texas Stand With Israel/Citizens Advocacy Day," organized by Texas State Representative Phil King. The gathering was to support the new bill, House Bill 89, and its companion bill in the Texas State Senate, SB 134. The bill was a victory cry over a movement called Boycott, Divest and Sanction, whose warfare wages against Israel's existence. The movement gained notoriety around the world in universities, governments, labor unions, and businesses, with some Christian denominations participating.[14]

"Looking at America from across the ocean here in Israel, it appeared that no one was going to be able to stop the U.S. from literally sliding down into a dark abyss—of atheism, politically correct authoritarianism, hatred, gross pornography, murder and violence, with a barrage of laws that would attack religious freedoms from every direction," Sorko-Ram noted. "That, together with a steadily growing influence of Islam, which, by its own mouth declares its goal to conquer America and the world, made America look irretrievable."[15]

---

13. Maoz Israel Staff, "Texas Stands With Israel," para. 9.
14. Maoz Israel Staff, "Texas Stands With Israel," paras. 1–2, 5.
15. Sorko-Ram, "Trump, God and Israel," para. 61.

Supporting Israel aligns with God supporting his covenants. One for Israel, an initiative of native-born Israelis proclaiming salvation to Israel, opened a college in 1990. For the first time in history, an Israeli-Korean forum was held on February 16, 2017, and became an annual event. Messianic Jewish and Evangelical Arab theologians and Bible scholars met with Korean Bible leaders and scholars on the campus of One for Israel in Netanya, Israel. "Our generation has seen not only the prophetic rebirth of the modern state of Israel but also the miraculous spiritual re-birth of thousands of Israelis who have recognized the ONE of whom Moses and the prophets wrote," One For Israel reports.[16]

When Hagar, the Egyptian woman, was sent away with her son Ishmael, she wept for him. Abraham wept too. He loved his son. Hagar put her son beneath a tree. He was dying. But God heard the cries of their suffering. Hagar opened her eyes to experience promise at a well of water, which would keep them alive (Gen 21:8–21). Earlier she calls the Lord El Roi, "the God who sees me" (Gen 16:13).

Hagar had been exiled, forcibly removed from her house. There in the wilderness she is told her son is not excluded from God's covenant promise. His people are part of the dialogue with Israel. "As for Ishmael, I have heard you; behold, I will bless him and make him fruitful and multiply him exceedingly; he shall be the father of twelve princes, and I will make him a great nation" (Gen 17:20). He will dwell apart, but beside, his brother Isaac. God calls Ishmael a wild donkey of a man, unbridled, a word in Hebrew meaning "fleet-footed" or "sturdy." He would thrive in the wilderness as a prince.

As the Jews return to Israel, they are blessing nations once thought to be excluded from God's desires. Maoz Israel partners with Dor Haba Worship Training Camp, bringing together about a hundred Arab, Jewish, and gentile youth to be met by the light for five summer days. "Dor Haba" means "Next Generation." Leaders from across the land come to guide the new generation to draw near to the cross, which was intended to kill God's Son, but instead opened the door to the tree of life.

By March 1, 2017, TJCII had an office in Jerusalem, and the vision booklet about being one body in Jesus was translated into Hebrew for the first time. Wisdom to move the way the Lord wants in order to expand the unity of church and Israel in Ireland is being sought at the mercy throne in heaven. For the first time, the Roman Catholic Bishop invited the Messianic Jewish community to participate with other denominations in an exhibition

---

16. One for Israel, "Who Is One for Israel," 2.

in Oradea, in northwest Romania, that included a table of items used for Passover.

In North America, the NOW Generation takes up the mantle as they continue bimonthly Erev Shabbat dinners, growing in fellowship and relationships. All are leaders in their own field of ministry, depending on the living waters of prayer. In Argentina, believers pray for government actions to favor Israel in their investigations of attacks on the Jewish Embassy, AMIA, and the killing of Dr. Aolbert Nisman in 2015. TJCII has been brought into contact with Presbyterian, Pentecostal, and Catholic communities, as prayer strengthens understanding of the roots of faith in Israel and the one Lord of all.

Reconciling with the nations, turning them toward Israel in God's word, intercessor Paula Leitner, who is co-coordinator for TJCII European intercessors, attended the Netherlands Open Days for new students at the end of August 2017. TJCII had a bookstand and held a workshop "with a very positive response," she said.[17] Another Open Day in November concluded with a Shabbat meal. The weekend offered messianic concerts, speaking on Shabbat morning, as well as singing songs on Sunday morning in a church service. It was a time given to sharing and worship.

Reverend Brian Cox visited Africa in March 2016 with other TJCII team members. He writes,

> Crucially, healing is not forgetting. . . . It begins with the members of a community examining their suffering at the hands of their enemy. The next, more dramatic step is their acknowledgment of their enemy's suffering. This recognition can, often to surprising degrees, lead to the change of heart, the repentance, and the embrace of the other in which healing begins.[18]

A member of TJCII's international leadership team, Reverend Cox developed faith-based reconciliation practices in his work in Africa, Asia, Europe, Latin America and the Middle East in political conflicts, as a religious framework for peacemaking and conflict resolution and as an alternative to religious extremism.

As director of the PACIS Project in Faith-Based Diplomacy at the Straus Institute of Pepperdine, he emphasizes the process of reconciliation happens with the assistance of divine power.

"It is not surprising that most religious traditions give prominent place to these practices," he says. "The Abrahamic faiths understand them as direct responses to God's mercy." Many missions have been sent to Africa over

---

17. Leitner, "Open Days."
18. Cox and Philpott, "Faith-Based Diplomacy," 35.

the years, but this meeting was for reconciliation between Israel and the nations.

As Fr. Peter Hocken, a Catholic theologian and member of the TJCII International Leadership Council, wrote in "Twenty Years of TJCII,"

> The elders of TJCII have known from the beginning, when we first heard of the vision, that we were participating in something that was truly given to us by God. This truth is so profound that we as mere humans often have to reset out perception of TJCII and ask the question: Do we assume that we fully understand this vision and its implications? My prayer is, as we ask that question, we will have the mind of Christ and the courage to act on his answer.

The stories call them home; the pomegranate and the figs, the calming scent of olive gardens and barrels of spices that the Lord provided to set the table when he designed the architecture of creation. Here the promises are reminiscent of ancestors struggling for them to have this knowledge of God, echoing from the places where they walked and passed away. Here the gathering excites, with each person returning, bringing them collectively nearer to the Messiah's return. The waves continue to pour in, moving the largest population of Jewish people in the world from America to Israel.

Palms lift their branches across Israel, as if in welcome. The temple was decorated with pairs of the trees, male and female, on both sides of doorways. They are also thought to be reminiscent of Eden, which the temple represented in its way back to relationship with God. Palm trees adorn the doorframes in Ezekiel's vision of the third temple, continuing the story to its destination of the Messiah's return. God said he would stretch out his hand to gather Israel from the four corners of earth (Isa 11:11). He would do this in the last days (Hos 3:4–5). They will never again be separated from their land (Amos 9:15).

The writer of Hebrews brought a message concerning the faith of Abraham, Sarah, Isaac, and Jacob:

> These all died in faith, not having received what was promised, but having seen it and greeted it from afar, and having acknowledged that they were strangers and exiles on the earth. For people who speak thus make it clear that they are seeking a homeland. If they had been thinking of that land from which they had gone out, they would have had opportunity to return. But as it is, they desire a better country, that is, a heavenly one. (Heb 11:13–16)

They were still believing when they died. Others were tortured, willingly holding faith, knowing that God had planned something better that he would bring about together with his people. Some faced jeers, flogging, chains, and imprisonment. Believers held in the palm of the Messiah's hand were stoned to death, sawed in two, and killed by the sword. They wandered in deserts and mountains, living in caves and in holes in the ground just to survive, in a state of destitution, persecution, and being mistreated. The Lord says the world is not worthy of them (Heb 11:38).

This is a very old message. Through all of human history, there have been those who felt the power of the world to come. None of them had yet received what had been promised. Presenting their burdens to the Lord for many years, waiting, wondering if he heard them, if he forgot his promise. Paul said that there were times when it was too much to bear, and her pleaded with God to take accusers away. God answered, "My grace is sufficient for you." Paul responded, "For the sake of Christ, then, I am content . . . for when I am weak, then I am strong" (2 Cor 12:8–10).

We must realize that the path laden with obstacles, perfectly placed to institute needed growth and pruning, is what attains the aliyah that enables man to bless his enemy. Seeing how the path clears in the Lord's inexplicable joy, moving with the power of a wild river, surpassing every wind, flowing over us, lifting us, and carrying us with him to enjoy God forever; this is the fruit of faith.

He shares his peace for the Shabbat to glow for us through every day, asking us to pray, especially for leadership. "First of all, then, I urge that supplications, prayers, intercessions, and thanksgivings be made for all men, for kings and all who are in high positions, that we may lead a quiet and peaceable life, godly and respectful in every way" (1 Tim 2:1–2).

"If the Lord has asked us to pray, he means to answer our prayers," Sorko-Ram said.[19]

---

19. Sorko-Ram, "Trump, God and Israel," para. 81.

BIBLIOGRAPHY

Aaron, David. "Secrets to Powerful Prayer." https://www.isralight.org/freemp3s/RDA/Secrets_To_Powerful_Prayer.mp3.
Apple, Raymond. "Jewish Attitudes to Gentiles in the First Century." http://www.oztorah.com/2008/07/jewish-attitudes-to-gentiles-in-the-first-century/.
Athenagoras. "Athenagoras of Athens." http://www.earlychristianwritings.com/text/athenagoras-plea.html.
Ballard, Donna. "Messianic Jewish Leadership Essential to Prayer Journey." *TJCII Communique*, Spring 2016. http://tjc2.org.br/wp-content/uploads/2013/04/Spring-Newsletter-Europe.pdf.
Barna Group. "Meet Those Who 'Love Jesus but Not the Church.'" https://www.barna.com/research/meet-love-jesus-not-church/.
———. "Tired & Stressed, but Satisfied: Moms Juggle Kids, Career & Identity." https://www.barna.com/research/tired-stressed-but-satisfied-moms-juggle-kids-career-identity/.
Ben-David, Lenny. "Winston Churchill's Defense of the Balfour Delcaration in 1921." http://jcpa.org/article/winston-churchills-defense-balfour-declaration-1921/.
Bilezikian, Gilbert. *Beyond Sex Roles: What the Bible Says about a Woman's Place in Church and Family*. Grand Rapids: Baker Academic, 2006.
Bornstein, Carrie. "The Mikveh as Our Spiritual Tool." *The Times of Israel* (blog), November 16, 2016. https://blogs.timesofisrael.com/the-mikveh-as-our-spiritual-tool/.
Bowman, Jaimie. "Why Women are Leaving the Church." http://pastors.com/why-women-are-leaving-the-church.
Braverman, Emma. "Father Patrick Desbois: One Man's Fight to Uncover the Holocaust." http://www.aish.com/jw/s/Father-Patrick-Desbois-One-Mans-Fight-to-Uncover-the-Holocaust.html?s=searchres.
Chosen People Ministries. "Did Jesus Celebrate Christmas or Hanukkah?" https://www.chosenpeople.com/site/did-jesus-celebrate-christmas-or-hanukkah/.
Cohn, D'Vera, et al. "Barely Half of U.S. Adults Are Married—A Record Low." http://www.pewsocialtrends.org/2011/12/14/barely-half-of-u-s-adults-are-married-a-record-low/.
Cox, Brian, and Daniel Philpott. "Faith-Based Diplomacy: An Ancient Idea Newly Emergent." *The Brandywine Review of Faith & International Affairs* 1.2 (2003) 31–40. http://users.clas.ufl.edu/kenwald/rpp/Cox2003.pdf.

De Groote, Michael. "Christian Killed Every 5 Minutes." *Deseret News*, September 2, 2011. https://www.deseretnews.com/article/700175766/Christian-killed-every-5-minutes.html.

Eichner, Itamar. "New System to Identify Anti-Semitism on the Web." *Ynetnews*, January 22, 2017. http://www.ynetnews.com/articles/0,7340,L-4910922,00.html.

Green, Joel B. *The Gospel of Luke*. The New International Commentary on the New Testament Series. Grand Rapids: Eerdmans, 1997.

Guignebert, Charles. *The Jewish World in the Time of Jesus*. New Hyde Park, NY: University Books, 1959.

Hocken, Peter. "The Church of the One New Man." *Toward Jerusalem Council II Communiqué*. Spring 2010.

———. "The Marranos: A History in Need of Healing." *Toward Jerusalem Council Communiqué*. 2006. http://www.peterhocken.org/mc/home.nsf/0/26CD0D955655FDBFC1257DBB006C5FA6/$FILE/Article.pdf?open.

"Jewish Student at UNC Charlotte Told to 'Burn in an Oven.'" http://archive.jns.org/news-briefs/2014/9/9/jewish-student-at-north-carolina-charlotte-university-told-to-burn-in-an-oven.

Jewish Virtual Library. "Jewish Practices & Rituals: Sacrifices and Offerings (Karbanot)." http://www.jewishvirtuallibrary.org/sacrifices-and-offerings-karbanot.

———. "Jewish Prayers: Aleinu." https://www.jewishvirtuallibrary.org/aleinu.

Juster, Daniel. "Is the Church Pagan?" http://www.tikkunministries.org/newsletters/dj-mar04.htm.

Kaplan, Aryeh. "The Soul." http://www.aish.com/jl/sp/bas/48942091.html.

Leitner, Paula. "Open Days in the Netherlands." *Toward Jerusalem Council II Communique*, Winter 2017.

Lewis, Naphtali. *Life in Egypt Under Roman Rule*. Oxford: Clarendon, 1983.

Maoz Israel Staff. "Texas Stands With Israel—Signing of Anti-BDS Bill." *Kehila News Israel*, July 30, 2017. https://kehilanews.com/2017/07/30/texas-stands-with-israel-signing-of-anti-bds-bill/.

Miller, Yvette Alt. "Anne Frank, European Soccer and Anti-Semitism." http://www.aish.com/jw/s/Anne-Frank-European-Soccer-and-Anti-Semitism.html?s=mm.

One for Israel. "Findings Of New Research On The Messianic Movement In Israel." https://www.oneforisrael.org/bible-based-teaching-from-israel/findings-of-new-research-on-the-messianic-movement-in-israel/.

———. "The Meaning Behind the Menorah." https://www.oneforisrael.org/bible-based-teaching-from-israel/the-meaning-behind-the-menorah.

———. "Who Is One for Israel?" https://www.oneforisrael.org/overview2016.pdf.

———. "Why Does Israel Mark Holocaust Remembrance On A Different Day?" https://www.oneforisrael.org/bible-based-teaching-from-israel/israel-mark-holocaust-remembrance-different-day.

Roach, John. "'Methuselah' Palm Grown From 2,000-Year-Old Seed Is a Father." *National Geographic*, March 24, 2015. http://news.nationalgeographic.com/2015/03/150324-ancient-methuselah-date-palm-sprout-science.

Sorko-Ram, Ari. "Anti-Semitism: Where Did It Come From?" https://kehilanews.com/2017/04/14/anti-semitism-where-did-it-come-from/.

———. "Guest Speaker: Richard and Carolyn Hyde, Ari Sorko-Ram." https://my.pcloud.com/publink/show?code=XZvBofZF605jK2N1dhIBmeTgt6nERj3TgX7.

Sorko-Ram, Shira. "Trump, God and Israel." *Maoz Israel*, January 2017. http://maoz.convio.net/site/News2?page=NewsArticle&id=11757&news_iv_ctrl=-1#1.

Stone, Roxanne. "Why Are Women Leaving the Church?" *Christianity Today*, June 2015. http://www.christianitytoday.com/women/2015/june/why-are-women-leaving-church.html.

Toward Jerusalem Council II. "Toward Jerusalem Council II: Vision, Origin and Documents."

"UCF Student Finds Swastikas Carved into Walls of Her Apartment." April 30, 2014. https://www.clickorlando.com/news/ucf-student-finds-swastikas-carved-into-walls-of-her-apartment_20151107093708309.

Williamson, Sandra Crawford. "Why Are Working Women Starting to Unplug from Their Churches?" *Institute for Faith, Work & Economics*, December 5, 2014. https://tifwe.org/working-women-unplugging-from-church.

Zion, Ilan Ben. "Ancient Temple Mount 'Warning' Stone Is 'Closest Thing We Have to the Temple.'" https://www.timesofisrael.com/ancient-temple-mount-warning-stone-is-closest-thing-we-have-to-the-temple/.

"The Zohar." http://www.sacred-texts.com/jud/zdm/zdm012.htm.

www.ingramcontent.com/pod-product-compliance
Lightning Source LLC
Chambersburg PA
CBHW050818160426
43192CB00010B/1803